The Conundrum of I

The Conundrum of Russian Capitalism

The Post-Soviet Economy in the World System

Ruslan Dzarasov

PlutoPress
www.plutobooks.com

First published 2014 by Pluto Press
345 Archway Road, London N6 5AA

www.plutobooks.com

Distributed in the United States of America exclusively by
Palgrave Macmillan, a division of St. Martin's Press LLC,
175 Fifth Avenue, New York, NY 10010

British Library Cataloguing in Publication Data
A catalogue record for this book is available from the British Library

ISBN   978 0 7453 3279 6   Hardback
ISBN   978 0 7453 3278 9   Paperback
ISBN   978 1 8496 4909 4   PDF eBook
ISBN   978 1 8496 4911 7   Kindle eBook
ISBN   978 1 8496 4910 0   EPUB eBook

Library of Congress Cataloging in Publication Data applied for

This book is printed on paper suitable for recycling and made from fully managed
and sustained forest sources. Logging, pulping and manufacturing processes are
expected to conform to the environmental standards of the country of origin.

10   9   8   7   6   5   4   3   2   1

Typeset from disk by Stanford DTP Services, Northampton, England
Simultaneously printed digitally by CPI Antony Rowe, Chippenham, UK and
Edwards Bros in the United States of America

Contents

List of Figures	vi
List of Tables	viii
Acknowledgements	ix
Introduction	1
1. Global Accumulation and the Capitalist World-system	15
2. From Central Planning to Capitalism	42
3. Russian Big Business: Corporate Governance and the Time Horizon	80
4. Rent Withdrawal, Social Conflict and Accumulation	133
5. Insider Rent and Conditions of Growth in the Russian Economy	175
6. The Accumulation of Capital by Russian Corporations: Some Empirical Evidence	196
Conclusion	255
Notes	261
Bibliography	269
Index	290

List of Figures

1.1 Net dividends plus net share buybacks as a percentage of
internal funds in US non-financial corporate business,
1951–2011   25

1.2 Foreign direct investment in developing and transition
economies, 1970–2010   26

1.3 Net dividends as a percentage of net investments in fixed
assets in US non-financial corporate business, 1960–2010   30

1.4 Investment in fixed assets and net acquisition of financial
assets as a percentage of US internal funds (book) in the
US non-financial corporate sector in 1945–2011   31

1.5 Total financial assets as a percentage of nonfinancial assets
in the US non-financial corporate sector, 1951–2011   32

2.1 Consumer price index in 1991–95   73

2.2 Inflation and slump in the Russian economy in the 1990s   74

3.1 The shares of ownership concentration of Russian firms   103

3.2 The 'Mejprombank' ownership network   109

3.3 A typical ownership structure scheme   111

3.4 Infrastructure of insider control over assets   121

4.1 The cash scheme of rent extraction   140

4.2 Ownership and control of Evrazholding   145

4.3 Price structure and rent distribution among the large and
small insiders   170

5.1 Price indices for Russian industries, 1990–2003   184

5.2 Profitability of industries' output in 2003   187

5.3 Profitability of organisations' assets, by kinds of economic
activities   188

5.4 Price structure and rent distribution among the large
insiders of a) the privileged sector and b) the industries
disadvantaged by price disparity   193

6.1 Private and public investments in fixed capital in Russia,
1990–2010   199

6.2 Distribution of the industrial organisations, according to
the period of purchases of machinery and equipment   205

6.3   The share of enterprises abstaining from any investments   209
6.4   Affirmative replies to the question 'Does the current level
       of investment in your enterprise secure necessary
       modernisation?'   210
6.5   Factors limiting production   211
6.6   Negative responses to the question 'Is there available
       Russian-produced machinery, necessary for your enterprise,
       which is not inferior to their imported counterparts?'   215
6.7   The share of enterprises which management thinks that
       competition from non-CIS producers in their markets is
       increasing   217
6.8   The share of companies introducing globally innovative
       business practices, technologies and products   218
6.9   Responses to the question 'What kind of services do banks
       provide to your enterprise?'   219
6.10 The ownership system at JSC Petchoraneft   232
6.11 Struggle of big insiders for control of Volgograd
       JSC Chimprom   240
6.12 The struggle of the Mazepin and Levitsky-Vekselberg
       groups of big insiders for control of the chemical industry   245

List of Tables

1.1 Relative import prices of manufacturers, average annual
     percent change, 1986–2006   29
1.2 Prices and money supply, average annual growth   36
2.1 Dynamics of the main social-economic indicators in
     Russia, 1990s   75
3.1 Ownership concentration in Russian big business   98
3.2 Ownership structures of companies in selected
     transitional countries, 1999   99
5.1 Producer price indices by kinds of economic activities   186
6.1 Dynamics of the value of fixed capital in industry   200
6.2 Origin of the machinery and equipment purchased by
     Russian firms   213
6.3 Sales and profit of Volgakabel   224
6.4 Major buyers of Petchoraneft on the world market   233
6.5 Some of Petchoraneft's debt commitments   236
6.6 Profits and losses of Chimprom   247
6.7 Value, structure, and wear and tear of Chimprom's
     fixed assets   250

Acknowledgements

I owe an enormous debt to the supervisors of my PhD thesis at Staffordshire University (UK), on which this book is based, Professors Peter Reynolds and Nick Adnett, for their continuous support and encouragement. They patiently worked with me over eight long years. I benefited enormously from their high academic standards, tolerance and understanding.

I also wish to express my profound gratitude to the staff of the department of economics at UMKC (Kansas City), who accepted me as a Fulbright visiting scholar. My special thanks to Professor Frederic Lee from the same department. He not only kindly invited me to stay at UMKC, but shared with me his enormous knowledge of post-Keynesian economics and the history of American business. Together with his wife Ruth, Professor Lee introduced me to American culture and way of life and the Missouri environment. I am grateful to Professor John Henry (UMKC) who discussed with me various topics which facilitated my research. Professor David Kotz (UMASS, Amherst) provided his valuable comments of my model. Professor Tae-Hee Jo organised discussion of my topic in Buffalo State College (New York) from which I gratefully benefited. I am much obliged to them and to all their colleagues who participated in the discussions.

My special thanks to consultant Dmitry Novojenov, who generously shared with me his wide knowledge of modern Russian business and was my indispensable co-researcher in Russia. I am also grateful to Dmitry Kuvalin at the Institute of Forecasting of Russian Academy of Sciences, who provided me with the results of his surveys and his advice. I owe a special debt to my colleagues from the Russian Academy of Sciences – Professors Valery Grebennikov, Vitaly Manevitch, Vladimir Khoros and Viktor Krasilschikov – and from Moscow State University – Professors Viktor Cherkovetz, Alexander Buzgalin, Andrey Kolganov – who provided invaluable advice content of my research, paving the way for its completion.

I am very obliged to a teacher of English from UMKC, Stephen Holland-Wempe, and to a sociologist and an interpreter, Renfry

Clarke, for their help in editing my manuscript. I want to thank as well the former Chair and Commissioning Editor at Pluto Press, Roger van Zwanenberg, who encouraged me to embark on this project and supported the idea. I want to express my gratitude to the team at Pluto Press, especially David Shulman, including the managing editor Robert Webb, the copy-editor Jeanne Brady, Melanie Patrick, responsible for the cover design, Jon Wheatley, Jonathan Maunder, and Chris Browne, all of whom brought the manuscript through the complex process of production with a high degree of professionalism, cooperation and support and worked on marketing and publicity.

I want to thank my parents Inna and Soltan Dzarasov, who were a constant source of support and encouragement for me during all my years of work. My dear friends Christine and David Cole, Barbara, Jim and Edward Granter, Tricia and Alan Jones, Ishbel and Douglas Mair deserve a few words here for their help in improving my English and introducing me to English culture and the way of life, and, of course, for their magnificent hospitality which was a great relief from the hardships of my work in the UK. I am grateful to my schoolteacher Irina Voloshko who patiently taught me English when I was a teenager and not so easy to deal with.

Unless otherwise indicated, translations from Russian sources are my own.

It goes without saying that I am the only person to be blamed for any deficiencies in the work.

Introduction

On the eve of the market reforms in Russia in the early 1990s, the prominent Russian television journalist Vladimir Pozner organised a talk-show with the provocative title 'Do We Need Capitalism?'. The broadcast was seen as a triumph for liberals over supposedly backward opponents of the new system. Stanislav Shatalin, a highly regarded economist of the time, explained the essence of the new 'one true doctrine'[1] to viewers in a simple analogy: 'Imagine a small pie, cut into equal pieces. That's socialism. Now imagine a big pie, cut into unequal pieces. Even the small pieces of the second pie are much bigger than in the first. That's capitalism.' Another guest on the programme then pointed to the simple, straightforward road said to lead to the promised consumer paradise: the state should get out of the economy. This, it was argued, meant that the state should make way for ordinary citizens.

During the same period, Russian television was also running an advertisement informing viewers of the 'democratic purpose' of the changes that were under way. Shown first was a map of Russia, covered with smoking factory chimneys and electrical transmission lines. For the benefit of the dim-witted, the voice-over explained: 'This is the entire wealth of the country.' Then a piece of a factory was cut from this map; 'And here's your share!' The piece was transformed into a voucher which in the hand of an anxious Russian, who proceeded to scratch his head energetically while the voice-over asked, 'What do you do with a voucher?'

On Pozner's talk-show, he had explained with enthusiasm that privatisation opened the way to rapid enrichment for every Russian citizen: 'Get together with your family and decide how to use your vouchers. You might open your own business. Remember, you can now decide your future and that of your children and grandchildren.' Pozner's last words here turned out to be the only morsel of truth uttered in this and numerous other broadcasts, though his words were true in a sense completely different from the one he intended. Before long, ordinary Russians who had obediently accepted the reforms were to witness an unprecedented decline in production and fall in their living standards, the criminalisation of society, the collapse of the education and health care systems, and the transformation of Russia into a semi-dependent state. The national income 'pie' had not only been divided into highly unequal pieces, but had also become stale and hollowed-out.

The collapse of the hopes which Russians held for capitalism has a significance that extends far beyond Russia and its people. Studies are now being published which argue that the former Soviet bloc countries as a whole, not just the sometime republics of the USSR, are resuming their earlier status on the periphery of western Europe.[2]

The greatest hopes held out for the future of Russian society were connected with private entrepreneurship. This, it was anticipated, would set right the evils and inefficiencies of the state bureaucracy. Under 'socialism', it was widely accepted, property belonged to no one. Now, with the transfer of the former state enterprises to private owners, the latter would properly look after their newly acquired assets, introducing efficient management, making long-term investments in modern technologies, and maximising their businesses' long-term growth and that of the economy as a whole. This would improve Russia's competitiveness in international markets for high-tech products, and would usher in the society of abundance that western-style consumerism was believed to represent. The reality of Russian big business proved, of course, to be utterly different.

Here, it is revealing to examine one of the Russian oligarchs' personal history (Klebnikov 2000). When economic reforms began opening up opportunities for private entrepreneurship in the late 1980s, Boris Berezovsky was a mathematician in his forties working for the Russian Academy of Sciences. As a Russian '*biznesmen*', Berezovsky abstained from creating any new productive business structure. Instead, as early as 1989, he founded a trading company named Logovaz, associated with the giant Russian enterprise Avtovaz. The latter produced cars whose popularity was attributable to their low price. Two elements of his auto trading were crucial in Berezovsky's rapid transformation into one of the wealthiest people in Russia: a personal connection with the managers of a major Russian enterprise, and an international financial network constructed so as to bleed that enterprise of cash flow (ibid.: 72). Logovaz bought cars very cheaply, and then resold them at market prices. Huge sums were embezzled, using a chain of financial institutions including reputable foreign firms and shell firms established in offshore tax havens. Eventually, revenues were accumulated in private accounts held by Berezovsky and a few top Avtovaz managers.

With the Soviet Union's demise in 1991 and the launching of Yeltsin's radical economic reforms in 1992, Berezovsky rapidly expanded his empire. He moved into the commodity export business, exploiting the different domestic- and world-market prices for oil, timber and aluminium. To conceal his growing control over some of the most lucrative former state assets, he established a Swiss-registered company, Forus Services SA. Among the company's other founders were a representative of Avtovaz and a Swiss commodities trading company. Forus Services' ownership structure was anything but transparent. Screening the true owners' identity were other foreign companies, including Forus Holding (Luxembourg), whose shares in turn belonged to other corporate bodies. In formal terms, Forus Services SA was a financial company that provided services to Russian companies operating abroad. But in reality, it was a holding company, owning the most important enterprises of Berezovsky's growing empire (ibid.: 89).

In 1993, Berezovsky set up Avva, an infamous investment structure which became a textbook example of a Russian-style Ponzi scheme. This joint venture between Avtovaz and General Motors was widely reported as preparing to manufacture a 'people's car', a project that would allow ordinary Russians to obtain a car cheaply, would bring good returns to investors, and would ensure prosperity to all of Russia. General Motors eventually quit the agreement after realising the level of criminality in the Russian car industry. Avva's finances were blatantly embezzled, the whole scheme collapsed within a few years, and private investors lost their money (ibid.: 140–43).

Unlike most of the future Russian oligarchs, Berezovsky did not participate in the early 1990s voucher privatisation. The smart former mathematician was among the first to realise that under the conditions of nascent gangster capitalism, what one needed to obtain was not so much formal property rights as firm control over the enterprises involved. '"The first stage" [and the most important one] of doing business in Russia', Berezovsky explained, 'is privatisation of profits' (ibid.: 170). Although Berezovsky would later consolidate his control through share acquisition, his hold over financial flows would remain of prime importance. To achieve 'privatisation of profits', one needed to do exactly as Berezovsky did at Avtovaz, that is, establish special relations with top managers at a targeted enterprise, or promote one's own team to these positions. As explained earlier, such a tacit takeover could put powerful intermediaries in a position where they could withdraw a significant portion of the firm's financial flows for private appropriation. This strategy worked regardless of whether the firm was in private or state hands. The same approach was applied later at an even more lucrative enterprise, a Russian crown jewel, the state airline Aeroflot.

In this case, Berezovsky managed to oust the old general director, a veteran of the industry, and replace him with his own protégé. In 1994, a new profit centre was established, a Swiss-based financial company known as Andava SA, whose main owners were Berezovsky himself and his partner at Logovaz; but Andava was affiliated with a number of other companies in offshore tax havens. Andava was entrusted with managing the revenues from Aeroflot's entire world network. After passing through a chain of financial intermediaries, these finances were eventually accumulated in private accounts held by Berezovsky and his accomplices (ibid.: 170–87).

Berezovsky was one of the first to realise that under the conditions of Russia's emerging capitalism it was impossible to survive in big business without strong political support. The Russian tycoon succeeded in establishing close ties with the country's first president, Boris Yeltsin, providing him with valuable financial services. To strengthen his political positions, Berezovsky sought and attained control over one of the most influential television channels in Russia, ORT. In 1996, he rallied other Russian oligarchs to help Yeltsin win what became acknowledged as the most corrupt presidential election campaign in post-Soviet Russian history. Yeltsin paid handsomely for this financial aid. In the course of the inglorious loans-for-shares auctions, the privatisation programme's biggest fraud, Berezovsky obtained a big stake in the oil industry for virtually nothing. Furthermore, he was rewarded with the influential position of deputy chairman of the National Security Council. This was in brazen violation of the law, which prohibits state functionaries from being involved in business.

It is impossible not to mention Berezovsky's extensive ties with the criminal underworld. For many years, his closest business partner was the notorious Georgian gangster Badri Patarkatsishvily, the association ending only with the latter's death under obscure circumstances. With help from this network of connections, Berezovsky emerged victorious from a series of appalling mob wars. Literally hundreds of people perished in a struggle for control of Avtovaz from which the tycoon emerged triumphant. Berezovsky took over the lucrative advertising business at the television channel ORT after his rival Vladislav Listyev, at that time the most popular journalist in Russia, was shot dead in the lobby of his block of flats. For many years, including during his tenure at the National Security Council, the oligarch maintained ties with Chechen warlords involved in kidnappings for ransom. Aleksandr Litvinenko, a former KGB officer allegedly poisoned by Russian spies in the UK, was for years involved in criminal violence in Russia and served as an agent for Berezovsky within the secret services. This is a far-from-complete list of the Russian oligarch's criminal activities, which were the prime sources of his fabulous wealth.

In the years after 2000, fortune at last turned its back on Berezovsky. Hoping to strengthen his own political influence, the tycoon personally aided Vladimir Putin in his rise to power. The new Russian president, however, was reluctant to share this power with anyone, and in a masterstroke of Byzantine politics, drove his former supporter into exile. Finding a safe haven in the UK, Berezovsky has never reconciled himself to losing his position at the top of the Russian oligarchy, remaining consumed with personal hatred for his arch-rival and continuously pursuing a clandestine anti-Putin vendetta. Not surprisingly, the Russian population generally approves of Berezovsky's expulsion from Russia, as well as that of several other oligarchs, viewing the protection given by the British to the outrageous 'robber baron' as a sign of western hypocrisy.

Putin, however, has never challenged the foundations of the oligarchic regime in post-Soviet Russia. Other tycoons who do not meddle in high politics are permitted to indulge in the same activities as Berezovsky's, striving to control the management and financial flows of enterprises, bribing state functionaries, occasionally murdering their business rivals, and above all siphoning off revenues to offshore tax havens. As a result, empirical evidence shows Russian big business to be oriented strongly to the short term (see Chapters 3 and 4), that is, seeking to extract current monies rather than to maximise long-term growth (see Chapter 5). The average age of the machines used in Russian industry now exceeds twenty years, while in the Soviet era it was less than ten. The condition of fixed capital stock (see Chapter 6) indicates that Russian big business frequently prefers to invest in low-quality obsolete equipment, and that it often fails even to maintain current production levels. Contrary to the Russian public's expectations, the Russian economy's structure has changed dramatically in favour of extractive industries, to the detriment of high-tech and even traditional industrial sectors.

Here, the conundrum of Russian capitalism finds its expression. Why do Russian enterprise owners show so little interest in long-term investment, and why is the investment they favour so inferior? To what extent is this situation a hangover from the degeneration of the Soviet system, and to what extent does it reflect the impacts of global, financialised capitalism? These are the core topics this book will explore.

In the author's view, two major formative influences have shaped modern Russia's social system: world capitalism at the present stage of its history, and the legacy of the Stalinist society that existed in the USSR. Chapter 1 will begin with a brief discussion of the first of these factors.

Following the collapse of the Soviet bloc, foreign direct investment by western transnational corporations (TNCs) and the industri-alisation of the periphery of world capitalism unfolded on a scale unparalleled in history. The labour pool available to global capitalism effectively doubled, with some 1.5 billion workers in China, India and the former USSR now available for exploitation, often at outrageously low wage rates (Freeman 2010). On the semi-developed margins of the capitalist world-system, a huge over-capacity was created as an unprecedented accumulation of capital took place. Even though wage growth was suppressed on a world scale, manufacturing profitability declined. Against this backdrop, the attractions of financial speculation increased, shifting the focus of capital from manufacturing to capital markets. The financialisation of the capitalist core proceeded apace.

The transformation of US corporations from managerial firms to financialised structures is one of the most notorious developments of recent economic history. Until the 1970s, a signal feature of corporate America was the separation of ownership from control. Shareholdings were too diluted to allow the domination by shareholders of day-to-day corporate decision making, a function which resided with the managers. The latter sought to maximise their organisations' long-term growth, since their own welfare depended on the growth of the firms they administered, not on current dividends. Nevertheless, major companies were always prey to the contradiction, underscored by Marx and Veblen, between their long-term interests as going concerns and the attractions of short-term financial gains: 'For thirty years after World War II, investment opportunities were good enough in general … that financial interests did not try to interfere with strategies to retain and reinvest' (Blair 1993: 5).

Accumulation of capital on a world scale, however, exacerbated capitalism's inner contradictions. Once western Europe and Japan had rebuilt their economies and emerged as effective rivals to the US, international competition exacerbated and undermined profits, leading to the 'stagflation' of the 1970s. This decline in the profitability of investment in productive capacity gave rise to the 'Shareholder Revolution' of the 1980s, with a wave of mergers and acquisitions rolling over the US economy (Ho 2009). The Shareholder Revolution overcame the separation of ownership and control and ended the relative independence of managers. US corporations were ruthlessly downsized, restructured and stripped of assets, while their investment funds were severely curtailed. The goal was to increase dividends and boost share prices. As the prime object of corporate strategy, increasing current shareholder value supplanted long-term growth.

Under the new conditions, a growing share of internally generated funds began to be directed to dividend payments and share buybacks (Milberg and Winkler 2010). This compelled US corporations to outsource production to regions with low wages, forming global production networks (Blair 2009). However, it was only labour-intensive chains of production with low levels of value added that were moved abroad; control by western TNCs over high value-adding processes was meanwhile strengthened. The results have included an increase in the exploitation of labour in both foreign and domestic settings. Among the prime vehicles of this process has been a redistribution of incomes through the mediation of financial markets.

This has created demand on the part of big business for financial assets at the expense of investment funds. In the 2000s, the share of financial assets came to exceed the share of productive assets in the capital structure of the US non-financial corporate sector (Orhangazi 2008).

Summing up the above, one can say that *the modern financialised capitalist world-system values short-term pecuniary gain much more highly than long-term growth of productive capacities.* As will be shown, this had a fundamental effect on nascent Russian big business. To really understand modern Russian capitalism's roots, however, requires a grasp of the manner in which the Soviet bureaucracy evolved in the environment created by global capitalism toward the end of the twentieth century. This is the main task of Chapter 2.

The Soviet system[3] arose out of the Russian Revolution of 1917, an upheaval which in essence represented a revolt by the periphery of the capitalist world-system against its core. As characterised by Trotsky (2004), Soviet society was strictly a transitional form; that is, it represented only an attempt at building socialism, and as such, it combined elements of socialism and capitalism in a contradictory manner. As a result of its low initial level of economic and social development, coupled with cultural backwardness, Soviet society gave rise to a new privileged ruling elite: the party and state bureaucracy. The ascendancy to power of the bureaucracy, reflected in Stalin's victories in the Communist Party during the mid-to-late 1920s, marked the 'Thermidor' or bourgeois degeneration of the Russian Revolution. This phenomenon distorted the development of the Soviet system in fundamental ways.

Soviet society accorded workers many important economic and social (though not political) rights, but at the same time generated inequalities of new kinds. Excessively centralised planning, reflecting the bureaucracy's power over society, brought with it the violation of economic proportions. An important manifestation of this distortion of central planning was the bureaucracy's arbitrary power to control income distribution. As its industries developed, Soviet society also experienced an increasing growth of informal control by the bureaucracy over economic resources, allowing the bureaucrats to appropriate private incomes on the basis of public property. The shift from an agrarian to a predominantly urban society brought with it an inner differentiation within the bureaucracy and intelligentsia, singling out diverse social strata and groups with differing and often conflicting interests. Under the conditions of an authoritarian state, this led to growing discontent among the bureaucracy and intelligentsia with the egalitarian aspects of the Soviet system (Lane 2011).

These social contradictions of Soviet society were exacerbated in the mid-1970s as the country's cheaper and more accessible sources of raw materials approached exhaustion, and as economic growth declined in consequence (Yaremenko 1997). Against the expectations of Gorbachev and the majority of observers, perestroika and democratisation in the late 1980s led to the formation of a powerful pro-capitalist bloc of social forces, made up of representatives from the ruling bureaucracy and intelligentsia. These forces succeeded in dismantling the Soviet system and central planning, and ushered in the transition to capitalism (Kotz and Weir 2007: 107–11).

The radical market reforms that were launched in early 1992 had their roots in the notorious 'Washington Consensus', devised by leading Washington-based financial institutions for application to developing countries. Through their main measures, the economic reforms contributed directly or indirectly to legalising informal control over Russia's productive potential by new owners who came from the ranks of the former Soviet bureaucracy (that is, the administrative class), intelligentsia (the appropriating class) and the criminal underworld.

In sum, the transition from the Soviet system to capitalism was a logical outcome of the Stalinist degeneration of the Russian Revolution. Through a process of interaction and mutual reinforcement, the Soviet bureaucracy's decadence and the influence of financialised global capitalism strengthened and entrenched the informal control exercised over productive assets by bureaucrats and criminals. This situation left an indelible imprint on the Russian business elite.

As Chapter 3 demonstrates, the actual forms of ownership and control that emerged in Russian enterprises were shaped by the wave of privatisation that began in the early 1990s. World 'best practice' in the field of privatisation includes distributing property rights over state enterprises to a range of their stakeholders, focusing on improving the performance of the former state enterprises, and close public monitoring of the whole process (Vuylsteke 1994). By contrast, the Russian reformers' primary goal was to guarantee that the dismantled Soviet system would *never* revive. Therefore, they aimed at creating a new business elite as quickly as possible at whatever the cost. This unscrupulous aim fitted perfectly both with the interests of the triumphant pro-capitalist coalition and with the needs of its western supporters. Privatisation in Russia was organised in a way that created widespread opportunities for abuses of the legal system by state bureaucrats and criminals, and enabled them to gain control over the most profitable enterprises (Freeland 2011). Large-scale undervaluation of former state enterprises was one of the principal means through which a handful of oligarchs acquired huge personal wealth. An increasing concentration of production and capital and the emergence of a corporate sector in the Russian economy then ensued.

At the initial stage of privatisation, the ownership structure of Russian enterprises was characterised by a predominance of insiders. Later, a redistribution of equities took place in favour of owner-outsiders (Dolgopyatova 2005), who began to dominate Russian enterprises and whom I describe as 'big insiders'. This situation shaped the Russian corporate governance model fundamentally (Dzarasov 2011a). Due to inadequate law enforcement, formal ownership rights in modern Russia cannot be exercised if they are not backed by control over the enterprises. The big insiders' power is based on the infrastructure of control – a network of formal and informal institutions that enables them to manage both the firm's internal and external environments. Criminal coercion and ties of corruption with the state are indispensable features of this infrastructure. Thus, the modern pattern of Russian corporate governance is characterised by the inseparability of ownership and control. This resembles the domination of shareholders in US corporations, but has a more direct and violent form.

Waves of redistribution of property among rival groups of big insiders sweep periodically across the Russian economy (Radygin 1999). The overwhelming majority of these takeovers are adversarial in character and are enforced through criminal coercion. Raiding has become a distinct sector of the Russian economy, with its own market for services and with a large annual turnover. Hostile takeovers primarily threaten big insiders who have failed to create an infrastructure of control strong enough to protect their dominant positions. Russian business is therefore characterised by a fundamental instability of ownership and control. This instability has very deep and far-reaching repercussions.

Threatened constantly with losing control over their enterprises, Russian big insiders are reluctant to commit themselves to long-term investment. The short-termism that stems from this uncertainty has an enormous effect on the objectives of Russian firms, which do not seek to maximise long-term growth, but rather 'insider rent'. This latter term refers to income which the dominant groups derive from their control over the firms' financial flows. Insider rent is appropriated from sources which include cuts to enterprise wage funds, depreciation funds and investments. Usually, insider rent is withdrawn from an enterprise and is accumulated in private accounts held by the big insiders in offshore sites. This type of income is short, or at best, medium term in nature, and the possibility of appropriating it is conditioned by the infrastructure of insider control over assets.

Insider rent is formed by surplus value, since its major part is ultimately reducible to the product of unpaid labour, and at times to the appropriation of wage incomes created outside the capitalist sector. Since insider rent is extracted using the infrastructure of control, it has certain features of feudal rent, along with the features of entrepreneurial profit. This dual character of insider rent reflects the ambiguous nature of Russian capitalism itself, with its origins in degenerate Stalinist society and global capitalism.

The Russian domestic market is stunted as a result of the increased income inequality caused by insider rent extraction. Investment by particular companies declines as funds are siphoned off by the dominant groups within these firms. The extraction of insider rent undermines the income of minority shareholders, of managers who do not belong to the dominant group, and of workers. Numerous corporate conflicts, increased opportunistic behaviour by employees, and worker unrest ensue, with the result that the dominant group is compelled to increase its investment in the infrastructure of control in order to supress these conflicts. All this undermines investment in enhancing capacity and product development. Insider control therefore curtails the supply of funds to Russian corporations.

Insider rent extraction also has the effect of raising the interest rates that apply to the internal generation and borrowing of funds, thus further diminishing the finances available for investment. At the same time, insider rent undermines the need for investment; due to growing inequality and the consequent shrinkage of the domestic market, the corporate profits expected from investing in productive capacity are low. As a result, Russian corporations often reject large projects with long pay-back periods. Since these projects are usually of crucial importance, long-term business prospects deteriorate sharply. The short-termism of Russian big insiders and their consequent propensity to rent extraction are exacerbated by the danger of hostile takeover attempts, a threat that increases to the degree that longer-term investment makes firms more profitable.

Insider rent extraction thus fuels corporate conflicts, increases the probability of hostile takeovers, and ultimately undermines the accumulation of capital by Russian big business. These effects have a profound impact on economic growth in Russia, as is discussed in Chapter 5.

Economic growth depends crucially on the price structures that exist within the national economy. Those industries in which the mark-up on unit costs of production is greater enjoy higher profits and, hence, better investment opportunities. Departing from his model of a typical corporation, Alfred Eichner formulates the 'value condition of growth, meaning the existence of a group of industry prices which covers both the costs of current production and the costs of expansion at the level of full employment' (Eichner 1991: 338). The relative size of mark-ups determines the distribution of financial flows among industries; sectors with greater mark-ups, and hence greater profits, obtain greater funds. The ability of prices to cover current production and expansion costs, and hence the value condition of growth itself, depends on the technologies applied in the national economy as well. Consequently, the price balance between different industries within the national economy is very delicate. In capitalist society, this balance depends not on the needs of different industries if full employment is to be achieved, but on the relative power of various industrial groups of capitalists.

Russia's economy provides a classic example of price disparity. The country has two unequal groups of industries, with prices growing relatively faster and slower than average. The first group includes the fuel-energy complex, ferrous and non-ferrous metallurgy, foodstuffs production, transport, and a number of segments of other industries. All other industries and segments are part of the second group. The companies of the privileged sector are in a position to limit the supply of their products to the domestic market since they can export their output abroad. This power over the domestic market manifests itself in the form of domestic price increases. Accordingly, manufacturing costs surge in uncontrolled fashion, and capital is transferred from this sector to the raw-materials and extractive industries (Dzarasov 2011a, 2011b). The Russian economy's price structure shows that big insiders in the privileged sector and in the industries that are among the victims of disparity appropriate revenues differently, both in amount and in kind. Mark-ups on unit costs in the first sector grow faster than in the second sector, because they include a greater share of insider rent. This difference in prices reflects the difference in market power of distinct industrial groups of big insiders. Due to their greater mark-ups, capitalists within the privileged sector redistribute capital from the unprivileged sector to their advantage. The fact that this privileged position with regard to price disparity accrues to big insiders within exporting industries that feature low levels of raw-materials processing reflects the semi-peripheral position of Russia in the world system.

Chapter 6 provides empirical evidence to substantiate the main propositions set out above. Since direct data on the informal relationships peculiar to Russian enterprises are lacking, and the official data on accumulation of capital in Russia are unreliable, I have relied on surveys of Russian enterprises and on three case studies. These provide insights, from different perspectives, into the intrinsic mechanisms of large-scale Russian 'biznes'.

All three case studies provide evidence that in Russian enterprises, informal control is associated with the inseparability of ownership and management. These studies support the idea that the fundamental instability of insider control leads big insiders to operate on a short-term time horizon. The case of Chimprom demonstrates that in the course of a fierce struggle for control, the rival groups of dominant owners did not concern themselves with long-term investment strategies. The case of Volgakabel suggests that even if the contending groups reach a temporary alliance, they are too suspicious of potential opportunistic behaviour on the part of their rivals to develop any sound long-term investment policy. However, the case of a relatively prosperous company, Pechoraneft, indicates that where insider control is stable, big insiders can adopt a longer time horizon.

Overall, the case studies and surveys of Russian enterprises show that the greater the portion of the firm's financial flows appropriated by big insiders, the more intensive intra-firm conflicts are likely to be; the greater the potential for intra-firm conflicts, the greater the infrastructure of control that is developed; and the shorter the time horizon of big insiders and the greater the portion of funds extracted as rent, the lower the volume and quality of the firm's investment. A further conclusion is that within the Russian economy's corporate sector, inferior investment strategies are dominant. Although the general evidence from the surveys implies short-termism, it does not establish a direct link to flawed investment strategies. Such direct links are demonstrated by the case studies. Volgakabel and Chimprom provide classic examples of short-termism, while Pechoraneft's history shows that even big insiders within the privileged sector are limited to a medium-term time horizon. The empirical evidence set forward in Chapter 6 indicates that the particular type of corporate governance peculiar to modern Russian corporations forms a major institutional obstacle to the investment required for effective growth of the national economy.

In sumary, I would like to emphasise that the present work seeks to explain modern Russian capitalism as an integral phenomenon. The ideas advanced have their basis in Marxist theory, which holds that the key features of capitalist society can be explained using the concept of surplus value. I identify insider rent as a specific form which surplus value assumes in modern Russian society. This concept allows researchers to comprehend the short-term aims of Russian corporations, their inferior investment strategies, the mechanisms of corporate pricing in Russia and the phenomenon of price disparity, the backward technological and distorted industrial structure of the Russian economy, and ultimately, the position of modern Russia as part of the semi-periphery of the world capitalist system.

1

Global Accumulation and the Capitalist World-system

1 Introduction

This first chapter provides a general framework for analysis of the Russian economy as part of the current capitalist world-system. A brief review of the main features of this world-system is necessary for discussing both the major formative factors of modern Russian society and its position in the world. The chapter begins from the Marxian perspective of capitalism as a society in which appropriation of value dominates over production of use-value. This approach is found to be in accordance with a Veblenian emphasis on a deep contradiction between the industrial and financial logic of the capitalist business enterprise. This contradiction finds its salient expression in the opposition that exists between the enterprise as a going concern and its share value. In the so-called 'Golden Age of Capitalism', from the late 1940s to the early 1970s, the typical US corporation was characterised by separation of ownership and control, the latter function residing with the managers. These were times when it was more or less possible to reconcile the contradictory interests of different stakeholders by paying relatively high wages and sound dividends, while at the same time making necessary investments in expanding and renovating productive capacity.

The 'Shareholder Revolution' of the 1980s transformed the US model of corporate governance: big business was compelled to sacrifice long-term growth for the sake of short-term benefits for the owners.

This drastic shift initiated deep changes in the capitalist world-system. Material production was largely shifted from the US and other core capitalist countries to their periphery, with the aim of exploiting cheap labour. Global production networks were established, in which high value-added processes resided with western multinational corporations and low value-added processes were moved abroad. Financial and speculative capital increasingly supplanted productive capital in the core countries, while state, corporate and consumer debt soared both in the core and on the periphery. From the emerging system of intensive global exploitation of labour, a growing gap appeared between global aggregate demand and global aggregate supply, thus engendering the current global economic crisis.

The second section of this chapter provides a brief review of the Marxian 'duality of labour' approach to analysing capitalism, and of Veblen's concept of the dual nature of the capitalist enterprise. The third section takes up the issue of the Eichnerian 'megacorp', which is characterised by a separation of ownership and management and having long-term growth as its prime objective. The fourth section focuses on the so-called 'Shareholder Revolution' through which the separation of ownership and control was overcome, and maximising shareholder value replaced long-term growth as the corporation's main goal. Various facets of the financialisation of the US non-financial corporate sector are examined. Using a global value-chains approach, the fifth section then examines the shifting of production to low-wage countries. This phenomenon is interpreted as both a result of financialisation, and an important factor in allowing it to proceed. The sixth section examines the shift of investment strategies of US non-financial corporations from productive to financial goals, with the corresponding changes in the structure of capital. The seventh section reveals how financialisation and growing exploitation of the periphery led to the current world economic crisis, while the final section provides some concluding remarks.

2   Marx and Veblen on the Duality of Capital and Enterprise

Marx's vision of the income of capitalists is based on his concept of the duality of labour (Afanas'ev et al. 1986) and on the 'ascent from the abstract to the concrete' (Dzarasov 2010a). The commodity – the point of departure of the Marxian system – embodies the dichotomy in which use-value is the product of concrete labour, and value is the product of abstract labour. These are opposing characteristics – as use-values, all commodities are different, while as values they are all identical.[1] At the same time, they do not exist without each other, since the only labour that creates value is that which creates use-value. This dichotomy of labour conditions duality as the main structural characteristic of capitalist economic relations at all steps of the ascent from the abstract to the concrete. Using this perspective, many obscure aspects of the question confronted here can be unravelled.

Capital thus has its material form, represented by an array of commodities (productive equipment, labour power, raw materials, output, inventories, and the like). But it cannot, as the neoclassical school assumes, be reduced to the property of yielding a return, the reason being that capital is represented by a definite quantity of value embodied in the capital goods.[2] Ostensibly, capitalist production is about supplying commodities or services. However, its main aim is the production of value, use-value being only a means to that end. Marx saw the nature of capitalist profit as being manifested in the phenomenon of surplus value, that is, in the product of unpaid labour appropriated by capitalists. From this source stem the other types of income that dominate in a mature capitalist economy:

> Up to the present, political economy ... has never separated surplus-value from profit, and never even considered profit in its pure form as distinct from its different, independent components, such as industrial profit, commercial profit, interest, and ground-rent. (Marx 1959 [1894]: 146)

Elsewhere, Marx adds taxes to the components into which profit is divided (see, for instance, ibid.: 32). Thus, the whole variety of the incomes accruing to capitalists is seen as resulting from a transformation of surplus value that takes place in the sphere of distribution and exchange, hence resulting from the exploitation of hired labour. The domination of value over use-value as the aim of capitalist production has important repercussions.

One of the most important is that appropriation of surplus value is not the only means of exploitation under capitalism. Marx also considered 'profit upon alienation or expropriation', 'resulting from zero-sum transactions that relate to money revenue or existing stocks of money, accruing through transactions in financial or real assets' (Lapavistas and Levina 2011: 8). In contrast to surplus value, this kind of profit is not predicated on the creation of new value, but supposes a redistribution of value that already exists. Marx demonstrated this through his theory of the 'primitive' or 'original' accumulation of capital, using such examples as the 'enclosures' through which commoners were deprived of their rights over the land and peasants were coerced into become hired labourers: the destruction of pre-capitalist modes of production, the plunder of colonies, slavery, and usury. In none of these activities was new wealth created, but redistribution of already existing values took place. 'All the features of primitive accumulation that Marx mentions have remained powerfully present within capitalism's historical geography up until now,' argues David Harvey in his persuasive account of the 'new imperialism'. This can be seen in the neocolonial exploitation of the periphery of the capitalist world-system, involving the displacement of peasants and their conversion into landless proletarians, the privatisation of public services and many other destructive activities (Harvey 2003: 145). Above all, this type of income appropriation is peculiar to modern finances. Since 'profit by alienation or expropriation' has marked not only the dawn of the capitalist era but its entire history, Harvey calls it 'accumulation by dispossession' rather than 'original accumulation'. These ideas are commensurate with Veblen's account of capitalism.

The founder of institutionalism distinguished between the logic of industrial and pecuniary business (Veblen 1936). The logic of industrial business requires understanding an enterprise as a going concern, and favours the 'uninterrupted interplay of the various processes which make up the industrial system' (ibid.: 27). Modern industry, Veblen argues, has become so intertwined on a world scale that disturbances to established supplies and deliveries cause increasing damage to the community at large. However, the aim of the so-called 'captains of industry' is pecuniary gain, not the common good. There is thus a deep contradiction between the industrial and pecuniary logic of capitalism, and the former is often sacrificed to benefit the latter.

Within Veblen's approach, it is not difficult to discern a modification of Marx's notion of the duality of labour. Indeed, Veblenian industrial logic corresponds to the processes of concrete and pecuniary logic – to the processes of abstract labour. The domination of value over use-value under capitalism engenders not only increases in production, but also from time to time 'a set-back to industrial plants'. This can be treated as accumulation by dispossession. Veblen related this type of enrichment to the vestiges of predatory behaviour in pre-industrial societies. Under capitalism, such behaviour resurfaces with the ascendancy of finances. The strategising of each capitalist 'is commonly directed against other business interests and his ends are commonly accomplished by the help of some form of pecuniary coercion' (ibid.: 31–2). Here the vital link between finances and coercion is established (Henry 2012).

Meanwhile, financial capital and its dynamics make up another important area in which the principle of the duality of labour applies at the new level of the ascent from the abstract to the concrete. The value of labour in its purest form is represented by money. Since capital in the form of money is central to the capitalist mode of production, finances take on an apparently independent existence in the form of interest-bearing and loanable capital (Lapavistas and Levina 2011). Taking economic relations at a superficial level, it may seem that money when employed in financial markets produces money. But nothing can sever financial from productive capital, because it is only in the sphere of production that new value is created, while financial markets merely redistribute it. The deceptive appearance of money creates 'a world of illusion' disguising fraud and alienation (Henry 2012).

In summary, the '"organic relation" between expanded reproduction on the one hand and often violent processes of dispossession on the other' may be said to have 'shaped the historical geography of capitalism' (Harvey 2003: 141–2).

3 The Megacorporation and Shareholder Power

Among the tacit assumptions underlying the Marshallian 'representative firm', one is particularly prominent: that it is owned and managed by the same individual. This expresses one of the most important neoclassical tenets: that the shareholder should be seen as an owner-entrepreneur: 'The neoclassical theory of the modern corporation, then, combined the notions of private property, ownership, self-interest, and profit maximization in the body of shareholder' (Ho 2009: 175). This presupposes a fusion of ownership and control that was characteristic only of the period prior to large-scale modern industry, when enterprises were small and owners oversaw their operations. Things changed dramatically with the concentration of production and centralisation of capital in the late nineteenth and early twentieth centuries. Business in the United States at that time was already remote from the neoclassical parable of the 'rational economic man'.

Since the publication of the classic text *The Modern Corporation and Private Property* by Adolf Berle and Gardiner Means (1932), it has been recognised that the emergence of big corporations in advanced market economies and the dispersion of shares among shareholders has led to the separation of ownership from control, with the latter in the hands of the managers. It is important that 'historically the rise of the corporation had been accompanied by a shift in power from the shareholders to the controllers of the corporation' (Lee 1998: 22), contradicting the neoclassical owner-entrepreneur model. Until the 1980s, and in stark contrast to the neoclassical position, it was widely believed that separation of ownership and control made the 'managerial firm' a long-term growth maximiser. The megacorp model of the American post-Keynesian Alfred Eichner (1938–88) provides a well-known example of such a vision (Eichner 1991, 1976, 1973).

The Eichnerian megacorp was the typical, representative corporation of the US manufacturing sector in the so-called 'Golden Age of Capitalism' from the late 1940s through the early 1970s. The defining features of the megacorp were: (a) separation of ownership and control, the latter function residing with the managers, (b) fixed production coefficients-constant average direct costs, and (c) an oligopolistic industry structure. Eichner believed that separation of ownership from management extended the megacorp's time horizon in the long run, making its prime objective the maximisation of long-term growth rather than short-term profit. This was held to be the case because the welfare of managers, when salaries and non-pecuniary privileges were determined, depended not on the size of dividends but on the firm's long-term market position. As a result, investment strategy became the prime factor underlying the megacorp's pricing decisions. Meanwhile corporate performance, even if apparently successful, could embody some important contradictions.

Berle and Means saw the reason for separation of ownership and control in 'the difference between the time for which the capital is needed by the enterprise and the period for which the investor desires to tie up his wealth' (1968: 248). An enterprise needs long-term investment to keep going, while an investor wants quick returns. This means that unlike the logic of industrial business, the logic of financial business is short-term and myopic. The needs of financial business are met using the liquid assets of financial markets.

Non-financial corporations, representing physical property, are essentially immobile, since they demand constant 'service of human beings, managers, and operators'. For the sake of financiers, they are therefore complemented by shares, which are nothing else but 'a set of tokens, passing from hand to hand, liquid to a degree, requiring little or no human attention' (ibid.: 251). Thus, to meet the different time horizons of the owners and other stakeholders, corporate property is split into liquid and non-liquid forms. Contrary to the neoclassical narrative of the shareholder-manager, liquid property can be priced by the stock exchange because it is separate from corporations. Consequently, the logic of financial business receives its own material expression and becomes partially independent of its industrial foundations. This assumes that opposed, contradictory social interests lie hidden behind the façade of the 'firm as a united family'.

This duality of the modern corporation is expressed in two sets of values associated with it: the price of productive capacity (fixed property) and the price of shares (liquid property), appearing 'one above the other, related but not the same' (ibid.: 250).

Veblen related the excess of share prices over the value of productive capacity to goodwill, seen as constituting the intangible assets of corporations as opposed to their tangible, productive property. Further, Veblen makes a very important point when he relates these assets to a monopoly position that a business enterprise may hold (Veblen 1936: 142–3).

Since the main aim of capitalism is to appropriate surplus value, financial interests represented by shareholders neglect the interests of managers and of society at large. It is goodwill, which reflects corporations' monopoly power, that inflates their stock over the value of immobile, productive property. Here we find the source of the tendency for the processes of abstract labour to free themselves from those of concrete labour.

4 Financialisation and the 'Shareholder Revolution'

As noted above, the Eichnerian model reflected the realities of the post-Second World War 'Golden Age of Capitalism'. In the decades from the 1980s through the 2000s, financialisation led to significant changes in the fundamental processes which determine the development of capitalism. Arrighi (2010) defined financialisation as a particular type of accumulation of capital in which profit increasingly is appropriated through investing money in financial markets, rather than in productive capacities. I will treat this phenomenon as an increasing substitution of fictitious capital (see below) for productive capital.

Financial capital seeks to stand apart from productive capital, but as explained earlier, it is tied to the latter by the simple fact that new value is created only in the productive sphere, and is merely redistributed by financial markets. The vital connection between tangible and intangible assets is explained by the Marxian theory of fictitious capital. If credit is extended to an enterprise to expand production, it is validated eventually through the creation of new value. However, if the amount of loaned funds systematically exceeds the labour product, financial capital becomes fictitious (Harvey 2006: 253). This is revealed painfully in times of crises when financial assets suddenly depreciate.

It should be remembered that the two aspects of labour are part of the same indissoluble phenomenon. This identity in diversity is necessary to establish the link between finances and coercion. When the intermediation of finances is incomplete, which is obviously the case with fictitious capital, new value is not produced and financial gain is obtained through dispossession (Lapavistas and Levina 2011). Why did financialisation in the above-mentioned sense come about?

Arrighi (2010) illustrates that there is always a point in the long cycles of accumulation when the capitalist world-system grows beyond the resource limits of a hegemonic country, be it Venice, Spain, Holland, Britain, or the US. At such moments of history, increased international competition in the market for goods depresses profits and engenders over-accumulation of productive capacities. Capital then relies increasingly on financialisation to boost profits (it will be recalled that financialisation implies accumulation by dispossession in addition to surplus value.) This historical account is consistent with Robert Brenner's findings (2003), who explains the post-Second World War boom in the US economy, that ushered in the 'Golden Age of Capitalism', as having drawn its sustenance from the earlier devastation of the European and Japanese economies. Only in this period was it possible to combine high incomes for workers, managers and shareholders with high rates of productive investment. Once the competitor countries had rebuilt their economies, international competition exacerbated and undermined profits, resulting in the 'stagflation' of the 1970s. With manufacturing profits shrinking all over the world, those inner contradictions of corporations identified by Veblen revealed themselves through the ignition of the 'Shareholder Revolution'.

'For thirty years after World War II, investment opportunities were good enough in general... that financial interests did not try to interfere with strategies to retain and reinvest' (Blair, 1993: 5). In conditions of plummeting profits and growing interest rates, shareholders demanded increased returns, taking their revenge during the 1980s in the form of a wave of mergers and acquisitions conducted mainly through hostile takeovers. Leveraged buyouts (LBOs) were introduced, implying wide use of junk bonds. These moves were substantiated by accusations that managers were responsible for their companies' poor performance and had allowed increased 'fat' in the form of non-pecuniary perquisites such as corporate jets. After being taken over, companies were ruthlessly restructured and downsized. Empirical studies have shown that the shareholder value of restructured companies usually increased (ibid.). The mere threat of a hostile takeover was a great incentive for managers to re-examine their companies, looking for opportunities to increase returns to shareholders. Sometimes this could be done by eliminating excessive perks and improving company management. However, 'in many cases improved returns could be achieved only by obtaining concessions from suppliers or customers, reducing the amount of taxes paid, extracting wage concessions, or cutting white-collar corporate staff' (ibid.: 5). These findings are supported by Lazonick and O'Sullivan (2000), who show that, while US corporations' profits in the 1970s tended to be reinvested so as to secure the growth of the firms involved (the Eichnerian megacorp), in the next two decades corporations increasingly downsized their labour requirements and distributed retained earnings to shareholders (for more on this, see below). This indicates that *the US corporate governance model had changed fundamentally. Corporate power had shifted from managers to shareholders, overcoming the traditional separation of ownership and control.* Increased shareholder value had replaced long-term growth as the prime object of US corporations (see below).

Two important indicators of this profound change in corporate objectives are growth in net dividend payments and increased share buybacks by US corporations. Equity buybacks have become so widespread and are so important a feature of investment behaviour that they deserve some special attention. Share buybacks help to boost share prices, and hence increase shareholder value. In modern conditions, the welfare of top managers is tied to shareholder value through options (Lazonick 2011a), which has a very important negative impact on corporate investment decisions and employment:

> Buybacks come at the expense of investment in industrial innovation and sustainable employment opportunities in the U.S. economy. The manipulation of the stock market through buybacks, the explosion of executive pay and the disappearance of middle-class American jobs all go hand in hand. (Lazonick 2011b)

An important dimension of the dominance of shareholder value is the ratio of net dividend payments and net share buybacks to the internal funds of the US corporate sector. Let us consider Figure 1.1.

It can be seen from the figure that, prior to the 1980s, net dividend payments and net share buybacks in the US non-financial corporate sector hovered around 20 per cent of internal funds, never reaching 40 per cent and at times approaching zero. From the 1980s, this share went through the roof, in 2007 reaching an absurd level of nearly 160 per cent (Q4). This figure plummeted in the crisis years of 2008 and 2009, only to recover quickly afterwards. The trend here demonstrates the motives behind the use of investment funds by the US non-financial corporate sector (see the next section).

As a result of increased shareholder value replacing long-term growth as the prime objective of US corporations, Wall Street (or rather its investment firms) obtained enormous power to reshape the

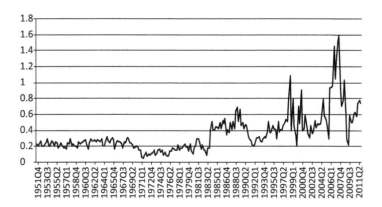

Figure 1.1 Net dividends plus net share buybacks as a percentage of internal funds in US non-financial corporate business, 1951–2011, quarterly (based on Milberg and Winkler 2010: 288)

Calculated from: Federal Reserve Bank, Flow of Funds Tables, 8 March 2012, Table F 102 'Nonfinancial Corporate Business' (Rows 3, 5 and 39). Net equity buybacks are considered as negative net equity issues.

corporate sector of the US economy in line with its own image and values. Karen Ho (2009) studied this process in her anthropological research into Wall Street investment banking. She found that among financiers a culture of smartness dominated, implying that the 'best and brightest' graduates from Ivy League universities seek jobs in investment banking. This is regarded as justifying the leading role of Wall Street in reshaping corporations. Meanwhile, the world of high finance is extremely hierarchical, segregated and oppressive. Job insecurity is rampant on Wall Street, with investment banks constantly being downsized, only to be expanded again later. This results in a motivation to earn as much money as possible in the shortest possible time span.

It is interesting to note that job insecurity is seen by investment bankers as a sign of merit. The bankers' skills are viewed as highly mobile, compared to the rigidity of the operatives in the corporate sector (Ho 2009: 244). This is an interesting case of the Veblenian logic of mobile and immobile property being extended to the whole economy. Investment bankers are themselves identified with liquid assets, their prime aim now becoming to cash out the outside world.

The Shareholder Revolution signifies the re-establishment of the law of surplus value as capitalism's main goal, in conditions where opportunities for extracting surplus value have been limited by over-accumulation of capital in the real production sector. Essentially, capitalism has reacted to the narrowing of opportunities to appropriate surplus value in the productive sphere by increasing exploitation on a global scale.

5 Value Chains and Accumulation by Dispossession

One of the most important repercussions of the profound change in the corporate governance model has been a reshaping by US big business of its investment strategies. From the 1990s onward, international capital has sought to benefit from the end of Communism by outsourcing production to regions with low wages. The vehicle for this process has been Foreign Direct Investment (FDI), carried out by transnational corporations (TNCs). Let us consider Figure 1.2.

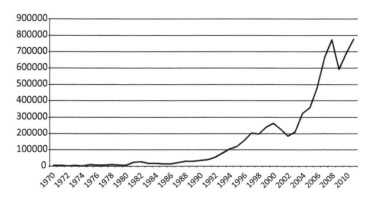

Figure 1.2 Foreign direct investment in developing and transition economies, 1970–2010 (US dollars at current prices and current exchange rates, in millions)

Calculated from: UNCTADSTART (UNCTAD Foreign Direct Investment database), Table 'Inward and outward foreign direct investment flows, annual, 1970–2010', <http://unctadstat.unctad.org/TableViewer/tableView.aspx>, last accessed 21 April 2012.

It can be seen from the figure that FDI began growing steeply from about 1990. The reasons are related to the fall of the Berlin Wall, the collapse of the Soviet Union and the corresponding eclipse of the world socialist and national-liberation movements. As a result, the threat of nationalisation was removed and conditions for FDI became much more favourable (Krugman 2009: 78–9). Maria Ivanova notes in connection with this that

> ... until the late 1980s, the relocation of production to peripheral countries remained a relatively limited phenomenon, confined to certain industries and countries. It was the disintegration of the Soviet bloc that ushered in a worldwide restructuring of production and social relations as it enabled transnational capital to surmount the last remaining obstacles to global inter-penetration. (Ivanova 2011a: 14–15)

According to the above data, FDI in developing and transition economies in 1990 amounted to $34.9 billion, while at its peak in 2008 it reached an astounding figure of nearly $779 billion, growing by 22 times in 18 years. It fell in 2001–02 following the dotcom bust, recovered from 2003, fell in the crisis of 2009, and started rising again in 2010 ($641.8 billion). The prime aim of FDI growth has been to tap the large workforce resources of the developing countries and emerging markets.[3]

The average worker in Jamaica today is paid half, in Bolivia and India a third, and in Nigeria a quarter of the wages received by his or her American counterpart (Rodrick 2011). This global outsourcing of jobs has led to the de-industrialisation of the core capitalist countries. The share of GDP made up by the value added in US manufacturing declined from 20 per cent in 1980 to 11.5 per cent in 2008, while the share of total employment represented by this sector fell from 20.7 per cent in 1980 to 9 per cent in 2009. In the latter year, nearly 86 per cent of non-agrarian labour was employed in the service sector, and only 14.3 per cent in the sphere of material production (Ivanova 2011b: 860). According to Blinder (2007), a further 30–40 million more jobs can potentially be moved abroad. The de-industrialisation of the core capitalist countries was accompanied by a dramatic expansion of the world labour market, as the labour pools of China, India and the former USSR joined the global market and doubled its size (Freeman 2010).

The global shift of production from North to South altered the nature of the modern corporation, rendering it 'weightless'. This process is analysed through the 'value chains' approach (Blair 2009), the essence of which lies in slicing the production process into separate chains according to the level of value added. Then the labor-intensive chains with low value added are moved abroad, while the so-called 'key competencies' with high value added – R&D, marketing, promotion and sales – are retained at home. Often, western TNCs nowadays do not carry on any production at all (Milberg 2008), or they may prefer to buy intermediate products (primary goods, parts and components, and semi-finished goods) from low-wage countries, bypassing the need for productive investment, personnel training, and so on. An important characteristic of 'value chains' is that TNCs enter the market for supplies as monopsonies, while their suppliers are compelled to compete with each other (which says a great deal about the ideological meaning of the free market doctrine). This phenomenon is of prime importance for reducing the relative prices of intermediate goods imported to the US from low-wage countries.

For a classic example of a global value chain, we may look to the production of the iPhone (Xing and Detert 2010), designed and sold by Apple in the US, but assembled in China. In 2008–09, the price of an iPhone in the US was cut by Apple from $600 to $500. Despite the price cut, Apple raised its gross profit margin from 62 per cent in 2007 to 64 per cent in 2009. This was accompanied by a decline of unit output cost from $229 to $178.96 over the same years (ibid.: 7). Apple, it follows, was marking up every iPhone by more than $300! One might think that Apple's Chinese partners still received a reasonable share of almost $179, but this was not the case at all. Only $6.50 accrued to China, while the other $172.46 paid for components which came from Germany, Japan, Korea, the US and other countries (ibid.: 9). Let us consider Table 1.1.

These data reflect the average annual per cent change in import prices paid by manufacturers relative to the US consumer price index in 1986–2006. They show that in an absolute majority of industries, the prices of imported supplies fell behind the US consumer index. This meant that US manufacturers enjoyed declining costs due to global outsourcing. Samir Amin (2010) uses the term 'imperialist rent' to describe the financial advantage that accrues to TNCs, due to

Table 1.1 Relative import prices of manufacturers, average annual percent change, 1986–2006

Sectors	1986–2006 average annual percent change (%)
33 Petroleum, petroleum products and related materials	7.45
28 Metalliferous ores and metal scrap	3.34
68 Nonferrous metals	3.14
25 Wood pulp and recovered paper	1.15
24 Cork and wood	1.07
67 Iron and steel	0.83
54 Medicinal and pharmaceutical products	−0.01
63 Cork and wood manufacturers other than furniture	−0.21
73 Metalworking machinery	−0.23
72 Machinery specialized for particular industries	−0.25
11 Beverages	−0.41
74 General industrial machinery, equipment, & machine parts	−0.55
66 Nonmetallic mineral manufacturers	−0.55
05 Vegetables, fruit and nuts, fresh or dried	−0.58
01 Meat and meat preparations	−0.62
52 Inorganic chemicals	−0.86
03 Fish, crustaceans, aquatic invertebrates, and preparations thereof	−0.91
51 Organic chemicals	−1.02
64 Paper and paperboard, cut to size	−1.03
69 Manufacturers of metals	−1.03
59 Chemical materials and products	−1.05
78 Road vehicles	−1.11
83 Travel goods, handbags and similar containers	−1.16
87 Professional, scientific and controlling instruments and apparatus	−1.36
65 Textile yarn, fabrics, made-up articles, n.e.s., and related products	−1.43
89 Miscellaneous manufactured articles	−1.49
82 Furniture and parts thereof	−1.60
55 Essential oils: polishing and cleansing preps	−1.63
85 Footwear	−1.64
84 Articles of apparel and clothing accessories	−1.84
81 Prefabricated buildings; plumbing, heat & lighting fixtures	−1.96
88 Photographic apparatus, equipment and supplies and optical goods	−2.13
62 Rubber manufactures	−2.23
77 Electrical machinery and equipment	−2.89
07 Coffee, tea, cocoa, spices, and manufactures thereof	−3.27
76 Telecommunications & sound recording & reproducing apparatus & equipment	−4.81
75 Computer equipment and office machines	−7.81

Source: Milberg 2008: 20.

the difference in real wage rates between the core and the periphery of the capitalist world-system. Thus, 'most large U.S. corporations, via outsourcing and delinking from manufacturing and product development, are moving toward the model of [the] "weightless" corporation which Wall Street interprets as enhancing shareholder value' (Ho 2009: 255). Dispensing with labour-intensive production means US corporations have become much more 'liquid', and have effectively been remodelled in line with Wall Street's financial banking standards.

6 Investment Strategies and the Structure of Capital

The Shareholder Revolution, Wall Street's dominance over the US corporate sector, and the shift of production abroad have led to sharp changes in the investment strategies that firms pursue. Let us consider Figure 1.3.

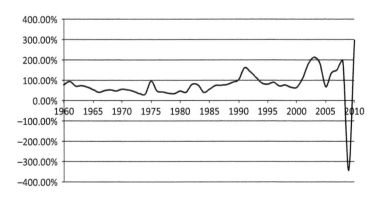

Figure 1.3 Net dividends as a percentage of net investments in fixed assets in US non-financial corporate business, 1960–2010[4]

Calculated from: Bureau of Economic Analysis, Integrated Macroeconomic Accounts for the United States, Table S.5.q Nonfinancial Corporate Business, 13 March 2012.

From the figure, it can be seen that in the 1960s and 1970s, net dividends were on average much less than the value of net investments in fixed assets, hovering around a level of about 50 per cent. For the Eichnerian megacorp, development of productive capacity was of greater importance than dividend payments. All this changed in the 1980s, when the Shareholder Revolution reversed corporate priorities.

In the 2000s, net dividends reached sums twice those for investment in fixed assets. The first of these values plummeted with the onset of the Great Recession of 2009, only to recover and reach a point triple the second value in 2010. Shareholders, no doubt, were demanding compensation for their losses during the slump. These data show unambiguously that long-term growth is no longer the prime objective of US corporations. *Increasing shareholder value is now much more important for US big business than developing productive capacity.* This conclusion is supported by the evidence, presented in Figure 1.4, which shows US corporations' investment priorities.

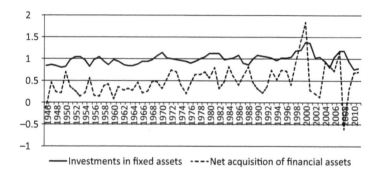

——Investments in fixed assets   ----Net acquisition of financial assets

Figure 1.4 Investment in fixed assets and net acquisition of financial assets as a percentage of US internal funds (book) in the US non-financial corporate sector in 1945–2011 (annually)

Calculated from: Federal Reserve Bank, Flow of Funds Tables, 8 March 2012, Table F 102 'Nonfinancial Corporate Business' (Rows 5, 12 and 16).

From Figure 1.4 it can be seen that, until the 1970s, funds generated internally by US non-financial corporations were invested in fixed assets to a much greater degree than in financial assets. Since the late 1990s, the shares of the two indicators have become more nearly equal, with net acquisition of financial assets at times even exceeding investment in fixed assets as a percentage of internal funds.

As a result of such investment strategies, the ratio of financial to real assets in the US non-financial corporate sector has changed dramatically. Let us consider Figure 1.5.

It can be seen from Figure 1.5 that in the era of the Eichnerian megacorp (that is, from the 1950s through the 1970s), financial assets

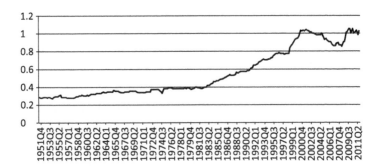

Figure 1.5 Total financial assets as a percentage of nonfinancial assets in the US non-financial corporate sector, 1951–2011 (quarterly) (based on Orhangazi 2008: 866)

Calculated from: Federal Reserve Bank, Flow of Funds Tables, 8 March 2012, Table B 102 'Nonfinancial Corporate Business' (Rows 2 and 6).

as a share of tangible assets in US non-financial corporate sector fluctuated between 30 and 40 per cent. From the 1980s, this figure climbed steeply. In the early 2000s, it exceeded 100 per cent, meaning that *financial assets surpassed fixed assets in value terms*. This represents an increase of Veblenian intangible assets, based on goodwill. There is thus a close link between financialisation and the formation of global value chains. As Serfati puts it, 'TNCs have become more oriented toward the generation of revenues based upon their financial and intellectual property rights than on the production process proper' (2008: 44). The rise of the issue of copyrights, together with the increase in the quantity of patents for innovations and technologies, reflects the growing use of tools aimed at strengthening corporations' monopolistic positions from the core countries in global production networks. This monopolistic power, embodied in intangible assets, accounts for the growing surplus of the value of shares over the value of corporations' productive capacities.

It is worth noting that after the dotcom bubble of 2000–02 burst, the ratio of financial to non-financial assets declined, and this trend increased following the 2007 crisis. From 2009, however, the ratio once again began to grow, quickly recovering its level of the late 1990s. This indicates that the US non-financial corporate sector has returned to its financialised practices, recreating the preconditions for the bursting of a *new* bubble.

As the data suggest, the Shareholder Revolution's impact on investment strategies has been devastating. The preoccupation with shareholder value as the prime measure of corporate performance has led to decreasing investment in productive capacity, to the manipulation of shares in attempts to boost their price, to the neglect of innovations and of workplace safety conditions, and to the risk of ecological disasters. All this can be seen in the performance of British Petroleum in the past 20 years.

In April 2010, the largest oil spill in US history occurred, following an equipment failure on the Deepwater Horizon oil rig in the Gulf of Mexico, where BP was engaged in a drilling project. The accident caused the deaths of eleven workers and an enormous environmental disaster – 200 million gallons of oil were spilled into the sea (Lustgarten 2012a). Experts related the disaster to changes in corporate governance in the late 1980s: 'Delivering shareholder value was by no means the only measure of a successful oil company; it may not have even been the most important one. But it's the one that mattered most on Wall Street, and it was becoming a driving force for British Petroleum's new, young management' (Lustgarten 2012b: 3).

In the 1990s, BP underwent a major expansion through mergers and acquisitions (M&A), sharply increasing its oil reserves. Top management had to persuade shareholders that money spent on M&A activities was money put to good use. The only way to do this was through boosting the company's share prices. 'Delivering shareholder value' demanded so-called 'lean' production methods, meaning all-out efforts to cut operating costs and reductions in spending on equipment. As a result, safety norms were neglected and equipment became increasingly obsolete. Workers and managers at the company's drilling sites and refineries tried to draw the attention of their superiors to the growing risks of accidents. However, their signals were ignored and whistleblowers were persecuted. None of BP's upper-tier managing executives, one source remarks, were deliberately malicious, but their decisions were driven by money: 'Neither their own sympathies nor the stark risks in their operations – corroding pipelines, dysfunctional safety valves, disarmed fire alarms and so on – could compete with the financial necessities of profit making' (Lustgarten 2012a).

The 2010 Gulf of Mexico oil spill provides a vivid example of the deep conflict, underscored by Veblen, between the financial logic of capitalism and the logic of an industrial enterprise. Lustgarten mentions something which the Shareholder Revolution had left deeply ingrained in BP's culture:

> People who knew [John] Browne [BP's chief executive] said that precision and exacting attention to operational detail bored him; that making sure the company ran safely, and that there were channels of communication, bored him. At the same time, Browne was clear, opinionated, and forceful about the priorities he did set, mainly financial ones. (2012b: 132)

7 Accumulation by Dispossession, and the Global Crisis

The neoclassical vision of the current economic crisis is a striking manifestation of positivism, together with fragmented thinking. Proponents of orthodoxy see the causes of the current world turmoil as lying exclusively in the financial sphere. On the surface, the crisis might indeed seem to be essentially a monetary-financial phenomenon. In 2009, Nobel Prize winner Paul Krugman produced a remarkably concise and popular explanation of the crisis from this mainstream standpoint (Krugman 2009). Despite providing an interesting review of turbulent events in Mexico, Argentina, South East Asia, the US, and so on, Krugman in his article puts forward only a very superficial explanation for this all-embracing process. At the heart of the crisis, he sees the development of a network of non-banking financial institutions, exempted from state regulation and prone to so-called 'moral hazards'.[5] He believes that when coupled with erroneous policy on the part of the US monetary authorities (excessively low interest rates facilitating a surge of financial 'bubbles', and the like), this led to a decline of investor confidence in financial instruments, inducing panic and eventual slump. Robert Shiller, another popular author writing from a conventional standpoint, seeks the causes of financial and mortgage bubbles in the psychology of financial speculators (Shiller 2008). He applies a model of epidemic disease to analysing the 'psychological contamination' through which risky financial operations spread from one speculator to another in the course of a capital-market fever. To prevent such fevers, Shiller calls for a democratisation of finances so as to make this sphere transparent to the general population. Krugman's, Shiller's and other conventional economists' arguments make a certain sense. That is, modern capitalism has created the problem of moral hazards; meanwhile, speculative fevers spread in epidemic-like fashion, monetary authorities make mistakes, and the democratisation of finances would serve the interests of the common people, if only the non-common people would agree to it. However, the views described share one important feature: they consider only the crisis's external aspects, as these are displayed at the surface level of economic relations in the monetary-financial sphere. Conventional economists fail to explore the deeper roots of the world's current economic dilemmas. Indeed, all the above problems – financial speculation, moral hazards, 'bubbles', and so forth – have existed more or less forever, or more precisely, as long as capitalism itself has existed. Why, then, have they produced a global crisis only now? Mainstream economics is unable to answer this question, because such an answer requires moving from a description of capitalism's external appearance to analysis of its nature as a social system.

The main thrust of the Marxian interpretation of the current world economic crisis lies in the emphasis it places on the over-accumulation of capital in the real sector, and the corresponding decline of the average rate of profit on fixed assets. A speculative surge of financial bubbles is seen as a temporary means of transcending the limits of accumulation of capital in the real sector.

As was mentioned earlier, international capital seeks to benefit from shifting production to regions of the world where wages are low. This very fact strongly contradicts the major tenets of the neoclassical mainstream. If corporate profit is only a marginal product of capital, and if capital makes no claim on the compensation received by labour, then why is capital not indifferent to the remuneration workers obtain?[6] If a capitalist shifts production to places where workers enjoy minimal rights, then he or she in fact rejects marginal productivity theory, and acknowledges that in practical matters one should be guided in a business-like manner (but, of course, tacitly) by Marx.[7]

As the developed capitalist countries underwent de-industrialisation, the workforce serving the world capitalist market experienced explosive growth.[8] During the 1990s, 1.47 billion workers in China, India and the former USSR joined the world economy, effectively doubling its size (Freeman 2010). It was due to this development that the massive decline of material production in the core capitalist countries, often interpreted as a shift to post-industrial society, became possible.

The export structure of the world-system periphery underwent radical change. Traditionally, exports from the periphery had been dominated by raw materials and agricultural produce, but the share of manufactured products in these exports grew from 20 to 80 per cent between 1980 and 2003 (Razmi and Blecker 2008: 22).

As mentioned earlier, a critical feature of the modern value chains, or global production networks, is that TNCs are represented on the world market as buyer-monopolists or monopsonies, while suppliers are compelled to engage in cut-throat competition with each other for access to the markets of the core countries. The position of peripheral societies is reflected in the 'fallacy of composition' thesis, which observes that 'if a number of developing countries simultaneously try to increase their exports in a range of similar products, many of them could end up losing from insufficient foreign demand and possibly depressed international prices' (ibid.). This process has become the most important factor determining the above-mentioned relative decline of prices for intermediate and final products imported by the core countries.

In the US, this relative decline of import prices has led to low inflation. Let us consider Table 1.2.

Table 1.2   Prices and money supply, average annual growth

Years	1986–90 %	1991–95 %	1996–2000 %	2001–06 %
Consumer price index	0.04	0.04	0.02	2.14
Import prices	0.05	0.02	−0.01	0.70
Money supply (M2)	0.06	0.02	0.09	6.19

Source: Milberg 2008: 13.

The data show that the consumer price index declined sharply at the point when restrictive monetary policy was eased (see row 3), and when import prices were decreasing relative to domestic prices (see row 2). These calculations demonstrate that restrictive monetary policy was not the prime factor determining the unprecedentedly low inflation rates in the US in the 2000s. Prime importance should be attributed to the exploitation of the world periphery (recall the 'fallacy of composition').

As a result, the profit share in the GDP of the developed countries, an index which had declined during the 'stagflation' of the 1970s, started to grow again. The same cannot be said of the share of wages. According to some estimates, the world labour market's drastic expansion during the last two decades has brought a decline in the capital:labour ratio of 55–60 per cent (Freeman 2010). This points to a radical change in the relationship of forces between capital and labour, to capital's advantage. More workers now compete for each job, and the position of hired labour has been undermined throughout the world. This has obvious implications for trade unions and for the social guarantees enjoyed by workers. In essence, western society has broken the social contract that was concluded with workers in the period of the post-Second World War 'Golden Age' (Kapstein 1996).[9] This development has found particular expression in the stagnation of real wages in the core countries. Thus, in 2005, the average wage of non-supervisory workers in the US was 8 per cent lower than in 1973 (in 2005 prices). Over the same period, the average productivity per worker in US industry grew by 85 per cent (Pollin 2007: 122)! (From this fact alone, readers can judge whether wage rates in the real world are governed by marginal productivity or by the law of surplus value.) In line with such processes, the share of the wage fund in the GDP of OECD countries has declined sharply (Ellis and Smith 2007: 4). It was noted earlier that workers on the periphery have much lower wages than their counterparts in the core.

Demand for hired labour is generally acknowledged as a prime factor determining the volume of the domestic market, upon which ultimately the demand for capital goods depends. A regular shortfall of wages from the growth of productive capacity generates a shortage of aggregate demand relative to aggregate supply on the world market. Low rates of capacity utilisation ensue (Mohun 2009: 1032). Accordingly, the rate of net profit in the developed capitalist countries declines. This naturally leads world savings and investment in productive capacity to fall as a percentage of world GDP (Brenner 2009: 10), and brings a reduction in the growth rates of world GDP itself (ibid.: 8).

The decline in profitability of real assets provides striking proof of the over-accumulation of capital that has resulted from intensive industrialisation in the peripheral countries. As in Marx's time, this over-accumulation is only relative. It stems from the shortage of aggregate demand which has emerged as a result of increased exploitation of the world's working class. It is against this backdrop that the global shift of capital from the real to the financial-speculative sector has taken place.

This problem has already been discussed with relation to the US economy's corporate sector. It was noted that financialised corporations, sharply decreasing their investment in productive capacity, have been compelled to shift production processes abroad. Apart from obtaining 'imperialist rent' from the difference between real wage rates in the core and the periphery, the developed capitalist countries also benefit from the capital flight that occurs on an enormous scale from developing and transition economies. The business elites of the core countries, especially the US, keep their personal wealth predominantly within their own national boundaries, while rich people on the periphery send it abroad (Aerni et al. 2007: 14). The main area of investment of 'free' capital, in a world dominated by the US dollar, is US securities.

The mechanism underlying the process of capital flight is rooted in global capitalism's very essence, based on exploitation of the periphery by the centre. To enhance its position in the highly competitive markets of the core countries, any peripheral nation needs to keep its national currency undervalued. A trade surplus with the US, however, generates an inflow of US dollars to the peripheral country, and the supply of dollars relative to the national currency increases. The result is a rise in the national currency's value relative to the dollar. This means that when measured in dollars, wages (and consequently production costs) in the peripheral country rise as well. Accordingly, the country's competitive edge declines *vis-à-vis* nations with lower foreign exchange rates. To prevent this adverse chain of events, 'excess' dollars must be bought up and withdrawn from the national market, stemming the rise in value of the national currency. Since it is impossible to invest these finances in the national economy without worsening the current account balance, the alternative usually resorted to is to invest them in interest-bearing US securities. Hence after enriching itself through the import of cheap products, the world-system's core, and above all the US, benefits further through exploiting the same workers indirectly, appropriating the savings created by their toil.

With real wages in the US stagnant or even declining, growth in consumption can be secured only through an all-round increase in all kinds of debt: state, corporate and private. An important source of growth of this kind has been financial flows from the periphery. Data show that in the developed capitalist countries in recent decades declines in savings and investment have been accompanied by increasing foreign trade deficits (IMF 2005: 92). This situation reflects the de-industrialisation of the core, which increasingly imports industrial products from the periphery. As explained earlier, the periphery creates savings which are appropriated by the core. This perverse system of financial relations is designed to overcome the limitations, engendered by the current capitalist world-system, on accumulation of capital by the core countries.

The Chinese economy has entered into just such a contradictory symbiosis with the US economy. The data show not only an impetuous growth of Chinese investment in US financial assets in the 2000s, but also a predominance of investment in so-called 'government-sponsored enterprises', above all Freddie Mac and Fannie Mae, organisations which invest their clients' money in the mortgage market (Jagannathan et al. 2009: 16). After the meltdown of the US dotcom market, China began to invest more money in US real estate. The inflow of Chinese funds became the prime source for the rapidly expanding US mortgage bubble. Comparing the dynamics of the US current account and of American household debt is instructive. It was in the period of US current account deficit that household debt started growing intensively (ibid., p. 17), because, as previously explained, funds earned by the periphery through exports to the US were largely directed by the financial system into financing household consumer credit.

It can thus be seen that the financialisation of US corporations and the subsequent shift of production to the world-system's periphery have given rise to an increase of capitalist exploitation unprecedented in scale and scope. Here we have the key reason behind the world economic crisis.

8 Conclusion

The transformation of US corporations from managerial firms to financialised structures is one of the defining developments in recent economic history. It cannot be explained on the basis of inner organisational development per se. To comprehend this shift, one needs to analyse the capitalist mode of production as a whole. The duality of labour, modified at every point in the Hegelian-Marxian ascent from the abstract to the concrete, becomes the 'Ariadne's thread' by which researchers need to be guided. Of its essence a self-aggrandising value, capital posits the increase of value as capitalist production's prime goal, reducing use-value to the secondary position of a means to this end. This, in turn, engenders a Veblenian opposition between the industrial and pecuniary logic of capitalism. Always inherent in corporations has been an inner contradiction between their long-term interests as going concerns and their striving for short-term financial gain.

The conditions idealised in the Eichnerian megacorp existed only temporarily during the post-Second World War 'Golden Age'. By the 1970s, the accumulation of capital on a world scale had exacerbated capitalism's inner contradictions, leading to stagflation. As the profitability of investment in productive capacity declined, the capitalist class responded by unleashing the Shareholder Revolution of the 1980s, overcoming the separation of ownership and control peculiar to the megacorp. As a wave of mergers and acquisitions swept across the US economy, corporations were ruthlessly downsized, restructured and asset-stripped, while their investment funds were severely curtailed – the goal being to increase dividends and boost share prices. Long-term growth was supplanted as the prime object of corporate strategy by the aim of increasing current shareholder value.

As a growing share of internally generated funds came to be directed to dividend payments and share buybacks, US corporations were compelled to outsource production abroad to low-wage paying regions. Global production networks were formed. As a rule, it was only labour-intensive production chains with low levels of value-adding that were shifted to the periphery; the chains marked by high added value remained in the core countries, in the hands of western TNCs. The exploitation of labour, both foreign and domestic, increased not only through the appropriation of surplus value, but also as a result of accumulation by dispossession, with income redistribution through the medium of the financial markets a prime vehicle. So it is that the modern corporation, unlike the Eichnerian megacorp, creates demand for financial assets at the expense of investment funds. During the 2000s, the share of financial assets came to exceed the share of productive assets in the capital structure of the US non-financial corporate sector. In this splitting of the demand for funds, the domination of value over use-value finds its modern expression.

With growth in the wage fund falling behind the expansion of world productive capacity, a classic over-accumulation of capital took place on the periphery of the capitalist world-system. To overcome this problem, capitalism used increased indebtedness to artificially stimulate consumer demand in the core countries; the results included the absorption of a large part of the savings generated in peripheral economies. This contributed to financialisation, and created still more of the preconditions for the current world economic crisis. From this it can be seen that beneath the current world economic turmoil lies the modern form of exploitation of labour, expressing itself through core–periphery relations. The roots of the modern crisis, it follows, are not to be found solely in the financial sphere, but must be traced to the very foundations of capitalist society.

2

From Central Planning to Capitalism

2.1 Introduction

A discussion of the essence of the modern capitalist world-system provides us a framework for analysing the emergence of modern Russian capitalism. It was shaped by two major influences: the degeneration of the Stalinist system and the impact of global capitalism. The former is rooted in the history of the Russian Revolution and Soviet society. Tsarist Russia exhibited the typical features of a periphery society, which viewed western capital as a major driving force for its own industrialisation. These services were paid for by relentless exploitation of the peasantry and the workers. The Russian Revolution opened the first wave of struggle of the periphery against the core of the capitalist world-system. Liberation from dependence on foreign capital resulted in high growth rates for the planned economy of 1929–75. However, Stalin's grip over society and the formation of a totalitarian state led to the ascendancy of the state bureaucracy, reproducing the hierarchical social relations of domination and subjugation. The new ruling elite enjoyed material privileges and sought private benefits from informal control over economic resources. This undermined the efficiency of the Soviet economic system and eventually led to its demise.

When Mikhail Gorbachev introduced democracy and perestroika into the USSR, the already existing bureaucracy used these ideas of democracy and perestroika to form a powerful pro-capitalist bloc which rejected socialist values and began to dismantle central planning in order to convert its social position into lucrative material assets. This process resulted in the dissolution of the Soviet Union, Gorbachev ousted from power, and the ascendancy of Boris Yeltsin as president of Russia and leader of radical capitalist reforms. Western influence was decisive in forming the character of the radical market reforms in Russia, which were based on the principles of the 'Washington Consensus'. The ensuing privatisation helped to convert state functionaries' positions in the Soviet hierarchy into that of private property overseers, which made a lasting impression on the character of private proprietorship. In Russia, private proprietorship entrenched informal control over assets which state bureaucracy had controlled in Soviet times. This legacy, in combination with the impact of global capitalism, exerted the major formative influence which shaped the current Russian model of corporate governance, discussed in Chapter 3.

In the second section of this chapter, there is a brief discussion of the essential nature of the Soviet social system, which emerged as a result of the Russian Revolution with all its achievements and contradictions; the third section takes up the issue of the evolution of Stalinist bureaucracy and its consequences for central planning; the fourth focuses on the impact Gorbachev's perestroika had on the management of the Soviet economy; the fifth deals with the radical market reforms of Yeltsin's Russia, with particular emphasis on privatisation, and concluding remarks are presented in the sixth section.

2.2   The Essence of the Soviet System[1]

Modern Russian capitalism, which is the primary subject of this book, appeared as a result of the dissolution of Soviet society. Its legacy played a crucial role in the formation of the modern social system in Russia in the conditions created by current global capitalism. This is why we take a brief look at the main features of the Soviet system, identifying its rupture and continuity with present society. It is natural to begin this discussion with the 1917 Russian Revolution.

2.2.1   The Russian Revolution: A Rebellion of the Periphery

Soviet society came into being as a result of the 1917 Russian Revolution, which was in turn a rebellion of a peripheral society against the pattern of historical development imposed by the core of the capitalist world-system. Reviewing Russian history from ancient times, Kagarlitsky (2007) shows that Russia always pursued a path of 'catch-up' development. A classic example of such an attempt is provided by the reforms of Peter the Great, initiated in response to the mortal threat to the country's existence posed by the Swedish invasion at the turn of the seventeenth century. It is characteristic that in violently imposing Europeanisation on the Russian nobility, Peter the Great completed the peasantry's enslavement. Thus, the westernisation of the upper classes was accompanied by the lower classes' 'easternisation'.

Paradoxically, the socialist path of development was opened for Russia not by the success, but on the contrary, by the failure of efforts towards modernisation, as attempted by the Tsarist regime of the late nineteenth and early twentieth centuries. Industrialisation at that time was a response to the increasing gap between Russia and the West in terms of both military and economic strength. The unfortunate results of the Crimean War (1853–56) had illustrated to Russia beyond any doubt the reality of its loss of independence. In the late nineteenth and early twentieth centuries, the expanding Russian empire encountered its British counterpart in Turkey, Persia, Afghanistan and the Far East. 'The Great Game' or the rivalry between the two powers is seen as the Cold War of its time (Hopkirk 1990). Conflicts for control over the colonies and economic competition between Britain and Germany quickly led the world to war (Tarler 1958). In such circumstances, industrialisation assumed the character of an imperative necessity for Russia's very survival.

Modernisation, through the imposition of capitalism from the top-down of government hierarchy rather than from the bottom-up cooperation of the common people, proved disastrous for the Russian peasantry. The highest bids of the government to attract foreign capital were made under the preservation of archaic, semi-feudal forms of land ownership and authoritarian political rule. The peasantry was forced to sell their corn for less than its real worth. It was then resold in Europe at negligible prices (in order to compete with cheap US and Argentine supplies). With the proceeds, the government bought gold and silver to secure the notorious Vitte's 'golden rouble'.[2] Now foreign capitals building enterprises in Russia were able to obtain profits in a sound currency. To this, the state's external borrowing at inflated interest rates must be added. Railway construction, mineral and coal extraction, metallurgy, timber and engineering were developed at the expense of the systematic plundering of the Russian peasantry and workers. Naturally, the gap between Russia and its chief competitors only widened.[3]

Specifics of the peripheral societies, as they were grasped by the theories of Lenin and Trotsky, were manifested in particular in the dependence of the bourgeoisie on the state, and its consequent inability to lead the so-called bourgeois-democratic changes.[4] That is why revolution would not be stoppable at the bourgeois-democratic stage and would inevitably lead to socialist changes. The Mensheviks, considering mature capitalism to be a necessary precondition for the socialist revolution, argued that the big bourgeoisie (the 'right-wing' Mensheviks), or the petty or middle bourgeoisie (the 'left-wing' Mensheviks) would lead the move to democracy (T'ut'ukin 2002). The Mensheviks' overestimation of the bourgeoisie's revolutionary potential was matched only by their notorious underestimation of the peasantry's determination. The major difference in the Bolsheviks' strategy lay in their awareness of the crucial role destined for the peasantry in the future revolution (Shanin 1986).

The inability of the national bourgeoisie to reconcile its interests with the peasantry and the workers, and its inability to lead society in the struggle for democracy (both of which factors are obviously interconnected), were the two salient features of Russian capitalism at the turn of the twentieth century. These features were related to Russia's position as a country at the periphery of the capitalist world-system. That is why these peculiarities are common to the majority of other peripheral societies. This is emphasised by Samir Amin who writes that the Russian Revolution opened the 'first wave of awakening of the South' in the twentieth century (Amin 2011: 59–64).[5] As will be shown in the subsequent section, these features are pertinent to modern Russian capitalism even more than to its historical ancestor.

2.2.2   Stalin's 'Thermidor' and the Nature of Soviet Bureaucracy

The victory of the Russian Revolution depended on the interplay of global and national histories and its future fate also depended on this same interplay. In the absence of a victorious world revolution, contradictions appeared between the European-Marxian and traditionalist currents in Bolshevism. The opposition beween Lenin and Stalin in 1921–23 was probably grounded not so much in personal antipathy as in the incompatibility of the two political cultures and two visions of achieving socialism.[6] With Lenin's death in January 1924, this contradiction assumed the character of an open split. Trotsky and Bukharin expressed, although in different ways, the values of a European Marxism,[7] while Stalin expressed those of traditionalism. With Stalin victorious in the intra-party struggle, the latter had triumphed.

I will not dwell here on the essence of traditionalism in any detail, but will only mention that by 'traditionalism', I mean the pre-capitalist societies' parochial values of the type identified by Amin as 'communal' and 'tributary' (Amin 2010: 41–6). That is, these societies are characterised by the dominance of communal (collective) interests over private, individual ones. The monarchical illusions of the Russian peasantry are an important manifestation of these values. There is a growing literature proposing that the Russian peasantry reacted to capitalism's intrusion into their traditional way of life by reviving its traditional communal attitudes and world outlook (Mogil'nitskyi 2009). This was an important resource which Stalin tapped into in order to achieve victory over party oppositions.

All sides participated in the contest for power in the 1920s, as all parties realised the urgent necessity for swift modernisation of Russia's predominantly traditional society. The optimal way of achieving this goal was industrialisation within the New Economic Policy (NEP) framework, advocated by Trotsky and Bukharin (with the emphasis on central planning and on the market correspondingly). Their model of development appeared to be unfeasible not because of economic circumstances as such (that is, taken from the standpoint of the interplay of the productive forces and production relations), but because of predominant values and psychological factors. Russian society, experiencing a headlong revival of traditional values, possessed only a limited potential for rational, European culture, so as to find the optimal combination of plan and market. This found its expression in Stalin's victory over his Bolshevik opponents with its fateful repercussions: the 'Great Leap' in industrialisation, enforced and often violent collectivisation, and, eventually, imposition of the shackles of the totalitarian state on society by means of terror.

Trotsky called Stalin's regime 'Thermidorian', under which term, referring to the French Revolution, he understood the regime to be 'a triumph of the bureaucracy over the masses' (2004 [1937]: 80). To be sure, any true revolution is characterised by the interference of the masses in the course of history, and this is definitely what had happened in Russia in 1917. But the essence of Stalin's terror was the opposite – in the subjugation of the masses to the totalitarian state's arbitrary power. The peasant character of the Russian Revolution was an important precondition for this, although it was the peasantry who became one of the new regime's primary victims.[8]

In the 1930s, Stalin, already a dictator whose opinion no one dared challenge in his own country, declared the successful construction of socialism in the USSR. Trotsky responded with his famous book *The Revolution Betrayed*, in which he refuted Stalin's assertion that the Soviet Union was a socialist country. He reminded the reader that socialism was understood in Marxism as a classless society capable to meet all material needs of the people. In this fundamental sense, one could not find 'a hint of socialism in the Soviet Union' (ibid.: 2); which is why Trotsky considered the Soviet regime as only transitional, that is, a preparatory stage in the transition from capitalism to socialism, and thus being neither the former, nor the latter. The exiled thinker emphasised that an indispensable feature of a socialist society was the 'dying away of the state', giving way to self-management of the workers. Nothing stood in such contrast with the repressive, totalitarian nature of Stalinism as the ideal of socialism.

For the benefit of his personal power, Stalin used the bitter consequences of the Russian Civil War (1918–22). Trotsky recalls the unfortunate chain of events to the initiation of which he was himself privy: 'The prohibition of oppositional parties brought after it the prohibition of factions. The prohibition of factions ended in a prohibition to think otherwise than the infallible leaders. The police-manufactured monolithism of the party resulted in a bureaucratic impunity which has become the source of wantonness and corruption' (ibid.: 79–80). Notwithstanding that all this was fair enough, the Soviet regime had other, deeper, reasons for its authoritarianism.

Trotsky recalled Lenin's teaching about the dual nature of the state under socialism, which is 'socialistic, insofar as it defends social property in the means of production; bourgeois, insofar as the distribution of life's goods is carried out with a capitalistic measure of value and all the consequences ensuing therefrom' (ibid.: 42). We should keep in mind that Lenin meant under socialism such a society which from its very beginning would supersede capitalism in labor productivity. And still he anticipated the need in distribution of commodities on the basis of some value measure. Taking into account that the Soviet society was only at the initial stage of its industrialisation in the 1930s, material want conditioned a much greater role of the redistributive state, and, hence, a much greater role for its 'bourgeois' functions. The bureaucracy, being the prime distributor of material commodities, is by definition a privileged stratum of such a society. Since Stalin severely suppressed not only political dissent, but also the most numerous social class – the peasantry – he naturally found the prime basis of his power in the bureaucracy. This single privileged caste of Soviet society he concurrently terrorised and awarded for complete compliance. Growing social inequalities stemmed from low labour productivity and from the difference in the social positions of the Soviet people. This situation was largely a result of there existing a ruling bureaucracy; at the same time, it provided a rationale for its expansion. Thus, the appearance and entrenchment of the privileged minority became the pivotal event determining the nature of Soviet society.

This raised the next question: was the ruling Soviet bureaucracy a new exploitative class like the bourgeoisie? Trotsky dealt with this complex and painful issue in such a thoughtful way which you would not anticipate from someone who himself and whose loved ones had been victimised by this same bureaucracy. The old Marxist revolutionary did not yield to the temptation to depict Stalin's bureaucracy as merely a new version of the exploitative class. Trotsky did not deny that workers and peasants in the USSR were suppressed and exploited by the state. While aware of this situation, Trotsky also recognised the many social rights obtained by the workers even in Stalinised 'socialism'. (I would add that the peasants were much more humiliated, but they were provided with a possible social advancement: the opportunity to become workers.) Hence, the USSR was still a workers' state, although largely deformed. The ruling bureaucracy was not a genuine 'new class', because it did not possess the means of production and did not derive its income from private ownership. The state functionary could be the commander of labour and enjoy privileges only according to their position in the hierarchy and only as long as their tenure lasted. Deriving the legitimacy of its power from socialist values, the bureaucracy could rule only by preserving the Soviet state's socialist elements, which limited its bourgeois aspirations (ibid.: 187–90). In the 1930s, heated debates on this point raged amonst North American and European Trotskyists. In 1939, an Italian adherent, Bruno Rizzi (1901–77), published his volume *The Bureaucratisation of the World* in which he compared Stalinism and fascism. After examining the rise of totalitarian states, Rizzi arrived at the conclusion that the new type of society which supersedes capitalism is not socialism, but a 'bureaucratic collectivism'. It seemed that even the US President Franklin D. Roosevelt's 'New Deal' fit this picture. Rizzi thought that the bureaucracy was becoming the new exploitive class. It differentiated from its antecedents in previous class-based societies in that the bureaucracy exploits those who toil not on an individual, but on a collective basis. The bureaucracy collectively owns the means of production, and collectively it appropriates profits. The influential US Trotskyists James Burnham (1905–87) and Max Shachtman (1904–72) agreed with Rizzi's criticism of Trotsky's views, pointing out the ascendancy of state bureaucracy in the US and the so-called 'managerial revolution'. Trotsky replied that the idea of 'bureaucratic collectivism' appeared as a result of disappointment in the revolutionary potential of the working class, which had failed to overthrow capitalism. However, Trotsky reasoned that the latter was still in deep crisis, the outcome of which was not yet decided by history. (See Deutscher 1963: 461–71, for a discussion of this debate.)

As a result of this controversy, one of the deepest insights regarding the Soviet Union's future was provided. Departing from the USSR's transitional nature, being neither capitalism, nor socialism, but including elements of both in a contradictory blend, Trotsky put forward two hypotheses concerning its possible fate. First, the workers can overthrow the bureaucracy in the wake of a successful socialist revolution in other countries, which can happen as a result of the impending world war. Secondly, in the absence of such a revolution, *bureaucracy itself can overthrow the Soviet system to restore capitalism.* In a masterstroke of historical materialism, he wrote:

Privileges have only half their worth, if they cannot be transmitted to one's children. But the right of testament is inseparable from the right of property. It is not enough to be the director of a trust; it is necessary to be a stockholder. The victory of the bureaucracy in this decisive sphere would mean its conversion into a new possessing class ... In reality a backslide to capitalism is wholly possible. (Trotsky 2004: 191–2)

The Marxian tradition of treating bureaucracy as a new suppressive and exploitative class has a history which actually started long before the Russian Revolution. Prominent, and divergent, intellectuals of the Russian and the world socialist movement such as Plekhanov, Bogdanov, Martov, Luxemburg and others warned that the Bolsheviks' authoritarian bias could transform the triumphant revolutionaries into the new ruling elite, who would suppress workers' freedoms. This process definitely started as early as the first years of Soviet power (Pirani 2008). In 1921, the Workers' Opposition among the Bolshevik Party, and, in 1929, Christian Rakovsky (1873–1941), a prominent left-oppositionist, voiced this problem (Deutscher 1963: 462). The aforementioned Burnham and Shachtman (and Milovan Djilas, to mention only one of many other critics) followed the path of treating Soviet bureaucracy as a new exploitative class. They added this or that additional detail to the analysis, but the picture was usually cruder than the one previously presented. The subtlety of Trotsky's insight stems from his recognition of Soviet society's transitory nature as being neither socialism, nor capitalism, which brought about the ambivalence and tenuous position of Soviet bureaucracy.

To appreciate the depth and acuteness of Trotsky's early prophecy, we should recall western Sovietology's shock at the completely unanticipated event of the Berlin Wall's collapse. After examining the nature of the Soviet system and its ruling elite, we are in a position to address the nature of Soviet planning.

2.2.3 The Centrally Planned Economy

All economic systems are susceptible to what John M. Keynes called the 'fundamental uncertainty'. This means a probability which cannot be measured numerically and, hence, whose adverse consequences cannot be deterred by insurance. Keynes used this notion to criticise the neoclassical (or neoliberal, in modern parlance) notion of market efficiency and self-regulation, based on the alleged ability of entrepreneurs to adequately calculate future economic variables.[9] The irrevocable presence of fundamental uncertainty dooms markets to failure at some point in time. That is why, Keynes asserted, markets should be regulated. The undeniable fact that capitalism is susceptible to periodical crises proves Keynes's thinking. However, his solution of state interference in economic life through indirect means is not the only answer to the problem.

Long before Keynes, Karl Marx also analysed the issue, but from a very different perspective. While the former treated fundamental uncertainty as a natural property of the human mind, the latter related it to the social conditions of production. The Marxian theory of 'commodity fetishism' maintains that competition amongst economic agents makes the path of economic development unpredictable, which gives rise to spontaneous processes not malleable to control by individuals. A salient example of this kind can be found in dispropor-tionate allocation of investments emanating from severe competition in the capital markets. As a result, the capitalist economy periodically undergoes slumps and contractions. Due to the growth of the concentration of production and rising accumulation of fixed capital stock, the damage inflicted on a society by economic crises increases disproportionately. From this, Marx derived the objective need of planning. Thus, the incessant accumulation of capital, rather than just the limitations of the human mind, makes economic planning necessary at a certain point in history.

In fact, planning became an instrument whose function was to decrease uncertainty in the economy. This was underscored by Vladimir Bazarov, a prominent pioneer of Soviet planning in the 1920s: 'being unable to *forecast* we are compelled to *forestall* the results of development in the form of a priori plan[ning] targets' (Bazarov 1989: 168–9) (original emphasis; author's translation).

The idea of planning as an alternative to the market was at the core of Soviet economic thought's worldview, for example, Tsagolov's school of political economy, developed at Moscow State University.[10] It attempted to develop a system of ideas reflecting the Soviet economy as a holistic entity. The point of departure for this approach was 'planomernost' (see below). All other categories of the Soviet economy were derived from this basic idea, in the same manner in which Marx derived his system of capitalism from the idea of commodity.

Tsagolov's school distinguished between planning as a process and 'planomernost' as a social relation, a property of a particular type of economy. *'Planned-ness' means deliberately reproducing a proportionality of the economy.* This notion stemmed from Marxian reproduction schemes which represented economic growth as a result of interrelation of the different sectors of the national economy. Proportionality means equilibrium, that is, the structural correspondence of all major industries and processes in the economy taken as a whole. An important external manifestation of this condition is the full employment of material resources and lack of unemployment. Proportionality corresponds to the notion of a general Walrasian equilibrium, but is not secured by the free interplay of market forces. The balanced state of the whole economy (*sbalansirovannost'*) is reached through securing a system based on particular balances of consumption and accumulation, incomes and expenditures of the population, industry and agriculture, and so on. This can be attained only if every industry has an output in exactly the quantity and quality which its customers need.

To ensure the 'planomernost' of the Soviet economy, a set of state agencies was created. In it is a simplified version of planning, which was organised as follows. The Politburo of the Central Committee of the CPSU, the highest level of the power in the Soviet hierarchy, developed the country's major development scenario for the next five years (*pyatiletka*). The document reflected some compromise between the contradictory goals of consumption and social development, investments, and defence needs. This scenario was passed to the USSR's major planning body – the State Planning Committee (Gosplan), which unfolded the scenario into 400–500 economic variables designed to meet the targets set by the Politburo. From this, the tasks were derived for the ministries in charge of the development of particular industries. They devised the plans for each industry's development, setting targets for the enterprises. Each industry's management would devise an enterprise development plan, requesting resources and investments to meet the targets. Then the proposed plans moved in an upward direction through the same hierarchy. Relying on this more precise information, Gosplan would fine-tune these planning details and targets, to produce a final five-year plan which would become law. This final five-year plan would be communicated down through the same ministries to the enterprises. According to the plan, the State Committee for Procurement and Supply (Gossnab) would allocate material and labour resources among industries and enterprises. The State Committee on Pricing (Goskomtsen) would set prices and the State Committee on Labor (Goskomtrud) would set wage rates for the different industries involved. Many other less important aspects of the central planning were fulfilled by a number of other state agencies.

All of this was intended to secure a well-balanced economy. For example, wage rate patterns should be set in such a way that the entire wage fund exactly corresponded to the value of output of consumption goods and services. However, the centrally planned economy's reality was very different.

The apologists for central planning largely resembled their opposites, that is, the staunch free-marketeers. Indeed, both camps took great pains to present 'their' social systems as devoid of conflict and inherent contradictions. This led to striking parallels in their ways of thinking. For example, faith in the omnipotence and wisdom of the so-called 'public centre' (an euphemism meaning the state) under socialism implies the absence of 'fundamental uncertainty' in the same way as faith in the omniscient market agent does. In both cases, the future is assumed to be transparent, predetermined and predictable, with supernatural computational abilities ascribed either to the state, or to an individual. This thinking allowed central planning's proponents to ignore the state bureaucracy's vested interests under socialism in the same way that this thinking allows free-marketers to ignore exploitation under capitalism.

The historical performance of Soviet central planning was contradictory. On the one hand, from 1929 (the year when industrialisation began) through 1975, the USSR's production rates were only matched by Japan. As Gur Ofer had succinctly explained:

Since the Bolshevik revolution of 1917, the Soviet Union has transformed itself through an intense drive for economic modernization, from an underdeveloped economy into a modern industrial state with a GNP second only to that of the United States. During that period the Soviet economy grew by a factor of ten and the level of GNP per capita grew more than fivefold. Its industrial structure had changed dramatically, from an economy with 82 percent rural population and most GNP originating in agriculture to one that is 78 percent urban with 40–45 percent of GNP originating in manufacturing and related industries. Furthermore, Soviet military capability is considered to be on a par with that of United States. (Ofer 1987: 1767)

Taking advantage of these high growth rates, the Soviet economy greatly increased people's living standards and life expectancy, provided the population with free housing, modern education and healthcare, conducted fundamental scientific research matched only by the United States, and made world-class technological advances in certain areas. This undeniable progress in economic and social development made the Soviet model appealing for many countries in their drive towards modernisation, particularly in the peripheries of the capitalist world-system.[11]

On the other hand, the Soviet economy suffered from constant shortages and deficits, poor-quality consumer goods, over-long construction cycles extending far beyond their original estimates. Significant benefits and social provision for workers, combined with their alienation from managing enterprises, led to poor workplace discipline and, hence, to poor productivity. Civil manufacturing and agriculture were notoriously backward in technological terms. From the mid-1970s, the previously high rates of Soviet economic growth began their remarkable decline.

The further fate of the Soviet economy, which had found itself at a crossroads, depended on the evolution of the Soviet elite.

2.3 The Crisis of Planning

It is very easy to misinterpret the reason for the Soviet system's breakdown as a failure of central planning, which the Soviet system was not allegedly able to reform. In fact, this understanding dominates western conventional literature on transition (for example, see Aslund 2007: chs 1 and 2). But this is only another manifestation of the famous 'end of history' thesis, the prime objective of which is not to evaluate all the complex factors of the Soviet system's dissolution, but rather to persuade the wider public how futile are any efforts to seek alternatives to capitalism. (This need becomes urgent in the times of crisis for the capitalist world-system.) This conventional and ideological approach ignores the evolution of the key social institutions and dominant social interests of Soviet society, which underlie its demise.

An alternative understanding of the USSR's declining economic growth rates can be suggested from the standpoint of the 'social structure of accumulation' (SSA) approach. This attempts to explain the long-term performance of capitalist countries (not only the core countries, but the peripheral ones as well) from the standpoint of the evolution of their main social institutions (see Kotz et al. 1994 and McDonough et al. 2010 for an introduction). The SSA theory appeared to be an attempt to comprehend Kondratiyev's 'long-term waves of economic growth'. In contrast to Kondratiyev's 'long-term waves', the SSA theory ascribed primary importance not to technological change, but to change in social institutions. The approach is focused on a particular set of institutions that create favourable conditions for the accumulation of capital. However efficient they may be at the initial stage of a given accumulation cycle, over time they inevitably turn from facilitating to impeding economic growth. This results in crisis and social turmoil, until a new social structure of accumulation is identified and established. From this standpoint, the very factors of success in economic growth over time lead to its breakdown. Although this approach was designed to comprehend economic growth under capitalism, the idea of a particular set of institutions, initially facilitating and then impeding development, is applicable to the Soviet situation as well. This section attempts to see the crisis of planning from this perspective.

Since the primary factor of economic growth is the social interests dominating the social system in question, one should start from the development of Soviet bureaucracy in the post-Stalin epoch.

2.3.1   Social Structure and the Ruling Bureaucracy

It is well known that Marxism bases its understanding of the social structure of the population on singling out large social classes defined by their relation to the means of production. This created problems for a Marxist analysis of the USSR's class structure since Soviet society eliminated private property or private means of production. On the other hand, as was previously demonstrated, Trotsky provided an insightful analysis of this problem as early as the 1930s, departing from the Marxian theory of classes. This was possible because Marxism recognises a more subtle differentiation of classes based on social strata and social groups. Marxism 'express[ed] more detailed characteristics of society in comparison with social classes'. Thus, the notion of class reflects the most general features pertaining to all strata and groups that comprise society (Semenov 1960–70). Such stratification was applied to Soviet-type societies as well (ibid.). However, their relations were depicted (with a few exceptions) as burdened only by minor contradictions, excluding the so-called 'antagonistic' ones which allegedly pertained only to capitalist societies. Notwithstanding, this approach can be used to study the evolution of the Soviet ruling stratum.

Alternatively, the Soviet bureaucracy can be analysed in terms of the theory of the elite (Gel'man and Tarusina 2003). However, this approach is focused on how the elite's interests affect policy making. It does not explain how these interests are formed and come to a dominant position. This is done by class analysis. David Lane suggests a synthetic approach: 'A strength of elite analysis is that it can distinguish between the political form and economic: class may articulate values, which shape institutions and motivate political actors (political elites)' (Lane 2011: 13). In other words, social classes, being complex structures comprised of different strata, produce an elite which in turn may contain different groups reflecting different and often conflicting interests. Hence, the dynamics of the elite reflect the underlying dynamics of the socio-economic system.

The record rates of Soviet economic growth ensured rapid changes in the social structure: urbanisation, the increase of the number of industrial workers corresponding with a decrease in agricultural workers, and the rise in the number of non-manual workers. The latter had grown from only one-sixth of the USSR's population in the end of the 1930s to one-third in the 1980s (Rutkevitch 1999: 22). This determined the change in the ruling bureaucracy's social base. Under Stalin, 'the major social prop of the regime' was the peasantry, while under Brezhnev and Khruschev, it was the manual worker: 'Under perestroika, the professional non-manuals became the ascendant groups and, it may be hypothesized, provided a social base which both pushed and was attracted to Gorbachev's policies' (Lane 2011: 56). Non-manual workers, or the intelligentsia, comprised a highly heterogeneous social group. The Soviet Union, we should remember, aspired to be the first 'workers' state'. That is why manual workers, although deprived of political rights, enjoyed many socio-economic privileges: full employment, high wages in comparison to other social groups (see below), public consumption funds (that is, state-subsidised housing, education, health care, and so on). This was reflected in wage patterns: in 1940, the average wage rate in education amounted to 97 per cent of the average industrial wage rate, in 1960, that percentage had dropped to 79 per cent, and in 1985 to 63 per cent. In the mid-1980s, a starting-level worker with only two to three years' work experience earned more than a starting-level associate professor (Rutkevitch 2004: 63). This produced growing social discontent, among both the manager-bureaucrats and different groups of the intelligentsia.

Lane (ibid.: 38) identifies two broad social groups which were destined to become the driving forces of the shift from central planning to capitalism. The first, which Lane labelled the 'administrative class', was populated by state functionaries controlling the economy, cultural life, law enforcement agencies and the military apparatus. This class was complemented by the 'acquisition class', consisting of individuals whose personal skills can be profitably utilised through the markets, and are regarded as the intelligentsia. A large proportion of both of these sizeable social groups were increasingly dissatisfied with the egalitarian practices which prevailed in Soviet society.

Hence, the rapid economic growth of the Soviet Union in the twentieth century produced radical changes in the social structure of society, making it more complex and potentially unstable, as it gave rise to diverse and often contradictory social interests. Rutkevitch (2004) identified a number of social conflicts burgeoning under the façade of Brezhnev's 'real socialism':

A salient feature of the gradually increasing tension in the relations of the groups and strata of the Soviet society as a social system ... took place in such a way that the whole process had not coincided with the fault lines of the class–social division, but originated inside the major social groups resulting from new strata coming into being. (Rutkevitch 2004: 62; author's translation)

Due to the Soviet political system's totalitarian nature, these growing social tensions were not alleviated by a search for social compromises and the corresponding reforms.

Summing up, one may say that as the result of modernisation and a prolonged period of economic growth which had profoundly changed the social structure of society, the Soviet system became susceptible to growing discontents of the different social strata, including the ruling bureaucracy. It is with this backdrop in mind that the crisis in central planning should be examined.

2.3.2   The Crisis of Central Planning

Despite the constant official boasting about the 'advantages of our social order', which was an indispensable part of their work, Soviet economists tried to understand this adverse process. A prominent Soviet specialist, Yuri Yaremenko (of the USSR's Academy of Sciences), recalled later that comparative studies of Soviet and US economic performances revealed a puzzle: for a few decades, the USSR had demonstrated higher overall growth rates, while the proportion of its GDP to that of its rival (the US) remained nearly the same (approximately 60 per cent) (Yaremenko 1997: 4–26). At the Moscow State University, Tsagolov's school of economics sought an explanation for the decline in growth rates which seemed to be in violation of the optimal balance of 'centralism' and 'self-dependency of enterprises'. In my student years at MSU (the first half of the 1980s), these labels were understood as obvious euphemisms for 'central planning' and 'the market'. It was maintained that 'centralisation was not identical to "planomernost".' The dialectics of the latter assumes that excessive centralisation can produce disproportions just as does insufficient centralisation. In other words, we should maintain a balance between the two contradictory sides of the economy to ensure 'planomernost'. Due to ideological reasons, the problem was discussed only in highly abstract terms and was never traced to its source: the Soviet bureaucracy's arbitrary power and specific vested interests.

An important insight into the inner mechanisms of the operation of Soviet-type economies is provided by Yaremenko (1997). Pondering the aforementioned comparison of the Soviet and US GDPs, he arrived at the quality of economic growth as being an important key to the problem. This led to the formation of the 'theory of the qualitative heterogeneity of resources'. Summing up the conclusions of this approach, we can say that it viewed the Soviet economy as a technologically non-homogeneous one. This means that the overwhelming majority of its high-quality resources – equipment, labour force, raw materials – were concentrated in the military-industrial complex, while the civil-sector economy was compelled to content itself with low-quality inputs. This fact had enormous and fateful consequences for both Soviet and current Russian economic development.

To ensure economic growth and an increase in consumption by the Soviet population, it was necessary to ensure an ever-growing supply of 'mass-produced' (low-quality) resources. This was achieved through increasing the rate of mineral extraction, the progressive urbanisation of the agrarian population and the recruitment of women into industrial labour, producing relatively simple equipment in ever-larger quantities. This type of economic growth presupposes a certain industrial structure. The sector supplying the intermediary products grows disproportionately. To ensure the same percentage of GDP growth in a larger technologically non-homogenous economy, we need more output of electricity, pig iron, capital construction, transportation, and so on. According to Yaremenko, this was the main reason why the USSR, for the few last decades before its collapse, could not catch up with the US; the latter had a more technologically homogenous economic structure, and, hence, greater quality of economic growth!

This technological non-homogeneity became the Soviet economy's Achilles heel. Many of the previously mentioned bottlenecks, such as the poor quality of consumer goods and low productivity growth, can be traced to this problem. In the 1970s, the reserves of cheap labour and raw materials extraction were virtually exhausted. This led to growing disproportions, which in turn produced an inevitable decline in the Soviet economy's growth rates. Meanwhile, détente's failure at the beginning of the 1980s, and the exacerbation of the Cold War, took their toll on the Soviet economy. From this, the necessity for the deep reforms in the Soviet system was increasingly recognised by a certain part of the country's leadership.

At first glance, at the bottom of the USSR's problems lay the 'non-economic burden' (in Yaremenko parlance) of the arms race. But further examination reveals the problem of over-centralisation of planning as a cause of these growing disproportions. It is my view that the aforementioned is only an economic dimension of the major catastrophe of Soviet history – Stalin's 'Thermidor'. Making traditional values triumphant over the values of European socialism, it attributed low value to individual freedoms. Reliance on mass resources as the main vehicle of economic growth was embedded in the 'Great Leap' of Stalin's five-year plans and in forced, often violent, collectivisation. This underpinned the over-centralisation of planning, denying society any legal right to participate in decision making. Summarising the aforementioned, we should agree with Kotz and Weir in that:

> The stagnation that set in after 1975 in the Soviet Union was due, not so much to the failures of the Soviet system, but to its successes. Nearly fifty years of rapid economic growth and development had changed the economy and society in ways that undermined the continuing effectiveness of the particular configuration of institutions which had generated the rapid growth. (2007: 49–50)

It is with this backdrop of increasing social tensions and the economy's slowdown that the development of the bureaucracy's informal control over the country's economic resources took place.

2.3.3 The Evolution of Informal Control

A number of analysts (see below) note that the emergence of a market economy in Russia was preceded by a gradual undermining of the state's control over enterprises as early as the late stages of the central planning period in the 1970s and 1980s.

Under both Khruschev's and Brezhnev's regimes, a number of attempts were made to reform the Soviet economy, designed to increase material inducements for enterprises to improve the quality of their work. Admittedly, these reforms failed to significantly improve the Soviet economy's performance; they were all executed within strict central planning frameworks without any introduction of market relations. But these attempts only produced new hierarchies or expanded the old ones. Andrew Barnes came to the conclusion that, as a result of the growing complexity of managing the national economy, enterprise managers grew more powerful, since they succeeded in resisting the reforms that sought to control them: 'Most important[ly], they and individual bureaucrats exploited the absence of a coherent command structure [in order] to enrich and empower themselves' (Barnes 2006: 35).

According to Blokhin (2002), some informal contractual relations between the state ministries and enterprises began to take place alongside administrative planning. A somewhat bureaucratic market gradually emerged, where a certain kind of informal trade was established between directors of the state enterprises and officials from the state ministries. If the latter demanded an increase in the planned targets, the former would demand more resources distributed by the state. Naturally, directors tended to decrease the level of planning tasks (that is, the level of activity required by the central planners), while at the same time trying to obtain more resources, 'the more sophisticated the production, the easier it was for the director to negotiate a more favourable bargain. He knew the subject better than the Gosplan officials: better even than the most professional of them' (Blokhin 2002: 52; author's translation). For a long time, Gosplan more or less managed to control the process, but gradually the role of the state management's central bodies became weaker, and the bureaucracy, including the directors, gained additional power (Yaremenko 1998).

This is confirmed by the data on ministerial bureaucracy mediating between the enterprises and the highest levels of the managerial hierarchy (that is, Gosplan, Gossnab and Goskomtsen). Allegedly, the ministries' top-level managers were promoted to their positions by the CPSU and their activities monitored and controlled by the latter. As a result of the economy's growing complexity and the corresponding growth in the number of ministries and their personnel, the reality increasingly became very different. Stephen Whitefield has studied the industrial ministries' role in the Soviet economy. After examining the training, promotion and assignment of ministry functionaries, he arrived at the conclusion that 'there is little sign that superior bodies, including the Council of Ministers both nationally and at republic level, were able to operate effective control over ministry personnel, in large measure because the ministries themselves were charged with the process' (Whitefield 1993: 87). Promotion of ministry officials was increasingly based on the mechanisms of informal relations rather than on selection of the best-qualified candidates. Moreover, the chaotic, over-complex structure of overlapping departments with often diffuse functions became a powerful tool enabling the ministries to resist their superiors' attempts to impose stricter control over their activities. In this milieu, informal groups of officials emerged which could 'manipulate various levers of intra-ministerial power to their own advantage' (ibid.: 93).

The Soviet economy experienced a simultaneous, rapid growth in the informal (that is, 'shadow', 'grey' or 'black market', or barely legal) sector, and the purely criminal sector. Such negative phenomena had always existed in the USSR, but in Brezhnev's and Gorbachev's times, their scale increased enormously. According to Karyagina's estimates (1990: 116–17), from 1960 to the end of the 1980s, employment in the illegitimate sector of the Soviet economy had grown from less than 10 to 25 per cent of the entire employed population. According to Rozmainsky (1999), the shadow economy's very rapid expansion can be attributed to the increasing cooperation between criminal structures and members of the ruling bureaucracy. Rutkevitch (1999: 27) notes that strictly regimented distribution of commodities in accordance with one's position in the bureaucratic hierarchy was often complemented by corruption, connections with the shadow economy and personal relations with influential people.

At the same time, the lack of private accumulation of capital, profit appropriation and the inability to bequeath a privileged position to one's heirs were accompanied by 'strict control "from above", on the part of higher echelons of power, and "from below", on the part of party and trade unions' committees, bodies of People's Control, mass media and so on' (ibid.). To this I would add the remaining, although already severely eroded, socialist values. I can say from my personal experience of association with members of the party hierarchy that they cannot be reduced en masse to a *nomenklatura* greedy for personal wealth. The older party functionaries, whose formative years were the 1930s and 1940s, still possessed a sense of historical mission and devotion for the Soviet state. (This sense was obviously much weaker in the next generation of party apparatchiks, who belonged to the Gorbachev generation.) These strong limitations of the abuse of power built into the Soviet system, especially in those who acted from below, are seldom mentioned in western literature, as they contradict the conventional view of the Soviet system as an unequivocally totalitarian state in which rank-and-file citizens were completely deprived of any rights. Meanwhile, these limitations were quite powerful. They represented the surviving legacy of the Revolution, vestiges of the 'dual character' of the Soviet state mentioned by Trotsky (see above). Due to the degeneration of a bureaucracy increasingly aware and jealous of the western elite's living standards and lifestyle, the barriers to personal enrichment started to be felt with growing, although for a time suppressed, discontent.

Thus, under the surface of an ostensibly monolithic planned economic system, processes were taking place which were to have significant long-term consequences. Expansion of the rights of control over material resources (finance played only a secondary role in the Soviet economy) provided the heads of state enterprises and their associates both pecuniary and non-pecuniary privileges. Together with the shadow economy's growth, this created the foundations for the development of private income generation based on manipulation of public property. It is important to note that despite the private nature of appropriating incomes from these activities, they were not essentially entrepreneurial, even in the shadow sector. They were based not on private ownership, but on administrative control over productive assets and material resources.

Hardly anyone in the Soviet leadership of the mid-1980s clearly understood their country's problems, but a vague and increasing anxiety that the country was lagging behind its Cold War competitors certainly had emerged.

2.4 Gorbachev's Perestroika and the Consolidation of Informal Control Over Assets

The final chapter of the USSR's economic history which takes place from 1985 to 1991, a period marked by Gorbachev's perestroika, is a sad story of rising hope, sporadic action and bitter disappointment. The era witnessed some genuine but ill-prepared attempts at reform, which led to a further deceleration of economic growth and an increasing sense of economic and social insecurity. Eventually these reforms, designed to strengthen the Soviet state, led to its disintegration. The only faction which benefited from what happened was comprised of those members of the administrative and acquisitive classes who sought to strengthen their informal control over resources as private property.

Gorbachev approached economic reform without any sound plan and clear understanding of what was needed. He relied on the advice of prominent academicians from the Academy of Sciences who proved to be too conformist and susceptible to rapidly changing external influences to provide solid and persistent intellectual guidance. At every new stage of reform, he would appeal to new specialists. Gorbachev's perestroika (economic restructuring) can be divided into three periods.

The first stage, carried out in 1985–86, witnessed some minor changes under the slogan of *uskoreniye* (acceleration). Its main effort was in the modernisation of the Soviet economy's engineering sector (Aganbegyan 1988). The manufacture of new production equipment was seen as the key precondition for the whole industry's modernisation and technological upgrading. The idea that technological advance depends on the quality of investment goods was correct. However, the protagonists assumed that little if any institutional changes needed to take place, and failed to take into account the technological non-homogeneity of the Soviet economy (see above). Preserving the situation where the best-quality resources were still reserved for military production made it impossible to modernise civilian engineering. Additional financial resources directed to this sector disappeared with little effect, which contributed mainly to an increase in consumer demand which remained unfulfilled, and to so-called 'inflation overhang'.

At the second stage, during 1987–88, some genuine reforms were undertaken. The major vehicle for change was the Law on State Enterprise (1987), which tried to achieve, to some degree, a new balance of central planning and market freedoms in the operation of enterprises. That is, the latter remained in state ownership, but control over them was significantly loosened. The actual plan, coming from above, was replaced by 'state order', and covered only 85 per cent of the output of enterprises. The sale of the remaining 15 per cent was permitted under market conditions. According to this law, enterprises obtained the right to establish direct 'horizontal' connections between each other without the mediation of Gosplan, and in some sections, even to make direct contacts with foreign firms. Enterprises were empowered with wider rights to determine wages and the range of products generated by a business. From 1990, state enterprises obtained the right to plan their activities themselves, fulfilling non-obligatory and approximate targets provided by the Ministries. The law assumed that there existed the possibility of state enterprises going bankrupt. In addition, the law introduced the right of personnel to elect their directors and established the Councils of the Workers' Collectives with vaguely defined rights of participation in decision making.

This reform introduced enormous changes in the operation of Soviet industry and the central planning system in general. It initiated a profound change in the fundamental institution of the economy, and was genuinely designed to find a proper balance of plan and market on a socialist basis. However, while all this is true, the law failed to take into account several crucially important circumstances. First of all, it left intact the environment in which enterprises operated. Meanwhile, the complete lack of market infrastructure – such as trade or financial intermediaries – in the Soviet economy meant that it was very difficult for enterprises to find a market for their products. In a society where workers had lacked not only actual experience, but even living memory of participation in civil society, they naturally failed to put their new rights to good use. For instance, the election of directors led to the advancement of populists, rather than efficient managers. Abstaining from any innovative activities in very uncertain conditions, enterprises greatly increased wages, while simultaneously increasing their products' prices, unaware of the true market-demand constraints. Bankruptcy proceedings were not applied, even to the growing number of firms showing losses. Probably, this law's most important consequence was that it greatly increased directors' powers in managing the resources of controlled enterprises (that is, those which were still considered to be owned by the state).

Another fateful measure of Gorbachev's reforms was the Law on Cooperation (1988), which permitted private initiative in the form of cooperatives free from state management. This was aimed at meeting the growing demand for consumer goods and services. At the same time, private initiatives were expected to compete with state enterprises, encouraging the latter to improve their own performance. The new entities, which grew very quickly, partially served these objectives. However, very soon the cooperatives were a focus for raised significant public anxiety and concern, because the new institutions greatly widened opportunities for embezzlement, fraud and pilfering in the state sector, rather than facilitating its normal activities. Top-tier enterprise managers began to establish their own cooperatives which funnelled away the assets of state-controlled organisations. This contributed greatly to the growing public discontent over reforms and central planning in general.

However deplorable these phenomena, they had been developing in the framework of what still seemed to be a guided process. In 1990–91, Gorbachev's reforms entered the third stage, when the central Soviet authorities were rapidly losing control over the economy. These were tumultuous years in Soviet politics, characterised by the open and perilous conflict between Gorbachev and Yeltsin, a steep decline in living standards, deep public dissent on the Soviet Union's future development, the emerging separatism of the Soviet republics and the surge of violent nationalism. While these conditions were prevalent, a completely new tranche of social forces was formed which succeeded in setting reform on a new trajectory.

Kotz and Weir challenge the conventional wisdom which holds that the Soviet system (which they label 'state socialism') disintegrated because it was impossible to reform central planning nor was it viable (2007: 71–2). They emphasised the fact that the Soviet economy did not contract and indeed continued to grow until the end of 1989. Only in 1990 did the USSR enter a period of economic slump, but that year also witnessed the dismantling of central planning. This was carried out by a new, powerful force, which appeared on the political scene: a pro-capitalist bloc of social groupings (ibid.: 107–11).

This bloc included broad circles of intellectuals, economists and businesspeople from non-elite backgrounds, but the pivotal role in this coalition was played by representatives of the party-state elite. Kotz and Weir believe that many members of the latter realised from their own, or their less scrupulous colleagues', experiences, what prospects of personal enrichment were opened by the market reforms of the late 1980s. This is why when Gorbachev's democratisation policy removed the threat of retribution for violation of party discipline, many members of the ruling bureaucracy decided to abandon the socialist world outlook in favour of capitalist values. They rallied behind Yeltsin and challenged Gorbachev's leadership and his reforms' apparently socialist aims. Never seeking support from below, Gorbachev found himself more and more abandoned and isolated, while the Soviet Union, the central planning framework and his own personal power increasingly disintegrated.

With this backdrop of the breakdown of the Soviet system, the previously mentioned informal control of the bureaucracy with reference to assets entered a new developmental stage. According to Radygin and Sydorov (2000), the late 1980s saw the onset of the spontaneous privatisation of state property. Lavigne (1999: 176) asserts that this is not a particular form of privatisation, but simply a way for the former state bureaucracy's members to 'become owners of the companies they managed before'. She argues that the process first took place in Poland and Hungary. Beginning in the era of the communist regime, state enterprises obtained more rights. Employees began to have an influence on companies' decision-making processes and even participated in elections for their directors. However, it was the managers rather than the workers who benefited from this transformation of enterprises into joint-stock companies. In the new legal framework, the managers began to split up state enterprises, hiving off their most profitable segments into limited liability companies or joint ventures. Later, the managers would move into positions at these newly established firms (ibid.). Something very similar happened in Russia: 'Heads of some enterprises obtained full control over the "managed" assets by lending them to their associated commercial structures; making some of the plants independent ... cooperating with state organisations on conditions favourable to their directors, and so on' (Radygin and Sydorov 2000: 46–7). This staged privatisation was led by different kinds of state bureaucracy: central, territorial, managerial, and so on (Radygin, 1992). Radygin and Sydorov particularly note that 'with the collapse of state control over production on the one hand and absence of the legal basis of the private property on the other, control over the assets was gained and retained largely by force, the use of criminal structures and bribery of government officials.' At the same time, 'the first foreign (and pseudo-foreign) pseudo-investors appeared, whose single aim was control over the financial flows' (2000: 46–7).

Informal privatisation at this stage can be illustrated by the story of the future Russian 'robber banker', Mikhail Khodorkovsky, who was always quick to spot new opportunities. Connections which he established when he was a middle-ranking official of Komsomol (the Communist Youth Organisation) helped him to create a students' café as early as in 1986 and later to obtain a licence to engage in foreign trade. However, one of his most lucrative assets was a business partner – Alexei Golubovitch, another Komsomol official, whose parents occupied important posts in the State Bank of the USSR (the Soviet Union's only bank). These connections were put to good use when in late 1989 Khodorkovsky created 'Menatep' – one of the first private banks in Russia. Relying heavily on its close ties with the state bureaucracy, the bank managed to benefit from diverting state finances to its own control (Sixsmith 2010: chs 4–6). The most significant wealth in those days was accumulated not through the hard labour of producing consumer goods and services, but through a close and mutually beneficial association with state structures.

The first cases of formal privatisation took part at the end of Gorbachev's tenure as well. Barnes calls this 'privatisation by exception', in which he includes 'the ever widening stream of decisions from the Council of Ministers to approve privatization of individual enterprises, networks of firms, or entire ministries' (2006: 58). He comments that such acts often started as leasing arrangements, with the assumption of manager and employee buy-outs. Unions at enterprises and even whole ministries were transformed into concerns and other kinds of market structures by decisions of the State Commission for Economic Reform, which had been established by the Council of Ministers (Whitefield 1993: 222–34).

Furthermore, the period of spontaneous privatisation previously discussed (and of 'privatisation by exception') still took place before this process was legally authorised, and discussions about the acceptability of the different, alternative property types were ongoing (Radygin 1992). It is important to note that in such conditions, the forms of control over assets, referred to previously – bribery, criminal connections, and so on, necessarily assumed an unofficial, informal character. This created important preconditions, which determined the character of *official* privatisation as it occurred after the Soviet system's collapse in 1991 and the onset of radical market reforms in 1992.

In summary, we may conclude that a genuine attempt to reform central planning based on socialist values was carried out only in the short period of 1987–89, after which it was dwarfed by a powerful pro-capitalist coalition originating from the milieu of the administrative and acquisitive classes. The most important result of Gorbachev's economic reforms for the nascent private businesses in Russia was the strengthening of informal control over state assets by some of the ruling bureaucracy.

2.5 'Shock Therapy' and the Emergence of Capitalism

In August 1991, Communist hard-liners attempted to stage a coup in an attempt to avert the impending dismemberment of the Soviet Union by Yeltsin's coterie and some Soviet republican elites craving power and property. The failure of this abortive attempt precipitated the Soviet system's dissolution – especially its central planning system, and many social rights of the common people – and ushered in a completely new epoch of capitalism. The triumphant pro-capitalist bloc, led by the former Communist functionary – Boris Yeltsin – had completely abandoned any socialist parlance and fully embraced the capitalist outlook in its neoliberal version. At the beginning of 1992, Russia embarked on a completely new course of economic reforms.

2.5.1 The Radical Market Reforms Agenda

Under President Yeltsin, an 'independent' Russia adopted a packet of radical market reforms known as 'shock therapy'. By no means were these reforms part of a plan designed by Russian economists to fit their country's unique conditions. On the contrary, the reforms were only an application of what is known in the West as the notorious principles of the 'Washington Consensus'. This term was originally coined in 1990 by the US economist John Williamson to designate the policy advice of the Washington-based international financial institutions, such as the IMF and the World Bank, when they were addressing the economic problems of Latin American countries. Over time, the term's meaning changed, and came to signify the neoliberal economic agenda promoted by the West in developing countries and emerging markets. Among other measures, the Washington Consensus includes a decrease of the state's role in the national economy through cuts in taxes and social expenditure, the privatisation of state enterprises, a move to free pricing, the deregulation of foreign trade, and restrictive monetary policy. The agenda can be summed up in the phrase: 'liberalisation plus stabilisation'. These principles are widely seen as promoting (or imposing) the vested interests of the core's capital (on) to the world economy's periphery, at the latter's expense. Washington Consensus scholars see it more as a vehicle of globalisation than as a way to achieve sustainable growth and development (Serra, Spiegel and Stiglitz 2008: 6). They note that the consensus 'called for opening of countries to the outside world. As a result, the fortunes of developing countries have increasingly depended on what happens outside their boundaries' (ibid.).

Russia's 'shock therapy' was only a slavishly followed version of the abovementioned principles. A useful insight into why the Washington Consensus was adopted by the Russian leadership is provided by Boris Jordan, a descendant of the Russian 'White Guard' émigrés and a US banker, who established the office of the Credit Swiss First Boston Bank in Moscow in 1992. Closely associated with the team of Russian reformers, Jordan recalls that at that time the Communists were still considered as a major threat (probably, by the pro-capitalist forces),[12] which is why 'Yeltsin's strategy was to break the totalitarian system. The only way to succeed in that goal was to free prices, transfer the assets to the public [for who actually obtained these assets, see Chapter 3], release market forces, and then make sure that the process was irreversible' (Desai 2006: 291). Thus, the main object of reforms was not to enhance the Russian economy's efficiency or improve the population's living standards, but to secure at all costs the victorious pro-capitalist coalition's interests. For this purpose, the principles of the Washington Consensus served perfectly.

That the former was the principle source of inspiration for Yeltsin's government can be easily seen from the list of the main objectives of the radical market reforms initiated in early 1992:

- State property privatisation
- Price liberalisation

- Reduction of state expenditures
- Restrictive monetary policy
- Liberalisation of foreign trade

To realise why these principles were adopted in Russia with such devastating results it is not enough just to refer to the Soviet bureaucracy's degeneration. While acknowledging its role in dismantling the Soviet system, Lane emphasises the global capitalism's influence as a driving force of transformation in the former socialist countries: 'The international political elites were decisive backers, initially, of the move to political competition and economic markets and, later, to privatization' (2011: 13). He singles out the 'global political class' who 'through the hegemonic governments of the West and international organizations' carried out its decisive impact, defining 'the course of transition and support[ing] the creation of capitalism and a bourgeois property-owning class' (ibid.: 43). Ostensibly, the prime role in carrying out the reforms was played by a group of senior Russian officials, led by Yegor Gaidar – the first deputy prime minister, and then prime minister of the Russian government in 1992. However, the reform process 'was advised, pushed and supported by senior officials of the US administration and a group of like-minded American economists' (Pirani 2010: 24). Neoliberal economists Jeffrey Sachs and Andrei Shleifer and lawyer Jonathan Hay played a prominent role in shaping the course of the radical market reforms. Their influence regarding Russian economic policy was unprecedented in the history of an independent state: 'The US advisers worked out policy measures with Gaidar, Chubais and their colleagues, which were written straight into presidential decrees. Every single significant economic decision of Yeltsin's presidency was implemented this way. Parliament was bypassed' (ibid.: 27).

This is vividly confirmed by Jordan (Desai 2006: 291–3). He recalls that in late September 1992, he was approached by Anatoly Chubais, who led the Russian privatisation programme. Chubais explained that the Congress of People's Deputies (the first democratically elected Russian Parliament), which had been scheduled for 9 December that year, was expected to call for a halt to privatisation, which is why he suggested that Jordan develop 'a fast-track privatisation programme'. A team of western specialists led by Jordan and his partner Steven

Jennings was set to work: 'We worked day and night, literally day and night, sleeping in our offices a few hours a night and working frantically', proudly recalls Jordan. They succeeded in omitting many important steps which were necessary to do the job with appropriate quality, and the process was launched on 8 December, exactly one day before the Congress was scheduled to gather in Moscow. 'What my grandfather could not achieve during the civil war between the White Army and the Communists, we were able to manage by getting the state out of property ownership', concluded Jordan, with great satisfaction (ibid., p. 192). It seems that it never occurred to him that, in bypassing the Parliament about privatisation which was such a vital issue for every Russian, he helped to undermine Russia's nascent, unsteady democracy. The whole episode is only another piece of evidence that under capitalism the elite's vested interests count more than democratic rights – it looks particularly sinister in the perspective of the outcomes of privatisation.

2.5.2   The Main Directions of 'Shock Therapy'

As privatisation is extensively dealt with in the next chapter, here I will only mention that it was widely promoted to the Russian public as an opportunity for anyone to become an entrepreneur, to secure their own future in the market economy. In reality, privatisation turned out to be a massive transfer of property rights from the state to the most unscrupulous representatives of the ruling bureaucracy, the acquisitive class and the criminal underworld, at the expense of the absolute majority of Russian citizens.

Allegedly, price liberalisation was designed to create preconditions for free market competition. It was assumed that free prices (that is, not prices set by the state) reflecting information on market demand would allocate economic resources in the most efficient way. In fact, as can be seen from Figure 2.1, price liberalisation engendered enormous inflation which in turn led to monopolistic pricing. To be sure, the data indicate that in 1992, the first year of the radical market reforms, consumer prices leapt by 2,610 per cent. No less impressive was the price surge in all other pivotal sectors of the national economy. Thus, in 1992, the price indices of industrial products had grown by 3,380 per cent, agricultural products by 940 per cent, producers in construction by 1,610 per cent, and the tariffs for cargo transportation by 3,560 per cent (Goskomstat 2001: 583). Essentially, price liberalisation turned out to be a monetary reform which confiscated labour incomes and savings and funnelled them to big business.

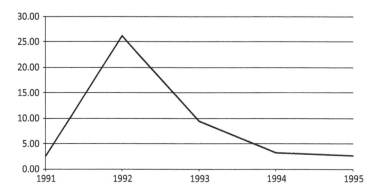

Figure 2.1 Consumer price index in 1991–95 (December to December of the previous year, in times)

Source: Goskomstat, *Rossyiskyi statistitcheskyi ezhegodnik, 2001* (Moscow: Gosudarstvennyi komitet Rossyiskoi Federatsii po statistike, 2001): 583.

With the backdrop of prices hitting the roof, the decline in public expenditures was no less significant in scale and scope. The enlarged budget, including the federal government's and regional authorities' finances coupled with the extra-budgetary funds, dropped from over two-thirds (69.1 per cent) of the country's GDP in 1992 to just over one-third (39 per cent) in 1998 (Morozov and Sundberg 2000: 1). If one takes into account that the Russian GDP declined in these years by nearly half in real terms (see Table 2.1 below), one can see how drastic was this public spending cut. The reduction affected all kinds of state expenditures: military spending, healthcare and education, enterprise subsidies and others.

This budget policy was complemented by a restrictive monetary policy. (See David Woodruff's classic work *Money Unmade* (1999) for a comprehensive study of this policy and its implications.) In order to bring a halt to inflation, the Russian government applied a very stringent monetary policy (Dzarasov, S. 2010b: 33–5), which was linked to the budgetary policy of suppressing wages and pensions, which affected both public and private sectors. To prevent the budget deficit from increasing inflation, the Russian government began to finance the deficit by issuing short-term bonds (GKOs) with extremely favourable interest rates. Since these opportunities were much more profitable, Russian banks drastically reduced their financing enterprises and turned instead to the GKO market. As a result, in 1993, the ratio of the money stock to the value of the annual commodity trade 'plummeted to [a] ridiculous 4.1 percent level' (ibid.: 33). Enterprises, being bereft of cash, had no other options than to resort to 'the barter of bankruptcy', to use Woodruff's expression. The results of this restrictive monetary policy, pursued by Russian government in the 1990s with enviable perseverance whatever the costs, turned out to be devastating for the national economy. Open inflation was suppressed, but, contrary to what was expected, this did not lead to economic growth. As Figure 2.2 demonstrates, suppression of open inflation facilitated the unprecedented slump in Russian economy in the 1990s. This was due to the growth of non-payments and barter trade (Woodruff 1999: 146–76).

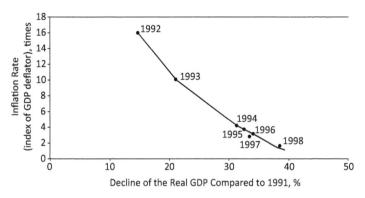

Figure 2.2   Inflation and slump in the Russian economy in the 1990s

Source: Dzarasov, S. 2010b: 34.

No less contradictory was the effect of the casual abolition of the state's control over foreign trade, which also backfired in an unexpected way. It was widely anticipated by Russian specialists and the general public that opening up to the world market would bring competition, which, in turn, would facilitate the modernisation of Russian businesses. In reality, 'raw materials became practically the only valuable economic assets', while Russian industry, 'without an insulated period for upgrading and modernization, could not be operated profitably in the face of superior foreign competition and the collapse of the domestic market' (Kotz and Weir 2007: 234). This is not a surprise given the Russian economy's technological structure. As Yaremenko explained, even as early as Gorbachev's term in office (see above), the Russian economy's civilian sector was based on mass-produced, poor-quality resources. When price controls were lifted, costs skyrocketed. As high-quality equipment for civilian production was produced only in meagre quantities and imported counterparts were far too expensive, Russian enterprises had no chance to withstand foreign competition. Instead, foreign trade deregulation provided opportunities for the export of hydrocarbons and for the flight of capital.

The data (see Table 2.1) show that following radical economic reform, Russia experienced a severe economic slump: GDP shrunk by nearly half and industrial production by even more; investment declined by four-fifths; inflation was very high; the average real income fell by half. As income inequality increased, the mortality ratio exceeded the birthrate by 4.9 (per 1,000 of population), and life expectancy fell by 4.3 years (Valtukh 2000, Kostin 2005, Rimashevskaya 2006, Yaremenko 2005).

Table 2.1 Dynamics of the main social-economic indicators in Russia, 1990s

Years	Base year	1998
GDP (% of the base year)	1989	55.8
Industrial production (% of the base year)*	1989	43.4
Agricultural production (% of the base year)	1989	54
Investment in fixed capital (% of the base year)	1990	21.1
Export (% of the base year)	1990	104.7
Import (% of the base year)	1990	70.9
Average per capita real disposable income (% of the base year)	1991	46.0*
Commodity prices increase	1990	1.16
Gini coefficient	1991 = 0.26	0.394
Population (% of the base year)	1992	99.3
Life expectancy of the newborn, years	1989 = 69.6	65.3**
Birthrate (per 1,000 of population)	1989 = 14.6	8.7**
Mortality (per 1,000 of population)	1990 = 11.2	13.6

Source: Grinberg 2007: 18.
* 1999; ** 2000.

Valtukh (2000: 7) maintains that at the turn of this century the level of Russian industry's development approximately corresponded to that at the end of the 1960s, which is why he thinks that a comparison of major industrial production output in 1998 with the 1970 level is the most appropriate measure of the slump's severity. Analysis indicates that the output of one-third of products decreased by more than 90 per cent, of another sixth of products by over 80 per cent, and so on. According to this account, on average, industrial output had fallen in this period by half. In 1998, Russia produced, for instance, fewer railway cargo carriages and textiles than in 1913; less agricultural machinery and textile equipment, as well as less sugar, flour and many other products than in the 1940s, and fewer steel tubes, and less footwear and other goods than in 1945 (ibid.). While GDP fell in 1992–98 by 39.4 per cent, investment in fixed capital at the same period declined by three-quarters (Kostin 2005: 224). According to the official data from 1995 to 1998, investment in fixed capital as a share of GDP decreased from 18.7 to 15.5 per cent (ibid.).

In 1999, the Russian economy began to recover (Grinberg 2007: 53–7). However, many specialists disagree with the official optimism expressed by the authorities in this connection. In the mid-2000s, at the eve of the global crisis of 2007–09, the real disposable per capita income and the real wage in Russia were still lower than prior to the 1990 reforms (Yaremenko 2005: 94); that is, the first major decline occurred in 1992–95, and then resumed in 1998–99. After that, a relative economic recovery followed and real incomes had grown in 2004 in comparison with 1999 by 1.7 times and real wage by 2.1 times. Despite this, in 2004, the former variable amounted only to about 80 per cent, and the second to about 70 per cent of their pre-reform level (ibid.). Only one-fifth of the Russian population benefited from the market reforms (Rimashevskaya 2006: 3). The official data suggest that, by the mid-2000s, the average income of the richest 10 per cent of the Russian population was 14 times higher than the income of the poorest 10 per cent and this disparity has remained roughly constant since 1998 (Yaremenko 2005, p. 98). According to independent estimates, based on the balance of monetary income and a mathematical model of the aggregate demand function, this figure was at least twice as high (ibid.). The post-reform period witnessed an enormous growth in poverty. According to the official data, the living standards of about 30 million Russians (about 20 per cent) were below the poverty line in the mid-2000s. This assessment is based on the value of the subsistence level, which is half that used in Soviet times. Estimates on the basis of the 1990 standard gives a figure of 30 per cent living in deprivation. If one takes into account not only commodities but also accommodation, then the proportion of those living in poverty amounted to 40 per cent of the Russian population (Rimashevskaya 2006: 13). (We deal with the shock of the 2007–09 world crisis for the Russian economy and its consequences in Chapter 6.)

2.6 Conclusion

Understanding the roots of modern Russian big business is predicated on comprehending the evolution of the Soviet ruling elite in the environment created by global capitalism at the end of the twentieth century.

The Soviet system appeared as a result of the 1917 Russian Revolution, which was the climax of the rebellion of the periphery of the capitalist world-system at the beginning of the previous century. The new society succeeded in industrialising, although at a great price. However, this society can hardly be termed 'socialist', since it reproduced social suppression in a new form. According to Trotsky's concept of 'Thermidor', with Stalin's victory in the intra-party struggle, the Russian Revolution experienced bourgeois degeneration. Soviet society was only transitional, that is, it was only attempting to build socialism and, hence, amalgamated the elements of socialism and capitalism. Due to economic, social and cultural backwardness, this society produced a new privileged ruling elite composed of the party and state bureaucracy. According to Trotsky, this elite was destined either to be overthrown by the victorious working class or to restore capitalism.

The idea of planning proposed securing a proportionality of the national economy, that is, a state where every industry's output is produced exactly in the quantity and quality as needed by its customers. In reality, Soviet planning's excessive centralisation, which reflected the power of the bureaucracy over the society, violated economic proportions. The Soviet economy was characterised by 'technological non-homogeneity', stemming from the concentration of the best-quality resources in the military-industrial complex. The civilian manufacturing sector had to rely on mass-produced, low-quality resources. One of the major inadequacies of central planning was the bureaucracy's arbitrary control over income distribution. Over time, this led to the bureaucracy and its representatives' increasingly informal control of economic resources. This allowed the bureaucracy to appropriate private incomes on the basis of public property.

As a result of the initially high economic growth rates secured by the planned economy in 1929–75, the structure of Soviet society had dramatically changed from a predominantly agricultural population to a modern urban one. This led to internal differentiation within the bureaucracy and intelligentsia, singling out diverse social strata and groups with differing and often conflicting interests. Under the conditions of a totalitarian state, these social contradictions could not be openly discussed and resolved. Due to this, discontent with the egalitarian nature of the Soviet society was growing among the administrative and acquisitive classes.

These social contradictions were exacerbated when in the mid-1970s the sources of mass resources had been largely exhausted and economic growth rates declined. With this backdrop, Gorbachev launched his perestroika project, aimed at modernising the Soviet system. Unexpectedly, for him and for the majority of external observers, democratisation had led to the formation of a powerful pro-capitalist bloc, consisting of representatives of the ruling bureaucracy and the intelligentsia and led by the former. This bloc succeeded in dismantling the Soviet system, and its central planning structure, and ushered in the transition to capitalism.

Radical market reforms, starting at the beginning of 1992, were based on the notorious principles of the Washington Consensus, which were devised by the Washington-based IMF and WTO financial institutions, for developing countries. Their modus operandi can be summarised in the formula 'liberalisation plus stabilisation.' Liberalisation of prices and foreign trade, privatisation, reduction of state expenditures and restrictive monetary policy contributed directly and indirectly to the legalisation of previously informal control over the assets on the part of new owners. This nascent proprietor class was formed from representatives of the former Soviet bureaucracy (administrative class), the intelligentsia (appropriating class) and the criminal underworld.

In summary, one should say that the transition from the Soviet system to capitalism was the logical consequence of Stalinist degeneration of the Russian Revolution, whose egalitarian and democratic essence has been forfeited in favour of the new ruling elite. Privatisation resulted from the interplay and mutual reinforcement of the Soviet bureaucracy's disintegration and global capitalism's influence. The emergence of the new proprietor class strengthened and entrenched the informal control of both the former bureaucracy and criminals over what had previously been the state's assets. This fact had left an indelible imprint on the Russian business elite.

3

Russian Big Business: Corporate Governance and the Time Horizon

3.1 Introduction

After reviewing the historical milieu in which the transition from the Soviet system to capitalism took place, we will now examine the institutional nature of already extant Russian big business. Particular attention will be given to understanding the relationship between ownership and control in Russian corporations. Identification of the major differences and similarities between the corporate governance patterns of Russian firms and typical US corporations provides further insights into the principle aim pursued by Russian firms. This chapter aims to develop an understanding of the Russian corporate sector's dominant mode of economic behaviour before discussing their investments in the next chapter.

Section 3.2 deals with the emergence of the Russian model of corporate governance. The nature of the privatisation of state enterprises is particularly emphasised. Section 3.3 explores the specific pattern of ownership and control in the Russian corporate sector, and the literature on this topic is reviewed. Research is focused here on the crucial role of aspects of this type of corporate governance. The concept of the infrastructure of control is introduced, that is, the network of formal and informal institutions which support the ownership of the dominant group. Section 3.4 considers the fundamental instability of property rights and control peculiar to Russian big business, and argues that the informal character of insider control puts the dominant groups in a vulnerable position. The major consequences of this, drawn from the above, are summarised in the final section.

3.2 The Privatisation of State Enterprises and the Formation of Private Ownership

3.2.1 Corporate Governance

Since this section is concerned with the particular type of corporate governance that has emerged in Russia, let us begin with a formal definition of this concept. The term 'corporate governance' is used by different authors in widely varied senses (Keasey et al. 1997: 2). In the first, narrow, sense, corporate governance means the system of accountability by a firm's top management to its shareholders. In the second, wider, usage, corporate governance includes all the formal and informal relations existing in the economy's corporate sector and its effect upon the society as a whole (ibid.). Keasey and Wright define corporate governance as 'the structures, processes, cultures and systems that engender the successful operation of the organisations' (1993: 292). From the standpoint of this book, the first definition is too narrow and excludes many issues relevant to the topic of corporate governance in Russia. For instance, such phenomena as the relationships between the dominant owners, other stakeholders and state officials are of crucial importance for a study of Russian big business, but this goes beyond the scope of Keasey and colleagues' narrow definition. The second definition is more relevant to this study, because it focuses both on the formal and informal institutions peculiar to the corporate sector, but it tends to stretch the term too far. For instance, concentration of production would be considered as an aspect of corporate governance and distribution of the national income as its consequence, while, according to the second approach, we should include these in the notion of corporate governance itself. The definition suggested by Keasey and Wright sets more appropriate boundaries for understanding of the term, as it relates to 'the successful operation of the organisations', although it seems that there is a certain ambiguity concerning what constitutes success. For example, current profit maximisation may be considered a success for a financial investor but may be a poor proxy of 'success' for the manager with an eye on the long term. Probably, it is assumed that organisations' success is related to the interests underlying their operation. For the purposes of this book, the second and the third (ibid.) approaches are the most relevant.

In my view, corporate governance reflects the methods by means of which power relations are shaped in corporations. At the bottom of this distribution of power lies the Marxian subsumption of labour under capital, although it includes divisions between managers and shareholders as well. Thus, we are concerned here with the mechanisms of formal and informal relationships which link the typical Russian corporation's aims to the interests of the dominating stakeholders. From this position, this book will discuss other basic notions of corporate governance which need to be clarified.

3.2.2 Insiders and Outsiders

'Insiders' are those individuals who control key decision-making within Russian enterprises, especially concerning these companies' finances, while 'outsiders' are stakeholders, who are blocked from contributing to these decisions. While this book does not give a formal definition of 'insiders' and 'outsiders', in conventional western understanding, the first term encompasses managers *and* employees, while the second signifies *a different* firm's stakeholders (see, for instance, Shleifer and Vasiliev 1996: 62, Blanchard 1998: 81, Keasey et al. 2005: 11, 423, Kuznetsova and Kuznetsov 2001: 96–7). For the purposes of this chapter, it is important to draw the main criterion which distinguishes between the two categories. The following studies provide important insights into the issue. Mallin refers to 'outsider' and 'insider' models differentiating between two types of ownership and control in Continental corporate governance systems. The first term is applied to firms with shareholdings dispersed amongst a large number of outside investors (as in the UK and the US). In such systems, institutional investors dominate, although they have little direct control, because normally they do not have significant parcels of shares. The second system, dominating Continental Europe, demonstrates a much more concentrated ownership 'with shares often being owned either by holding companies or families' (Mallin 2004: 124). Here, one has a significant expansion of the term 'insiders', embracing not only managers and employees, but owners with large shareholdings. Blair provides a further extension of the term. Describing securities market regulations, she explains that insiders' right to trade a corporation's securities is restricted. Here insiders are defined 'as corporate directors and officers and any individual or institutional investor holding 10 percent or more of the outstanding equity' (1995: 51). Blair makes an important point: that what is really significant is the shareholder's access to inside information and not the size of the share parcel as such. Access to inside information allows shareholders to extract additional fraudulent profits from the selling of equities. What features do employees, managers, holding companies, families and individuals with large shareholdings have in common? From the discussion of the various meanings of the term 'insiders', we can conclude that the different types of insiders discussed all have their say in the decision-making process. Thus in general, one can conclude that insiders are those stakeholders who, due to their formal and informal positions, are able to affect the company's corporate governance. Correspondingly, the concept of 'outsiders' refers to those stakeholders who do not possess such privileges. Corporate governance in Russia, including relationships among insiders and outsiders, has some important history which deserves a brief discussion here.

3.2.3   Privatisation and the Formation of the New Business Elite

According to the World Bank report *Techniques of Privatisation of State-Owned Enterprises* (Vuylsteke 1994), the experience of those countries which have been successful in carrying out a privatisation programme suggests that the distribution of a state enterprise's property rights to a number of stakeholders is the right route to take. Such an approach permits a diversity of privatisation methods and helps to take into account and reconcile differing stakeholders' interests. Vuylsteke describes a whole range of privatisation programmes: open equity sale to the general population, the sale of shares to particular individuals, new private investments in state enterprises, the sale of state assets, the division of state enterprises into separate parts, the repurchase of the state enterprise by managers and waged labour, and tenancy and management contracts. Often such schemes are applied simultaneously or in parallel. This allows the government to be flexible and take into account the peculiarities of different situations. For example, the government could sign a management contract of a few years' duration with an entrepreneur. If, during this period, the enterprise has not declined in terms of its performance, this state property could be sold to the entrepreneur. This means that an entrepreneur is entitled to purchase state property only after proving his or her ability to run that state enterprise effectively.

Apart from this situation, international privatisation standards presume that the whole process should be subjected to public supervision through an external, independent state audit. For example, the 'Guidelines on the Best Practice for the Audit of Privatisation', applied by INTOSAI,[1] maintains that 'what is being sold is a public asset, and the public needs independent assurance that the process has been properly handled and that the taxpayer has received value' (INTOSAI 1998: Guideline 3). According to the 'Guidelines', the state's controlling agencies should audit the whole privatisation process at every stage – from the pre-sale value assessment of the state assets to studying the results of the sales. The state's responsibilities should extend to observing the degree to, and timeliness in, which a new owner fulfils their commitments according to the agreement's conditions (ibid.: sections 2–8). Unfortunately, in the 1990s, the Russian government undertook privatisation on a very different basis than is depicted above.

Russian privatisation's basic principles and the major consequences of the privatisation process are explored in the official Report of the Russian Federation's Accounting Chamber[2] (hereinafter known as the Accounting Chamber) (Stepashin 2004). These official findings are consistent with other accounts of Russian privatisation, such as Radygin (1998, 1999, 2001), Radygin and Sydorov (2000), Menshikov (2007: 5–6, 9–11), Barnes (2006), Freeland (2011) and others. The official report was a collective work, undertaken by a group of the Chamber's leading specialists, headed by its chairperson, Sergey Stepashin. The report is based on a wide range of materials, including the reports by the Accounting Chamber's auditors, information requested from different government structures, data of state statistics, the results of scientific research in this field, and so on. Based on this evidence, the report provides 'an expert assessment of the results of the government bodies' activities in the field of state property privatisation in 1993–2003. It identifies the causes and consequences of the violations of legality, which happened during the course of this process' (Stepashin 2004: 2). The report was officially approved by a session in the Accounting Chamber's council (Protocol N 34(404) from 29 October 2004) (ibid.). To date, this report is the most authoritative document on privatisation in Russia.

The privatisation process in Russia went through three major stages. The first stage (1992–94) was a period of 'mass' privatisation. Every citizen was issued a voucher, with which it was possible either to sell or to invest in a former state enterprise, by obtaining its shares. The second stage (1994–99) was a period of cash privatisation, when state enterprises were sold for money. The third stage (1999–2003) was a period of limited monetary privatisation, when the whole process's mechanisms became more public. Privatisation of some particular state enterprises and partial quasi-nationalisation also continued beyond the period covered by the report (see below).

The report maintains that privatisation was not based on a comprehensive and specific approach to choosing the particular state assets where efficiency could be increased by transferring them to private owners. This suggests that improvement in the economy's performance was not among the Russian government's priorities. Privatisation legislation was often contradictory and deficient. In particular, it failed to provide equal opportunities for all social strata of the population to take part in privatisation; the new owners' commitments concerning the socially important aspects of an enterprise's activity were not clearly identified, and so on (ibid.: 16). This created preconditions for abuse of the law during the course of privatisation. From the current research's standpoint, one very important flaw of the privatisation process in Russia was the undervaluation of very profitable state enterprises and fraudulent organisation regarding their sale. This report contains a number of such examples.

One such example is the audit of the JSC Eastern Oil Company, undertaken by the Accounting Chamber in 2002, which revealed that the Russian government breached existing regulations during this organisation's privatisation. As a result, the enterprise's share value was underestimated and the state budget suffered losses amounting to US$250–425 million. When the sale price of JSC Tyumen Oil Company was calculated, the company's oil and gas resources values were not taken into account. Consequently, the share price depreciated to $920 million (it would have been $920 million more). Shares, constituting 7.97 per cent of the principal capital of the JSC Oil-Gas Company 'Slavoil', were sold to private owners in 1996–97 for $48 million, while its market price, according to the company's capitalisation at the end of 1997 was $358.1 million. In this sale, the state was therefore deprived of $309.3 million (ibid.: 59).

However, the most exemplary story is that of the famous shares-for-loans auctions of the mid-1990s. In 1995, a consortium of the leading Russian banks[3] proposed the provision of a sizeable loan to the government. This proposition was made with the condition of transferring, to the banks, shares of a number of the largest and most profitable state enterprises, to be held in trust. This deposit was demanded by the consortium as security for the money lent. On the basis of a few presidential decrees,[4] the Russian Federation's Ministry of Finances signed twelve loan agreements with the auction winners with the condition that the winners provide the above mentioned deposit (ibid.: 60). As early as the end of 1995, the Accounting Chamber sent an information letter to the government with a recommendation to repudiate these deals as unfavourable, but to no effect. The current report considers those deals as 'feigned', that 'actually [the] banks provided to the government its own money' (ibid.: 61). The Ministry of Finances deposited some funds, in advance, in the consortium members' private bank accounts; this money was then loaned back to the government, from whence it had originally come. Shares of the most profitable Russian enterprises – for example, oil company shares – were used by the government as collateral for the loan which the consortium gave the government. Next, the government deliberately defaulted on the loan from the consortium, so that the consortium could take possession (illegally, of course) of these very profitable Russian enterprises' valuable shares. In addition, these agreements had a provision under which debt redemption should be made by the government as per the 1995 budget. However, that budget did not provide financial resources for these transactions and the securities were transferred to the ownership of the banks. This meant that, in reality, the shares were not temporarily placed in trust management, but were disguised and then sold to the bank consortium. The auctions themselves were organised without any real competition. For only four of the twelve agreements from the auctions did the loan amounts increase through the bidding process; for these four, this process was most likely staged, to appear to have held a regular bidding process. The other eight agreements had the same price at the end of bidding as they had at the beginning. Participation in the auctions was limited to the consortium members and their controlled structures (ibid.). The Accounting Chamber arrived at the conclusion that, as a result of the 'shares-for-loans' auctions, appropriation of state property was undertaken with a depreciation significantly below their free market value and with only sham competition (ibid.: 62).

Another deep flaw in the privatisation process in Russia was its lack of independent external control over the preparation of state property deals. This contradicted the international privatisation standards previously discussed. The failure to create such a system until 1995 can be explained by the lack of a necessary federal controlling agency. However, after the Accounting Chamber was established, notes the report, such a situation indicated a 'desire of the executive authorities to preserve their privatisation options' (ibid.). Moreover, it was revealed that sometimes those businesses interested in privatisation deals had managed to use their affiliated organisations as allegedly 'independent' external experts (ibid.: 63).

Russian privatisation's most significant characteristic, with the most long-term consequences, was the strong impetus which it gave to criminality and corruption. The report maintains that, in the course of privatisation, a range of new, previously unknown crimes appeared in Russia: the forging of securities, fraudulent operations with vouchers, construction of so-called 'pyramid schemes',[5] and so forth. According to law-enforcement agencies' assessments during privatisation, the conditions emerged for the laundering of criminal capitals, a significant amount of state and municipal property being transferred to criminal and semi-criminal structures, an increase of the latter's influence on economic and political life, and state corruption. One widespread practice was for the directors of state enterprises undergoing privatisation to withdraw valuable assets from these organisations and place them into newly established firms of which the directors held a majority of shares. As a result, the former state enterprises' new owners obtained largely unprofitable assets. During the period 1993–2003, the Russian Ministry of Internal Affairs registered 52,938 crimes committed in connection with privatisation; of these violations, 11,045 ended up in court, and 1,526 people were criminally prosecuted (ibid.).

A wide range of researchers in the field of Russian privatisation support the evidence of the Accounting Chamber. For instance, Satarov (2004: 58) notes that about 30 per cent of all non-legislative regulations (that is, instructions interpreting the law and the underlying activities of the state officials) covering privatisation were not consistent with the original legislation. Among the registered law violations committed by state officials in 1994–97, a tenth took place during privatisation. In nearly half of the Russian regions, civil servants involved in privatisation were accused of criminal acts. To these criminal acts should be added the manifold actions of officials which are not directly regarded as crimes, for example, the artificial undervaluation of privatised property, the manipulations of the conditions for competition, the purchase of state enterprises by the state authorities through third parties (ibid.).

This significant undervaluation of state assets is also discussed by Menshikov and Volkonsky. According to Menshikov, from privatisation, the government obtained less than 5 per cent of its former property's market value. Even if one takes into account the later revaluation of assets, adjusting their price in accordance with the effect of inflation, receipts did not exceed 11 per cent (2004: 61–2). Volkonsky argues that state enterprises were sold at prices 20–30 times less than their real value, maintaining that, for instance, Uralmash (34,000 employees) was privatised for $3.72 million, and Chelyabinsk Caterpillar Plant (54,300 employees) for $2.2 million (1998: 12–13). However his arguments rely on using the number of employees as a proxy for an organisation's market value. As the experts of the Consortium on the Questions of Applied Economic Researches[6] observe: in the course of privatisation 'the formal property rights became only a screen concealing legalisation' of the misappropriation of enterprises' assets and resources (Consortium ... 2001: 24). After examining the first stage of the process (1992–94), Barnes concludes that:

> Most notably, managers of industrial and agricultural enterprises exploited their respective mass privatization programs; and ...

both proved enormously successful. Regional governments [and the federal bureaucracy as well] also played a role in property redistribution in this period ... allying themselves with the regional and local managers trying to take advantage of the new laws. Workers, farmers, and other citizens ... enjoyed few of the advantages of managers, and their influence declined as time passed. (2006: 69).

The advantageous position of the elite in this whole process was clearly admitted by the reformist government's leader, Yegor Gaidar, who had recognised that privatisation had been carried out in favour of private owners from the ruling bureaucracy, rather than the common people. However, he added that a privatisation process that was to the advantage of ordinary citizens had never happened anywhere and 'could never happen', because 'everywhere and at any time redistribution of property occurs only in the interests of the ruling elite' (Gaidar 1995). Meanwhile, as previously mentioned, other countries' experience of this process has been very different from that as understood by the former Russian premiere.

We can conclude from this discussion that Russia's privatisation process differed drastically from the world standard at least in two crucial aspects: first, it was not designed to find a balance of interests between the different stakeholders (as openly admitted by Gaidar); and, secondly, it completely lacked transparency and independent public control. In such conditions, the informal relations of private income appropriation, which were gradually emerging within the Soviet system, found their natural outlet in the privatisation of state property, particularly in its criminal and semi-criminal forms. As a result of these corrupted privatisation practices, the Russian economy suffered large-scale criminalisation. R.F. Gorodetsky, deputy head of the Academy of Economic Security attached to the Ministry of Internal Affairs (MIA), maintains that, according to MIA's data, Russia's shadow economy exceeds 40 per cent of GDP (Prokhorova 2005). This percentage was interpreted by some experts as indicating a 'high degree of criminalisation of the Russian economy'. Gorodetsky argues that operators in this area have been the cause of numerous legal abuses and crimes connected with money laundering. This money 'undermines the legal economy and hinders its further development' (ibid.). The crucial effect of these practices on the institutional nature of Russian big business will be discussed later. Here it is only mentioned that, according to Freeland, the reformers 'quickly defined' whom was their best bet in building capitalism in Russia: 'a new breed of aggressive, ostentatious entrepreneurs, eventually dubbed the New Russians' (2011: 69).

Privatisation had another important result: it greatly enhanced the formation of private ownership and the emergence of the so-called 'corporate' sector. According to Menshikov (2004: Chs 2, 3) and Papper (2000, 2002a), control over the most profitable assets in the Russian economy has gradually shifted into the hands of the powerful clans (business groups) of the 'oligarchy' (Menshikov), or Integrated Business Groups (Papper), beginning in the second half of the 1990s, which continues today. For instance, in 2004, the eight largest corporations produced the following shares of the industry's output: 44.5 per cent in fuel production, 53.1 per cent in ferrous and 40.2 per cent in non-ferrous industries (Rosstat 2005c: 76). In the later editions of the *Promyshlennost Rossii* (Industrial Statistics Yearbook), data on the concentration of production among industries are not provided. According to the yearbook, in 2011, the eight largest corporations produced the following shares of sectorial output: 59 per cent in raw materials extraction, 23.7 per cent in manufacturing and 28.42 per cent in production and allocation of electricity, gas and water (Rosstat 2012a: 63). The foundations of such groups were laid before 1998, and since then they have continued to expand, taking over private companies and privatised enterprises.

The results of this concentration of assets by the oligarchic clans have been estimated by World Bank specialists.[7] They studied 1,700 large enterprises in different industries, which provided jobs for 12.3 per cent of all Russian employees. It was established that in 2001–03, 22 main groupings of private owners controlled 38.8 per cent of sales and 20 per cent of employment in the industrial sector. As the former figure is double the latter, this indicates that the clans gained control over the most productive sectors of the national economy. For each of these business groups, their annual return exceeded $350 million and the number of employees exceeded 12,000. Among these organisations, the largest in terms of volume of sales was JSC Lukoil, with more than $16 billion, and the largest in terms of employment was the business group led by O. Deripaska with 169,000 employees (ibid.: 9–13).

For the majority of Russian corporations, Radygin (2001) notes their general organisational structure in the 1990s imitates the structures of Soviet territorial-productive complexes, and scientific-technological and trade-manufacturing units, which consisted of many interrelated enterprises. In a sense, such repercussions of privatisation, for example, the big state enterprises being split into a few independent entities, were reversed. Indeed, the current period has witnessed the actual restoration of former Soviet enterprises, but this time on the basis of private property and without their excessive subsidiaries[8] (ibid.: 36).

However, not everybody was dissatisfied with the results of the fraud previously described. Andres Aslund served as an economic adviser to the Russian government in 1991–94, and then in the same position to the Ukrainian government and to the president of the Kyrgyz Republic. He said, 'a decade after the loans-for-shares privatizations' he had difficulties in understanding 'the great emotions they aroused'. He reasoned that 'The Russian privatization scheme was never designed to be moral or egalitarian but to be functional, to privatize and generate able owners. The loans-for-shares did exactly that. Hardly any privatization scheme in world history can record such great economic success' (Aslund 2007: 164). While it is good that someone who played an influential role behind the scenes of the Russian reforms finally confessed that Russian privatisation 'was never designed to be moral or egalitarian', it is a pity that he waited for so long, failing to explain this at the dawn of privatisation, when Russian reformers claimed overwhelming moral superiority over the Communists and pledged to build the 'people's capitalism' in Russia (see the Introduction). That is to say, there are no doubts that privatisation drew to the forefront quite able people, but their skill at deception is certainly not commendable. This is discussed in the next section.

3.3 Ownership and Control of Russian Corporations

Due to privatisation, corporate structures emerged in the Russian economy, which ostensibly resemble western corporations. To identify the key differences, we must examine the institutional nature of the former in more detail.

Frydman, Gray and Rapaczynski emphasise that the corporate governance models, which are successful in advanced market economies, 'cannot be mechanically transplanted in Eastern Europe' (1996: 4). The reason for this is not only the difference in the cultural environment and historical heritage, but also the difference between established and evolving institutions. Frydman and colleagues argue that, in advanced market economies, the business environment experiences only marginal changes, while in transitional economies, such changes are rapid and fundamental. In the first group of countries, it is enough for an owner to make sure that their firm's value is maximised in the established framework. In a transitional economy, on the contrary, the owner is confronted with the need to restructure the firm, re-orientate its activities, and so on. And these multiple problems need to be solved in rapidly changing, and hence largely unpredictable, external economic conditions: 'Thus, instead of being mostly a passive monitor of a large part of its portfolio, a new East European owner is likely to have to be active across the board, stretching to the maximum its scarce human capital' (ibid.: 5). I have only briefly reviewed corporate governance in developed economies here because, as will be demonstrated below, the Russian experience is unique.

3.3.1   Investor Protection and Type of Control

The classical separation of ownership and control, which prevails in predominantly Anglo-Saxon countries, is not the only kind of corporate governance demonstrated by modern corporations. Different types of modern corporate governance have been studied by La Porta and colleagues (1999), whose survey embraced corporations from 27 countries. It was found that more than a third of organisations, mainly based in advanced market economies, belonged to joint stock companies (JSCs) with diffused property rights and a classic separation of ownership and control. Firms in many other countries, such as Argentina, Greece, Austria, Hong Kong, Portugal, Israel and Belgium, had a dominant owner – either family or the state (ibid.: 491–6). The family-owned firm is of most interest for us here.

La Porta and colleagues show that two-thirds of the families dominating corporations occupy positions in the companies' executive management (ibid.: 502), which is very different from the separation of ownership and control. According to La Porta and colleagues, the dominant families often secure a larger share of the firm's resources than they are legally entitled to, according to the volume of their share holdings. There are important reasons for this. Complicated pyramids of control are formed on the basis of complex intertwined relations in the firm's ownership. The dominant owner is at the top of such a pyramid and enjoys influence which significantly exceeds the role of the minority shareholders. Due to their particular position, the dominant families enjoy additional benefits, at a cost to other shareholders (ibid.: 473). However, in most of the countries surveyed, the legal system, and its enforcement, has been sufficient to marginalise the dominant owners' opportunistic behaviour. This study's major conclusion is that the type of control depends on the degree to which the minority shareholders are protected. If their protection is high, then a separation of ownership and control prevails and if not, the dominant owner prevails. The importance of investors' protection in transition economies is stressed by Grosfeld and Hashi, who analysed corporate governance in Poland and in the Czech Republic, emerging as a result of mass privatisation. These countries show a significant concentration of ownership since privatisation, suggesting that 'private benefits of control are large in both countries' (2004: 11). At the same time, Grosfeld and Hashi note the important difference between the two countries. In the Czech Republic, poorly performing firms demonstrate fewer tendencies to increase in ownership concentration than the better-off companies. By contrast, in Poland, performance does not affect this variable. The authors arrive at the conclusion that 'if Czech investors seem to be more risk averse and more concerned with diversification this is largely due to the weakness of the legal protection they face' (ibid.). This suggests that the legal environment is of prime importance for corporate governance, a conclusion that fits with Russian experience. Here, I attempt to view Russian governance problems from this perspective of international experience.

The literature on corporate governance in Russia embraces major topics such as the cultural context and ethical values of governance, legal environment, ownership structure, governance and companies' market value, governance and investment, and so forth. A classification of this literature with respect to the main focus of the publications is provided in Table 3.3. Thus, McCarthy and Puffer (2002, 2003) discuss foreign and domestic influences on emerging corporate governance in Russia in the context of the nation's culture and traditions. They find that the corporate governance systems in the US, Germany and France had a strong effect on the development of Russian corporate law. At the same time, these models were unintentionally modified by aspects of the Russian traditions, such as 'a tendency to circumvent laws and directives, low trust in transactions outside personal relationships, and reliance on personal networks to achieve objectives' (2002: 637). The authors conclude that eventually the Russian system will move to its own unique model, formed by its traditional culture. Fey and colleagues (2001) study the types of leadership style prevalent in Russian corporations, assuming that leadership efficiency strongly depends on the national context. Their research finds that Russian managers prefer task-oriented and relation-oriented figures as being more effective in leading their organisations, rather than their democratic and authoritarian colleagues. This volume emphasises the low level of trust and a reliance on personal networks in the Russian corporate sector. The aforementioned cultural traditions are put into the historical perspective of private income appropriation by Soviet bureaucracy (see Chapter 2) and are now embedded in the informal control of powerful 'insiders' over enterprises, particularly in the infrastructure of this control (see below).

A number of studies focus on weak law enforcement in contemporary Russia and on its influence on corporate governance. With the advent of radical market reforms in the early 1990s, the Russian government began to develop a new legal framework for economic agents, largely based upon the legislation in advanced market economies. The new laws contained some clauses which in theory protect the rights of minority shareholders. A number of categories of such rights can be identified: the right to take part in open meetings, the right to have access to information, the right to demand repurchase of shares, the right to initiate civil actions against company heads and other organisations controlling the company, and the right to initiate civil suits to declare as illegal deals involving the vested interests of individuals influencing company management (Symatchev and Drugov 1999: 39).

Radygin and Sydorov (2000: 56) argue that, in the early 1990s, many of these rights in Russia were purely theoretical, because it was impossible to enforce them through the court or by other legal means. By the end of the 1990s, the situation had changed greatly. In terms of implementing new economic legislation, Russia was in the leading group of transition economies. At the same time, Hashi notes that 'although the legislation of the countries in transition became more developed, law enforcement is still unsatisfactory.' He notes that according to the surveys 'Russia looks particularly bad' in this sense (2004: 56). Symachev and Drugov agree that currently in Russia the most pressing problem is not the quality of legislation but its practical enforcement. When abused by insiders, shareholders are usually passive and do not try to secure their rights in court. If they attempt to do so, they encounter corruption from government authorities. For most judicial disputes, the party with greater administrative[9] and financial resources appears to be favoured (Symachev and Drugov, 1999). This means that corruption has become a factor of prime importance, affecting the behaviour of economic agents.

As previously stated, according to official estimates, Russia's informal economy, which includes criminal activities, exceeds 40 per cent of GDP. Corruption in the public sector is an inseparable part of this problem. Systematic attempts to estimate quantitatively the scale of corruption have been undertaken by Voitsekh. In 2001, he found that the Russian population spent a sum equal to one-third of the federal budget on bribes. The 'market' for business corruption amounted to $316 billion, exceeding the federal budget revenues by 2.7 times. Corruption appears to have increased over time. Although in 2001–05, the average *quantity* of bribes declined by one-fifth, its average *amount* has grown by 13 times. For the same period, the Russian businessperson's average annual 'investment' in the so-called 'black cashier' (that is, a fund for illegal transactions) increased by 11 times from $23,000 to $243,000. To take into account inflation, researchers related the average bribe to the value of a square metre in a new flat. It was found that if in 2001, the average bribe would pay only for a 30-square-metre flat of mediocre quality; in 2005, it would pay for 200 square metres. In the later period, 87 per cent of these finances accrued to the state's executive branch of the state, and 7 and 5 per cent to the legislative and judicial branches respectively (Voitsekh 2005).

It can be concluded that the existing Russian legal environment is unfavourable for law-abiding business. The 'law of the jungle' operates: 'The reason, why particular economic agents neglect legal constraints, lies in the inefficiency of punishment (it is either weak in comparison to the expected benefits or has a low probability of realisation)' (Symachev and Drugov 1999: x). This weakness significantly influences the operation of Russian business.

This problem is analysed by Rozmainsky (2002) who thinks that widespread opportunistic behaviour has increased uncertainty and risks in the economic relations between market agents. Their mutual trust decreased dramatically, which gave rise to higher transaction costs:

> In order to overcome these problems Russian economic agents ... adopted two behavioural strategies – orientation on family and clan relationships. Some deals are made between people having family connections of varying degrees. But others are made between people under the protection of the same criminal or semi-legal (that is, connected with the state authorities) clan (in turn, the clans are formed on the basis of regional, professional, or ethnic ties). In other words, in the first case, enforcement of contracts were secured by the mutual trust of family relatives, and in the second – by coercion on the part of clans. Such coercion was much tougher than that on the part of the state (Rozmainsky 2002).

Rozmainsky speaks of the 'family-clan' type of capitalism in Russia. This situation undermines the idea of free competition for control over assets and of market efficiency based upon redistribution of property rights to more effective owners. In accordance with La Porta and colleagues' study (1999), the legal environment and this type of economic behaviour has greatly affected how business is conducted in Russia. Thus, Dyck explores the lack of corporate governance function in Russia. He traces this to the fact that dominant owners, be they managers or oligarchs, 'took advantage of their powerful position to enrich themselves' through theft (2002: 3). He partially attributes this crisis to the lack of institutions, such as corporation law, accounting rules, security regulations and others, but above all to the lack of regulatory enforcement (ibid.: 4). Heinrich and colleagues compare corporate governance in the oil industry in Russia and in a number of transition economies. Their study finds significant differences in the quality of governance between the Central European countries which joined the EU and the CIS countries. In the latter case, 'a weak rule of law and widespread corruption' has had a strong negative impact (2005: 23). Sprenger provides a survey of ownership and control structures in Russian industry. He concludes that 'monitoring and control are important features of Russian corporate governance' due to the lack of legal enforcement, which is why the 'strategic majority owners' dominate, as they depend on court solutions far less frequently than the minority shareholders (2002: 20). This book also emphasises the problems of enforcement and corruption (see below). However, unlike the papers cited here, I also argue that the external protection of large insiders' 'property rights' itself reinforces the corruption of state institutions.

Many papers concentrate on ownership and control in the Russian corporate sector and their consequences, for example: Abe and Iwasaki 2010, Desai and Goldberg 2000, Dzarasov and Novojenov 2003, Dolgopyatova 2002, Dorofeev 2001, Kapelushnikov 1999, Novojenov 2003a, Oman 2001, Papper 2000, 2002a, 2002b, Radygin 1998, 1999, 2001, Radygin and Sydorov 2000, Radygin and Entov 1999, 2001, Radygin et al. 2002, Skorobogatov 1998, Ustyuzhanina et al. 2010, and others. These studies expose the large differences between the formal distribution of 'property rights' and the actual relationship between ownership and control in the Russian economy. The previously mentioned sources arrive at the conclusion that in Russia it is difficult to exercise formal property rights if they are not backed by some kind of informal control over the enterprise. It means that the classical separation of ownership and control is not a characteristic of the typical modern Russian corporation.

At the early stages of privatisation, the former state enterprises' shares were widely distributed among the employees, and employee ownership was frequently predominant (Berglof and Thadden 1999). For the reasons previously discussed, this model of corporate governance was characterised by weak shareholders but strong managers (ibid.). The majority of new shareholders soon found that their property rights were a mere formality, giving them no source of real income; the majority of share prices were practically worthless and dividends were either negligible or not paid at all. Ownership could generate revenue only if it 'gave control over the cash-flows of an enterprise, in such conditions attaining and/or keeping control over the current activities of a company became the main motive for buying shares' (Dolgopyatova 2005: 4). As a result of this practice, and following the concentration of production and capital, mentioned previously in Section 3.1, the concentration of shares in the hands of big business owners began to emerge. According to Papper (2002a: 32) – a leading researcher into modern Russian corporate business, the current major business structures emerged in 1995–97. After the 1998 financial crisis, an even more substantial redistribution of property took place, but the formal picture of the distribution of ownership rights still looked fairly democratic (Radygin 1999: 60). However, under the surface, important changes in the concentration of ownership continued.

According to Dolgopyatova (2005: 4), the management's share in the companies' equities was persistently increasing to the detriment of the employees. The employee-ownership model increasingly receded into the past and the highly concentrated corporate ownership of either top managers or external investors now occupied its place. By becoming the dominant owner, the outsider becomes an 'insider', because he or she directly takes part in managing the enterprise or appoints the top-tier management, which operates under the owner's control (Dolgopyatova 2003a: ch. 2). The concentration of property rights in Russia at the end of the 1990s is summarised in Table 3.1 below.

Table 3.1   Ownership concentration in Russian big business

	End of 1998		End of 2001	
	Mean %	Median %	Mean %	Median %
The largest shareholder's parcel	36.7	30.0	42.2	39.5
Combined shares of three major shareholders	48.9	47.5	57.6	56.0

Source: Dolgopyatova 2003b: 15.

These results are based on a study of 220 Russian JSCs. As can be seen from Table 3.1, from 1999 to 2001, the largest shareholder parcel had significantly increased. By the end of 2001, 'two-thirds of the JSCs had a shareholder with a blocking parcel of shares (that is, normally about 30 per cent of the whole amount of shares – which permits its owner to determine major decisions), and more than 39 per cent of the companies had a controlling shareholder parcel (holding more than 50 per cent of the total shares)' (Dolgopyatova 2003b: 15).

Table 3.2 gives us the opportunity to compare ownership structures in Russia and in some East European countries, which reflects differences in their adopted models of corporate governance. These data show that the share of insiders in the ownership structure of Russian corporations is much greater, while the state's role is much less than in other three countries. At the same time, the share of outsiders is relatively similar, although there is an important difference in the constituents of the latter category. Among the Russian owner-outsiders, individuals and families occupy a much more prominent position than in other countries. At the same time, positions of the institutional outsiders are the reverse.

Table 3.2 Ownership structures of companies in selected transitional countries, 1999

	Czech Republic %	Hungary %	Poland %	Russia %
Insiders	3	11	10	40
State	51	53	26	8
Outsiders	46	29	55	45
Kinds of Outsiders:				
Individuals/families	6	8	31	40
Institutional outsiders	40	21	24	5
Others/no answer	0	7	9	7
Number of enterprises	35	38	84	214

Source: Mallin 2004: 151.

These observations reflect the differences in the corporate governance models adopted in the countries in question. Thus, while the Russian model of corporate governance is characterised by the domination of insiders, who gradually lose ground to 'new outsiders' (according to Dolgopyatova), in the Czech Republic, Hungary and Poland, state and institutional investments dominate.

It is important to note that, in Russia, 'qualitative in-depth interviews conducted on small samples show that real concentration of property is much higher than formalised surveys can reflect' (Dolgopyatova 2005: 6). Concentration of property occurs because, in a majority of cases, the dominant owners occupy the position of top-tier manager, which gives them additional power over decision making. Thus in 2003, two sets of interviews (about 50 JSCs in total) revealed that dominant owners of more than 70 per cent of these JSCs possessed more than 50 per cent of shares, and blocking share packages (more than 25 per cent of shares) existed in more than 90 per cent of these companies (ibid.). Another survey of 822 JSCs, conducted in 2005, discovered that this consolidation of shares by the largest owners was continuing. It was found that three-quarters of companies had blocking holders and about two-thirds were controlling holders (ibid.). These results are consistent with Abe and colleagues' 2007 study of internal control in Russian corporations, which found that the majority of Russian corporations are still closed joint-stock companies, lacking the mechanisms to attract outside investors. This happens, first of all, due to the control of dominating shareholders, either by directly occupying top managerial positions or by tightly monitoring top-tier management. Thus, ownership concentration becomes the major feature of the emerging corporate governance model. The hiring of top-tier managers is treated here as a separation of ownership and management, but this approach largely ignores the effect of separation on investment behaviour and the intensity of corporate conflicts. Although this hiring practice is partly consistent with the view suggested in this volume, it is hardly reasonable to consider the hiring of top-tier managers as 'separation of ownership and management'. Abe and Isawaki arrive at the conclusion that 'the presence of a dominant shareholder significantly increased the likelihood of turnover of the whole management team' (2010: 449), which assumes very strict control of the Russian dominant owners over management (see Section 3.3.3). Taking into account the argument that big insiders create an infrastructure of control, as developed in this volume, hiring top-tier managers is only a formality, which disguises tight informal control. This is the major reason why this book argues that such ostensible 'separation' does not effect investment.

This dominance of insider control in Russian enterprises does not preclude different degrees of ownership consolidation and a multiplicity of dominant owner types. Dolgopyatova (2001) identifies four models of corporate governance in the modern Russian economy. Model 1 is a 'private enterprise' in which the functions of ownership and management are united. The director is the dominant owner and other managers, employees and state authorities can be minority shareholders. Model 2 is the 'collective managerial property', which also unites the functions of owners and managers. In such a company, four to five top-tier managers headed by the director hold the controlling share parcel. Model 3 is 'concentrated external ownership', where the outside owners hold the controlling share parcel, while managers are hired personnel or minority shareholders. Model 4 is 'diffused ownership', where the actual control belongs to managers. Usually, in such a case the dominant manager (or group of managers) possesses a shareholding of medium size (5–15 per cent), with the other shares being distributed among the minority shareholders in tiny quantities. This model is usually unstable. Dolgopyatova notes that in the newly emerged institutional environment the models with diffused or moderately concentrated asset ownership (2 and 4) are unable to compete with the models based on strong concentration (1 and 3). This means that big business owners are relatively stronger than smaller ones, the reasons for which are subsequently explained in this chapter. Here, we should note that gradually the former models are replaced by the latter (ibid). This is peculiar for the majority of transitional economies, which 'experience has shown that, since the mid-1990s, there has been extensive reallocation of ownership rights between different ownership groups and a rapid concentration of ownership' (Hashi et al. 2004: 5).

Avdasheva and colleagues (2007) discuss the expansion and corporate governance of Russian holding companies (business groups). It is noted that the latter can be unstable if there are no additional tools to impose discipline on management. When available, these tools allow the holding company's dominant owners to maintain tight control over their subsidiaries' managers, even when the dominant owners do not have the ownership rights. Vernikov finds that ownership concentration is significant for corporate governance in Russian banks. He concludes that the 'blockholder model' of control prevails, minority shareholders are generally not represented, the allocation of capital through the stock market plays only a limited role, and outsiders' control over the company does not generally exist. Vernikov maintains that recent improvements in corporate governance, such as adoption of voluntary corporate control codes, disclosure of information, dividend payments and the like are nothing more than 'window dressing', necessary to attract investors. In reality, 'bank owners give low intrinsic value' to corporate governance (2007: 29). Mickiewicz compares the corporate governance systems of Russia and Poland. He finds that corporate ownership in the studied samples is highly concentrated in both countries, with 50–60 per cent of the dominant owners alone holding all, or almost all, company shares (2006: 5). The share of employee ownership is twice as large in Poland and institutional ownership is less significant in Russia (ibid.: 5–6). Mickiewicz concludes that unlike in Poland, 'corporate control by individuals emerges as a typical outcome of post-privatisation evolution in Russia' (ibid.: 12). This is explained by the interplay of economic institutions, policies and social attitudes, reflecting the relatively greater economic freedoms in Poland in socialist times, which complements the findings of McCarthy and Puffer (2002, 2003) and of Fey and colleagues (2001). Broadman believes that ownership concentration occurs due to lack of investor protection, although he notes that the main governance problem in closely controlled companies in Russia is not just shareholder protection, but the prevalence of 'crossholdings, holding companies and pyramid or other mechanisms that dominant shareholders use to exercise control' (1999: 7). Lazareva and colleagues also relate the mechanisms of corporate governance in Russia to ownership structures, adding financial markets and government policy to the list of determinants. Similar to Dyck (2002) as previously mentioned, Lazareva and colleagues conclude that high ownership concentration in conditions of a weak legal system leads to 'high private benefits of control' (2007: 4).

Thus, empirical studies show that in a majority of Russian enterprises ownership rights are concentrated, and insider control – meaning a merger of ownership and management – prevails. True, we should mention that according to some studies (for example, Avdasheva and Dolgopyatova 2010) up to the end of the 2000s, these features of the Russian economy became somewhat weaker, though by no means did they disappear. Avdasheva and Dolgopyatova see a decrease in ownership concentration, and an increase in the role of foreign investors. This is analysed as a shift to a separation of ownership and control. The National Council on Corporate Governance found that, in the 2000s, corporate law and law enforcement improved in Russia. In particular, this is characterised by the regulation of the interested party's transactions, struggles with corporate raiders, stock market regulation, and improvement in the work of arbitration courts (Shastitko 2008, 2009). Coupled with the economic recovery of the 2000s, opening new opportunities for longer-term investments and integration in the world markets increased the demand for the instruments of sound corporate governance in Russia. However, empirical evidence suggests that these positive tendencies still have not led to a profound change in the model of highly concentrated ownership and centralised control over enterprises. Let us consider Figure 3.1.

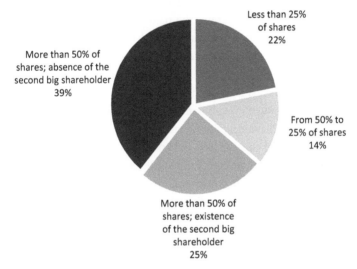

Figure 3.1   The shares of ownership concentration of Russian firms

Source: Avdasheva and Dolgopyatova 2010: 29.

As can be seen from Figure 3.1, at the end of the 2000s, ownership concentration in Russia was still very high. Indeed, among the firms surveyed, organisations in which the major shareholder held 50 per cent of shares or less comprised only 36 per cent. At the same time, the firms with the major shareholder owning more than 50 per cent of equities amounted to 64 per cent of the whole sample.

However, Dolgopyatova emphasises that the nature of insider control has changed since privatisation's early stages. At present, this group consists not only of managers, who became legal owners, but also of major outside owners who became '*new* insiders' (2003b: 20).

Kuznetsova and Kuznetsov support this conclusion. Mentioning that control in Russia is more concentrated than ownership, they argue that even if employees together own over 60 per cent of the company's shares, as separate individuals they each have only a small number of shares (2001: 96). What is more, 'As a source of control, ownership matters in Russia only to the extent it is underpinned with power associated with the position of authority in as much as extra-ownership control is highly effective' (ibid.). This means that individuals with relatively large shareholdings, to whom Dolgopyatova refers as to managers and 'new insiders', are much more important than the other shareholders.

Subsequently in this section, the nature of control over Russian enterprises will be examined in detail, though before this, it is necessary to emphasise the very important corollary of Dolgopyatova's point. It has been found that individuals who can formally be referred to as 'insiders' – that is, managers and employees – occupy very different positions in the Russian corporate sector. As will be demonstrated below, employees have insignificant influence on corporate governance. Hence, they can be equated with outsiders. From this point forward, the term 'insider' will be used to mean those individuals or groups of individuals who exercise control over the companies through specific means. This understanding of the term is consistent with the specific notions of insiders and outsiders introduced at the beginning of this chapter, relating their sense to the influence on corporate governance. The approach of this volume takes into account first of all the informal aspects of corporate governance, understanding insiders as individuals, or groups of individuals, who dominate enterprises has another important advantage. As was already shown, in modern Russia, dominant individuals may or may not be the formal owners of enterprises. This means that the term 'dominant owners' may be misleading in some cases. Another addition is necessary. In describing these dominant individuals or their groups, they are referred to as '*big* insiders' in this book. The reason for this is, as will be demonstrated in Chapter 4, that under certain conditions some representatives of the 'deprived' old insiders may challenge the control of the big insiders, although not in strategic decision making.

In contrast, with these works Guriev and colleagues (2003, p. 3) find that ownership concentration has a generally positive impact on corporate governance, but only if the largest blockholder's stake does not exceed 50 per cent. Further concentration of shareholdings either has no effect, or even worsens governance. The same point is made by Yakovlev (2004), who explores the evolution of corporate governance in Russia from the perspective of the interplay between government policy and economic agents. He arrives at the conclusion that traditional recommendations to improve enforcement are insufficient. Yakovlev believes that only consolidated owners can be strongly motivated to improve corporate governance and attract investors, which is why government policy should be based on the collective interests of entrepreneurs. I argue in Chapter 4 that consolidated owners (big insiders) are not interested in improving corporate governance as such, but instead suppress 'small insiders' by developing an infrastructure of control.

Other studies focus on the effect of Russian companies' corporate governance on their assets' market value (Black 2001, Black et al. 2006, Pajuste 2007). These studies generally find these relations are strong. Goriaev and Zabotkin (2006) study the risks of investing in the Russian stock market. They find corporate governance has a significant effect, along with political and macroeconomic risk factors, on the security market in Russia. From this standpoint, the positive changes in corporate law, which took place in Russia at the turn of the decade, are important. These are discussed by Iskyan (2002) and Mandel and Nougayrede (2004). Iskyan stresses that, in the 1990s, low levels of governance led to Russian companies being undervalued by stock markets. New developments in corporate law increased the following: minority shareholders' rights, required authorisation by shareholders' meetings of major deals, a wider disclosure of important information about the dominant owners, and so forth. Mandel and Nougayrede (2004) show that new legislation provides better regulation of mergers and acquisitions, creating obstacles to false bankruptcies. According to Iskyan, regulation of mergers and acquisitions should increase the market value of Russian companies' securities. In contrast to Mandel and Nougayrede as well as Iskyan, Belikov (2004) is much less optimistic regarding the increase of Russian companies' market value. He considers speculative investors as a threat to governance reforms, because they seek to invest in equities with a high potential for short-term growth. They take on significant risks connected to bad corporate governance. Since, according to the research, the majority of players in the Russian markets are foreign and Russian speculator-investors, companies will not gain much premium from improving their governance. This book is closer to Belikov's position (2004), but views the underlying problem from the perspective of the domination of big business insiders. Insider rent extraction is seen as the prime reason for the low valuation of Russian corporations' shares (see Chapter 4).

Previous discussions in this book relate the lack of law enforcement to poor corporate governance in Russia for corporate investment. Abe and colleagues observe that the Russian corporate sector's relatively closed character 'is inseparably linked to its poor corporate governance practices and its investment behaviour, which remains inactive regardless of a significant economic recovery in recent years' (2007: 3). Avdasheva and colleagues (2007) finds that the size of enterprises and the kind of corporate governance affect their investment. Smaller-size, closed joint-stock companies do not borrow money, relying on internally generated funds, while large public companies borrow more frequently. Lazareva and colleagues conclude that improvement of the legal system is 'crucial for building an environment that would help Russian companies attract external finance' (2007). In contrast to Abe et al., Avdasheva et al. and Lazareva et al., Guriev and colleagues (2003) maintain that ownership concentration has a positive affect on investment, disregarding the quality of corporate governance. This book shares the position of those studies which argue that ownership concentration leads to the abuse of power by dominant owners, poor corporate governance, as well as discouraging investment.

The majority of these studies (with exception of Broadman 1999) view the governance problem from a narrow standpoint of only minority shareholders' rights, thus ignoring its wider implications. Although some papers trace poor corporate governance to ownership concentration (Avdasheva et al. 2007, Vernikov 2007 and some others), the mechanism of control on the part of the dominant groups is not considered in any depth. Meanwhile, statistical surveys of this phenomenon provide only knowledge of its *apparent* form, neglecting that its *essence* is in informal institutions embedded in its infrastructure of control. Although some authors speak about 'high private benefits of control' (Lazareva et al. 2007: 4), Lazareva's vague formula fails to grasp the specific nature of the dominant owners' income, their time horizon, their extraction of income and so forth, which precludes demonstrating its effect on both corporate governance (intra-firm conflicts) and investment behaviour (short-sightedness) of Russian firms. The aforementioned studies do not explore the link between corporate governance and Russian corporations' time horizon. Only a very few papers (for instance, Abe et al. 2007) relate this low quality of corporate governance to Russian companies' poor investment behaviour, but even in these few papers the nature of this relationship is not exposed. Meanwhile corporate governance supports the position of dominant owners, whose interests underlie the accumulation of capital by Russian companies. This volume attempts to fill in these gaps in the analysis of corporate governance in Russia. To do this, I examine the nature of the large insiders' domination introducing the idea of the infrastructure of control (this section). In contrast with the previously mentioned papers, the influence of corporate governance on Russian companies' investment behaviour is viewed from the standpoint of the instability of insider control and the short-term time horizon of the big insiders (Section 3.4), insider rent extraction and the ensuing corporate conflicts (Chapter 4).

Thus, one may conclude from the preceding studies, relying on empirical evidence, that the Russian model of corporate governance is based on dominant 'insiders' (dominant owners) with control over enterprises. To understand the nature of this control, it is necessary to examine how it operates. The following analysis shows that the dominant insiders rely on a complete set of intertwined formal and informal institutions to exercise their control over companies. This set of institutions will be called the 'insider-control infrastructure' (or 'control infrastructure') over the assets. The main aim of the insider-control infrastructure is to secure opportunities to extract revenue from the controlled enterprises for dominant insiders. In relation to controlled enterprises, the infrastructure of control can be subdivided into external and internal elements. We will first examine the external elements of the insider-control infrastructure.

3.3.2   Chains of Firms

Radygin and Sydorov find that the principal owners, occupying positions as the top managers, obtain the largest incomes in their companies and frequently conceal their dominant role. Usually, they do not possess equity shares directly. As a rule, they own companies, funds, offshore firms, nominal shareholders and so on, which in turn are the owners of the controlled enterprise equities. Systems (chains) of the nominal firms are designed in such a way that the real owners are not present at all in any shareholders' lists: 'Such judicial forms of organisation as Joint-Stock Company (in the classical sense) exists only formally. Shareholders connected with the dominant group follow the common scheme developed by the actual owners' (Radygin and Sydorov 2000: 51). Dolgopyatova (2005, p. 8) agrees that non-transparency is a regular feature of Russian corporations, which usually conceals the principal owners. She notes that the ownership structure is often based on five to seven firms, all but one being phantom firms (shell companies), linked together for the purpose of concealing the real owners' identities and withdrawal of their funds; all the while, only one of these multiple, linked firms is actively productive. As such, it is important to note 'affiliated individuals and companies, offshore firms, nominal holders, as well as multistage company management systems, sometimes ... [use] ... cross-ownership' and 'so far there has [sic] been no visible reductions in the number of such levels' (with a few exceptions) (ibid.). Let us consider an example of the cross-ownership network of ostensibly independent firms. The scheme in Figure 3.2 is drawn from Latynyna (2002), an expert on economic criminality.

All the companies shown in Figure 3.2 belonged in 2002 ultimately either to Mejprombank (a very prominent Russian bank) or to its owners, top-tier managers, or their relatives. Take, for instance, Weststroyservice Ltd and Business-Master 2000 Ltd. According to the Moscow Registration Chamber, their principal capital amounted only to 8,400 roubles each (about $272 at the end of 2002). Both companies belonged to the same five firms on equal terms. Two of these firms, Pinfin and Korplast, are like twins, because they fall under the same umbrella organisation of Mejpormbank and are structured very similarly. Both were established by two organisations: JSC RTK-Sport and Mejprombank Bonds Center Ltd. JSC RTK-Sport had the same founder – KB Mejdunarodny Promyshlenny Bank – the structure affiliated to Mejprombank. Thus, only 40 per cent of Weststroyservice Ltd and Business-Master 2000 Ltd's shares belonged to Mejprombank. Nevertheless, were Skylock, Favn-1 and Van-Jude,

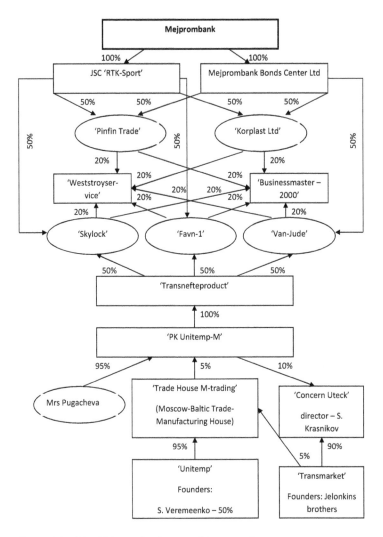

Figure 3.2   The Mejprombank ownership network

which owned the other 60 per cent of shares of Weststroyservice Ltd
and Business-Master 2000 Ltd, independent? Analysis shows that
Skylock, Favn-1 and Van-Jude were in fact not independent. All three
companies had been established by the same individuals with the
same principal capital of 8,400 roubles. When they were later sold,
half of their shares were appropriated by JSC RTK-Sport, as previously

mentioned, and Mejprombank Bonds Center Ltd, and the other half by Transnefteproduct.

Was perhaps Transnefteproduct independent at least? It was entirely owned by PK Unitemp-M, whose director, T. Makharashvily, was a member of the Mejprombank Board of Directors. PK Unitemp-M had two founders, and 95 per cent of its shares belonged to Mrs Pugacheva who happened to be the spouse of the Chairman of the Mejprombank Board of Directors. The remaining 5 per cent of shares belonged to the Trade House M-Trading. Its head was another member of the Mejprombank's Board of Directors. Ninety-five per cent of the Trade House belonged to the structure established by the Mejprombank executive S. Veremeenko and his spouse. The other 5 per cent of shares belonged to the Jelonkins brothers, one of whom was Mejprombank executive's deputy.

As we can see, literally all these various and allegedly independent companies were controlled by the same dominant group from the Mejprombank. How this control was used to appropriate income for the Mejprombank dominant group will be discussed later.

Papper (2002b: 89–90) provides a generalised scheme of ownership of the typical Russian corporate structure. There are a number of enterprises in the form of JSCs. Every one of them belongs to shareholders, which in a majority of cases, are organisations established by the dominant owners to hold equities. Most of these organisations established by the dominant owners are registered in offshore jurisdictions. They are also JSCs and belong to other offshore JSCs. Only at the end of this chain do the real owners appear. Let us consider Figure 3.3 which has been taken from Papper (2002b: 90) with some slight changes.

Figure 3.3 depicts the typical structure of ownership relations in the Russian corporation. Its first level consists of productive enterprises. Above the first level of productive enterprises in Figure 3.3, there is an 'offshore cloud' (ibid.) which holds the shares of enterprises and these enterprises are interconnected through cross-ownership to disguise ownership. At the top of Figure 3.3, we can see a group of individuals who own the offshore firms. They are the real dominant owners, the big insiders. At least some of them, or perhaps even all, occupy managerial positions at the first level, controlling day-to-day management.

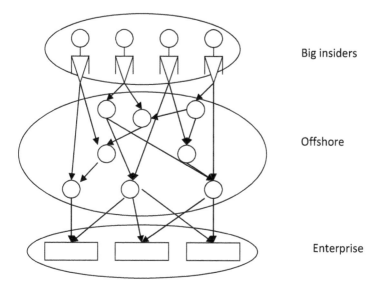

Big insiders

Offshore

Enterprise

Figure 3.3   A typical ownership structure scheme

Figure 3.3 illustrates how non-transparency functions across the whole system largely due to the fact that offshore companies help big insiders to escape from Russian legislation. Connected to the 'offshore cloud' disguising big insiders' ownership, Hashi (2004, p. 54) observes that in Russia 'big shareholders are offshore companies, whose real owners are unknown.' Dominant individuals also use the institution of 'nominal shareholders'. According to Russian corporate law, when such JSCs provide information to the market or the authorities, they are not obliged to reveal their actual shareholders (Papper 2002b: 90). The overwhelming majority of Russian corporations use this form of 'property rights defence'. According to E. Fedorov, head of the State Duma Committee on economic policy and entrepreneurship, 95 per cent of Russian big business is registered in offshore sites (Fedorov 2011).

Thus, the chain of the nominal firms – that is, the 'offshore cloud' – is the first element of the infrastructure of control. The function of the 'offshore cloud' is to provide big insiders with an efficient tool of ownership over ostensibly public companies. These property rights would be useless for big insiders if they were not supplemented by the next element of the infrastructure, the conjunction of ownership and control.

3.3.3 Direct Control Over Top Management

Concentration of property in the given legal environment significantly affected the Russian pattern of ownership and control. According to Papper, one of the inherent features of Russian big business structures became the 'inseparability of ownership and control. One and the same group of individuals is simultaneously both top-tier managers of the Integrated Business Group or company, and – directly or indirectly – its major shareholders' (2002a: 33). Radygin and Sydorov (2000) note that usually the group of big owners in Russian enterprises occupy the positions of the top-tier managers, who exercise maximum power over the firm. The following research supports this opinion.

Dolgopyatova (2003b: 15) argues that the control over an enterprise by the dominant owner can be traced through the analysis of the company's Board of Directors' membership. The previously mentioned sample surveys have shown that, at those enterprises without external dominant owners, nearly one in two directors had been working more than ten years at their post, and only 22 per cent of top managers had been replaced after the 1998 crisis. On the contrary, at enterprises with dominant external shareholders (new insiders), almost a half of the directors had been replaced after the crisis, and less than 19 per cent have survived since the early 1990s (ibid.: 19). These results suggest that if the director is also the dominant owner, then they preserve their top managerial team, while if an external figure becomes dominant, they replace the top-tier managers with their own people. A 2005 survey indicated that mergers of ownership and control were the most widespread – 82 per cent of individuals interviewed recognised the existence of an individual shareholder or group, who controlled their companies' management (Dolgopyatova 2005: 6). Abe and Iwasaki find that 'the presence of a dominant shareholder significantly increased the likelihood of turnover of the whole management team' (2010: 449). This is additional evidence in favour of the strong control of dominant owners over managers.

Abe and Iwasaki's observation can be supported by an analysis of data from around a hundred of the wealthiest businesspeople in Russia, as published by *Forbes* magazine in 2005. I have searched for information about the current position of every person from this list. In 70 cases, it was found that big insiders occupied top managerial positions: general directors, chairman of the Board of Directors, CEOs, and so on. Another 13 people occupied key political positions – presidents of the local republics, or governors of the Russian regions, senators and State Duma members. Though the law prohibits senators and State Duma members from holding managerial positions in business, this does not mean that they have actually relinquished control over their assets. Further on in this book, I discuss the crucial role of the links between Russian business and political structures. I failed to find information on the remaining 17 people on this list. Nevertheless, these findings suggest that Russia's biggest businesses consider direct management of its property as its prime task.

Dolgopyatova argues that a gradual separation of ownership and control emerges in big business structures, where the dominant owners entrust current decision making to the hired managerial teams. In contrast, she observes restrictions in that strategic issues are still left to the competence of the dominant owners: 'Boards of Directors of these companies are strictly controlled by the dominant owner.' She also mentions that the Boards of Directors often function simply as a formality, to endorse the decisions made by the dominant owners (2005: 19). All Dolgopyatova's observations (ibid.) mean that actually in these cases there is no real separation of ownership and control, at least in strategic matters, but instead the owners' informal control over the enterprises. The importance of her observations, especially this last point, will become clearer in Section 3.4.

Besides occupying managerial positions and directly controlling the Boards of Directors, many large insiders construct additional managerial structures, which are not connected with the property structures as previously discussed (Papper 2002b: 90). They establish independent organisations which concentrate on the executive functions of the corresponding enterprises, but do not possess any property. For instance, in 1998, UKOS established three such executive companies – UKOS Exploration and Production, UKOS Refining and Marketing and UKOS-Moscow – which managed oil extraction, production of oil products, and so on.

As will be seen in Section 3.4, direct control over management is necessary for the big insiders to exercise fully their 'property rights' over the assets. None the less, all this is insufficient to retain control over the assets without the next crucial element of infrastructure.

3.3.4 External Protection of 'Property Rights'

Given the unfavourable legal environment in Russia (see above in Section 3.2.1), and the permanent threat of hostile takeover (discussed below), Russian big insiders need strong guarantees of their 'property rights' to protect them from encroachment by rival groups. Such guarantees can be provided by state authorities. Papper (2002b: 86) emphasises a 'high degree of dependency on the state' as one of the key features of Russian big business. In these conditions, groups of big insiders try to establish strong connections with particular governmental bodies or officials. Radygin and Sydorov (2000, p. 55) speak about the 'privatisation of the state institutions', meaning the informal ties which connect big business and governmental officials, to their mutual benefit. The World Bank experts who have studied this system of relations, peculiar to some transitional countries, label this a 'capture economy' (Hellman et al. 2000). This type of economy is characterised by a company's ability to influence state officials through private payments and to shape the *rules of the game* to the company's advantage: 'In the capture economy, public officials and politicians privately sell underprovided public goods and a range of rent-generating advantages "a la carte" to individual firms' (ibid.: 2). Hellman and colleagues contrast the concept of the state-capture economy with those of influence and administrative corruption. Influence plays the same role as the state-capture economy, but is based on the large incumbent firms' close ties with the state and without recourse to payments. Administrative corruption reflects bribery connected with the implementation of laws and regulations. Hellman's study shows that new entrants are in competition with already established large firms, which exert significant influence on state officials; as such, the new entrants are compelled to turn to the state-capture economy, for the new entrants' capture of the state is a compensation 'for weakness in the legal and regulatory framework' (ibid.).

In Russia, privatisation of the state institutions at the federal level ensures the free export of financial resources abroad, paralysing the efforts of other governmental bodies and individuals trying to make state control stricter (Radygin and Sydorov 2000: 55). Privatisation also allows the gain of judicial control over state property at a minimum price, payment evasion on accumulating debts, the initiation of business-friendly changes in legislation, and so on. At the local level, the takeover of the state assures a multitude of concessions: tax allowances and payment delays, investment credits, subsidies, profitable loans given under the guarantees of the Russian Federation, subsidised licenses, state property leasing arrrangements at low or even no rental fees, and so on. Corporations manage to use the government to prevent competitors from entering controlled markets (the state has enough means to create problems for any enterprise), to suppress collective labour organisations, and so on. However, the most important advantage of state privatisation is, of course, that big business is protected from a redistribution of *property rights*. The main instruments of *taking over the state* are bribes and *rotation* between the civil service and private-sector employment (Radygin and Sydorov 2000: 55). A number of sociological studies support the above, for example, Zakharov 2004, Kolennykova et al. 2004.

The state-capture economy was pertinent in Yeltsin's Russia of the 1990s. In Putin's Russia of the 2000s, many changes occurred. Remarkably, from the authorities' standpoint, a few especially ostentatious oligarchs, trying to obtain *too much* power, were expelled from the country or imprisoned. This is emphasised by Pirani:

> On one level, this was a battle between power and money, but it is more accurately described as a reordering of their relationship. The state disciplined the oligarchs in the interests of the property-owning class as a whole, and restored to itself the functions it lost in the chaos of the 1990s. Its power is not an end in itself but a means of managing post-Soviet Russian capitalism and integrating it into the world system. (Pirani 2010: 1)

In fact, a kind of tacit collusion was concluded between big business and authorities: if big business does not meddle in the top structure of political power, it can enrich itself by all means traditional for Russian capitalism (see below). The state continued in its role as *property rights* protector.

The INDEM study treats state-capture economy and administrative corruption as mutually complimentary strategies (Satarov and Parkhomenko 2001: 11). One approach to interpreting their data is that state-capture economy hinders progress in transition economies. Surveys of corruption in Russia provide another interesting result (Stolyarov 2002): 80 per cent of people interviewed confess that they themselves initiated corrupt deals because they were *efficient*. In 98 per cent of the cases, individuals receive a favour for which they have paid (ibid.). Levina analyses the activities of state officials who have regular connections with big business structures. While in advanced market economies, lobbying means influence exerted by business groups on state bodies within the legal framework; in Russia, lobbying often goes beyond the law (2006: 4–5). Levina argues that a state official seeks to maximise their profit from the position they occupy by serving the interests of friendly firms. An official can even diversify their activities, and provide aid to a number of firms. If the official's business-friendly structures occupy solid positions in the Russian economy, they can expect in the future to obtain a prominent position in management (ibid.: 11). There is also movement in the opposite direction, that is, from managers to state officials. In both cases, such individuals operate in a whole network of commercial interests (ibid.: 9). Levina concludes that 'lobbying, based on a network of commercial interests, is one of the main determinants of the modern situation in Russia' (ibid.: 35).

Another type of guarantee of these *property rights*, growing in Russia today, is the so-called '*krysha*' ('roof' in Russian). This criminal structure provides protection against hostile takeover for usually significant remuneration. According to some publications (*Argumenty I Facty* 2000), 'roofs' appeared in the early 1990s as the most widespread type of protection racket. Usually such services are provided by private security agencies, which are established either by criminal groups or by the state's law-enforcement agencies. Law-enforcement agencies provide one of the most appreciated services in this market today, freeing big insiders from subjugation and enforced rack-rent payments to criminal groups (ibid.). The demand for the services of security agencies of *criminal* origin is created by organisations deeply involved in illegal activities. Remuneration for protection is usually paid in cash and in St Petersburg, for instance, it will usually cost a businessperson 10–20 per cent of their revenues (ibid.).

In the West, it is common to attribute the role of criminality in modern Russia to the legacy of communism. Without a doubt, criminality existed in the Soviet system and played an increasing role with the degeneration of the Stalinist bureaucracy (see Chapter 2). However, criminality was limited to the margins of economic life and was never able to penetrate the Soviet system's core. In her study of rent-seeking behaviour in the Soviet Union and modern Russia, Nell (2011) finds that central planning kept this phenomenon at the system's periphery, while decentralisation in the course of market reforms allowed rent-seeking behaviour to penetrate the core. As a student of the origins and the role of criminality in the Russian economy, Rawlinson finds that

> ... what is designated 'gangster' capitalism in Russia *is neither a derivation from nor an aberration of the free market*, but rather, when taken from a harm paradigm, a micro-version of capitalism as it operates on a global level. A closer examination of the social consequences of Russia's adoption of *laissez-faire*, the responses by Western advocates of shock therapy to political objections raised against fulfilling the programme, and the legal and ethical slack given to those supportive of the free market, expose a raft of harms to rival any of those attributed to organised crime. (Rawlinson 2010: 4, original emphasis)

Thus, external protection of the *property rights* (the official definition and practice of which frequently diverge) may be necessary to preserve a firm control over profitable assets. The external protection of property rights, as a crucial element of infrastructure, currently has a predominantly informal character. This is worth noting, because it shows that Russian dominant owners' mechanism for control over enterprises goes beyond the limitations set by the law.

3.3.5 Internal Protection of 'Property Rights'

The infrastructure of control has both external elements and internal elements. Here we focus on the internal elements of the infrastructure of control.

The unfavourable character of the legal environment in which Russian business operates, finds its manifestation not only in external threats to ownership but also in possible encroachments on the firm's financial flows on the part of managers and employees. The reasons why employees widely exhibit opportunistic behaviour will be explained later. Here we should note that in order to preserve their control over these assets, big insiders are compelled to create very developed and sophisticated internal elements of the infrastructure of control.

The Russian corporations' organisational structures were formed as a result of the evolution of institutions in the post-reform period, beginning in 1992. As discussed above in Section 3.2.1, the majority of Russian corporations appeared through mergers and acquisitions of enterprises made by big-insider groups in the course of privatisation. With the increase in conglomeration, the dominant group would establish a managing company, concentrating part of the production management's functions. If the big insiders kept acquiring new assets, the managing companies' structures became more complicated, containing two to three management levels. For instance, a managing company established by a dominant group and situated in Moscow acquires a few more companies, situated in different regions, each of which in turn owns production enterprises. In such a case, the first-level managing organisation (the core of the group) runs the enterprises (on the periphery) indirectly, but through the mediation of a few second-level managing structures. Such conglomerates' core had weak control over the periphery, where the previously entrenched managers dominated. In the 1990s, many Russian corporations went through the stage of creating weakly connected companies and later decided to eliminate them to improve the quality of decision making. Gradually, the position of the dominant groups strengthened and they started to centralise management for securing income redistribution in their favour. Currently, advanced corporations continue to increase their degree of centralisation (Novojenov 2003a, 2003b), while their managing companies tend to set more detailed investment parameters (Dzarasov and Novojenov 2005: 279–80).

According to Bochkarev and colleague (1998), big insiders established new and initially informal codes of behaviour, which included rules designed to prevent their personnel from behaving opportunistically. Later, these norms were improved and formalised through the development of different organisational structures, standards for business processes, rules, instructions, and so forth. Since this book is focused on the accumulation of capital, apart from strict control over the day-by-day production activities, we should discuss in more detail the centralisation of the investment management process. Novojenov (2003a, 2003b) studied systems of investment management at eleven large Russian companies – Tumen Oil Company, Oil Company YUCOS, Oil Company Rosneft, Magnitogorsk Metallurgy Combinat, Siberian-Ural Aluminium Company, Norilsk Nickel, AvtoVas, Aeroflot, the Ministry of the Russian Railroads (a large state-owned company), Transnefteproduct and Transneft – and found the following typical features:

1. In all eleven firms, the central managing companies made decisions regarding the main characteristics of corporate investment activities as a whole, the key parameters for the production divisions' investments and parameters for the groups of projects. Central companies also determined the conditions for external borrowing.

2. In the majority of corporations, decisions about the particular characteristics of projects were made by the same central companies, which formed investment portfolios. Sometimes the right to determine parameters for a part of those investments with a relatively low cost was given to the middle-ranking managing companies. In the frameworks for total budgets, these organisations independently formed small investment portfolios, but decisions concerning the majority of projects were still under the central managing companies' authority.

3. In ten of the surveyed companies, decisions on finance for the majority of investment contracts were made by departments at the highest level of the corporate hierarchy. These divisions were integrated into the specialised functional blocks in the central managing companies or in purchasing-logistics companies strictly controlled by big insiders, rather than being part of the lower levels of the managing hierarchy.

4. The companies' regional divisions and subdivisions had the right to influence the quantity, technical characteristics and timing of the materials and services purchases for investment activities. However,

even these decisions were controlled by a multitude of high-rank subdivisions.

In Russian corporations, big insiders personally make decisions concerning both the main aspects of corporate investment activity as a whole and particular significant projects. Other decisions are usually in the competence of the highest administration level and are made by the core managing company's managers. Usually these managers are loyal to the dominant group because their salaries are much higher than other managers' salaries. In practice, this means that big insiders share their rent with this group of managers.

Incidentally, this group of managers is strictly controlled by the controlling-revision services and private security services of the enterprises (ibid.). The security services are often provided by independent firms established by big insiders allegedly to maintain order but actually to keep an eye on personnel who might be inclined to opportunism. These security firms' employees not only protect property and material values from outside theft (sometimes all contracts with outsiders must be endorsed by the security service), but also struggle against opportunist managers and employees. In one sizeable wholesale firm, the internal security service used to overstock goods in the delivery service vehicles to test employees' honesty (ibid.).

These phenomena mean that such Russian companies create sophisticated internal protection systems to maintain big insiders' control over their assets. This discussion of internal infrastructure of control suggests that there are three key elements of these systems: centralised decision making (not only regarding strategic issues but also a multitude of minor questions); sophisticated control and internal auditing procedures, and internal security structures.

3.3.6 Infrastructure Scheme

Based on this discussion of infrastructure of control, it is possible to depict the typical scheme of the infrastructure of insider control over assets in Figure 3.4.

We may conclude that, in modern Russian conditions, the infrastructure of control largely underpins a firm's power over the market. Elements of this infrastructure are the formal and informal

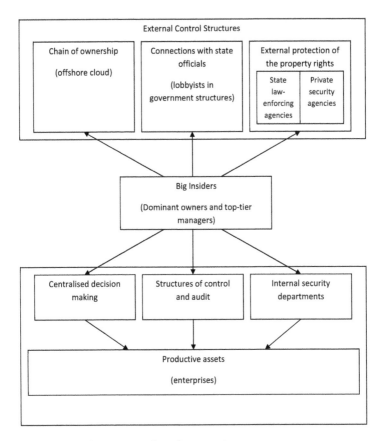

Figure 3.4 Infrastructure of insider control over assets

institutions created by big insiders to secure their market positions, and their control over their enterprises' external and internal environments. Under current conditions in Russia, only this infrastructure ensures control over assets and, consequently, enables owners to maximise the income generated from their property. As we will see, the amount of income obtained by big insiders and, often the very opportunity for profit itself, depends on the efficiency of their infrastructure for control over assets. It should be particularly stressed that due to the crucial role of informal institutions for the infrastructure of control, big insiders' real power greatly exceeds their legal rights based on their official status. Thus, they exercise supra-property rights over their controlled enterprises. The infrastructure of control clearly indicates the lack of separation between ownership and management, which is one of the prime characteristics of the modern Russian business. This set of institutions is a logical consequence of the informal relationships of private income appropriation which began early in Soviet times (see Chapter 2) and became institutionalised during the course of privatisation. We can better understand the significance of this infrastructure, taking into account the instability of control over the assets in the modern legal environment in which big Russian business operates.

3.4 The Fundamental Instability of Insider Control

Studies of modern Russian business practices conclude that the struggle for redistribution of property rights among the dominant groups is its permanent feature (Radygin and Sydorov 2000, Radygin 2001, Kapelushnikov 2001, Deryabina 2001, Abe and Dolgopyatova 2010, and others).

3.4.1 Hostile Takeovers

Radygin and Sydorov (2000) argue that periodic waves of property rights redistribution among the dominant groups in Russian business are a recurring phenomenon. If in 1996 a struggle for control was completed at 25 per cent of Russian enterprises, and in 1998 at 50 per cent, the years after the 1998 crisis witnessed a renewal of the mass redistribution of property rights, as shown by registration data. This is supported by a number of quantitative estimates (Kapelushnikov 2001; Kapelushnikov and Demina 2005).

Since acquisition of an enterprise usually leads to a change in the top-tier managers, it is possible to make the corresponding statistical inference from the frequency of such appointments in the corporate sector. According to Kapelushnikov, from the beginning of the 1990s until 2000, the general director was changed at more than half the industrial enterprises (43.6 per cent of general directors had worked more than ten years in the same company), while for nearly 10 per cent of organisations, the executive director was changed during the previous year (at the date of research) (2001: 110–11). Another research study shows that, from the mid-1990s, on average, an annual change of the principal owners took place at 6–8 per cent of industrial enterprises. Redistribution processes annually affect up to one-sixth of the stock capital (Kapelushnikov and Demina 2005). This figure seems persistent, since Avdasheva and Dolgopyatova give exactly the same percentage range as an estimate of the annual share of the Russian JSCs which changed ownership. They argue that this process 'speeded-up rather than slowed down with the increase in ownership concentration' (2010: 25).

These data suggest that *despite the existence of a highly developed infrastructure, big insiders' control over Russian enterprises is fundamentally unstable.* Such conditions in large measure arise from the importance of the informal elements of insider control. For instance, if a prominent political official leaves or is ousted from his or her position, the sophisticated network of personal connections created between that official and his or her business counterparts may crumble. This instability is even more acute because, in the majority of cases, big insiders' informal positions are of a criminal or semi-criminal nature, which means they can always be challenged. Hence, big Russian business is always in a vulnerable position; due to the given legal environment and to big business's largely criminal nature, privatisation laid the foundation for a permanent struggle between rival groups of big insiders for control over profitable assets.

Kapelushnikov (2001) shows that conflicts inside an established dominant group can arise due to either a business's rapid expansion or decline. In the first case, a corporation faces growing problems with the distribution of incremental income, when certain big insiders want to increase their share and thus challenge others within the company. However, in modern Russia, such situations are not observed very often, because there are not very many increasingly prosperous companies. The decline of a company's income decreases the potential rent available and as a result, some dominant group members will try to eliminate their fellow-insiders. Such situations are widespread and have been substantiated by empirical investigations (ibid.: 119, 123). The worse the enterprises's position, the higher probability that the majority of shares will pass to a rival group of big insiders, and thus the more unstable the general director's position. It is also found that conflicts are generally preceded by a deterioration of the business (ibid.). Indeed, in the short term, conflict amongst the big insiders drastically shrinks the time horizons of managerial strategies. Threatened by the complete loss of their control rights, the dominant groups undertake only the repairs necessary to shield the production process from breakdown. All available income is withdrawn to finance the 'hostilities' and to fill the accounts of those who are at risk of losing control. In such conditions, the struggling adversaries may well appropriate even the funds borrowed by the enterprise in the external capital market. There is empirical research to substantiate this conclusion about the deterioration of the businesses' unstable position. Kapelushnikov establishes that the worst situation is characteristic of those enterprises where the general director and the chairman of the Board of Directors were replaced within the last year of the research undertaken. The whole range of the examined performance variables show that these companies fell behind those with a stable top-tier management (ibid.: 122).

Another cause of struggle between the big insiders is identified by Radygin and is connected with high profitability and relatively weak control (2001: 32–3). If, in an enterprise, current big insiders fail to establish an infrastructure of control that is capable of assuring their positions, a potential raider will be sorely tempted. In this case, stronger outside groups may be induced to challenge the established big insiders' claim to ownership. Usually such situations occur when a company becomes the object of an adversarial acquisition attempt on the part of some oligarchies' clans. Challenged by such an organisation, which enjoys powerful 'administrative resources', even big insiders in control of significant financial flows, may lose their assets. Describing the mergers and acquisitions in Russian business, Dolgopyatova argues that 'transactions are taking place outside the organised markets' (2005: 8). Among the tools frequently used in this process, she mentions bankruptcy procedures, hostile takeovers, and equities manipulations.

The scale and mechanism of adversarial business takeovers helps us to understand better the nature of ownership and control in Russian enterprises and should therefore be examined in more detail. First of all, it is necessary to clarify the notion of the 'hostile takeover' in modern Russia. In western literature, this term usually means the legal act of acquiring the controlling parcel of a company's shares followed by replacement of that company's managerial team. It is regarded as the operation of the market for corporate control which hinders expropriation of shareholders by managers (Keasey et al. 2005: 4). The sense in which this term is used for the description of property redistribution in modern Russia is very different. As will be seen below, in Russia, a hostile takeover means the appropriation of enterprises using violent, coercive methods.

Such criminal practices are widespread. According to Popova, corporate governance department director of the Russian Federation's Ministry of Economic Development and Trade, in just the first half of 2005, 70 violent (that is, using physical force) business takeovers took place in Moscow alone (Novikova 2006). In other regions, the situation is similar. Pleskatchevski, the chairman of the State Duma Committee on Property Ownership, informed the public that the Russian Federation's Trade Chamber had counted about 5,000 hostile takeovers in Russia during the period 2000–04, while in 2005 there were a further 1,900 (Kondratyeva 2006). These data were confirmed at the hearings at the State Duma Committee on Security Issues, where the following estimation was presented (Deitch 2006). Of the total figure of 1,870 acts of mergers and acquisitions, which took place in Russia in 2005, 75 per cent were of an adversarial nature. It was mentioned that even the so-called 'special regime' enterprises, that is, those pertaining to national defence, are not protected from violent takeover (ibid.). This figure can be related to the aforementioned statistical estimates of the average percentage of Russian enterprises which change their principal owners annually. The calculation gives us the figure of 4–6 per cent of businesses on average which are subject to hostile takeover in Russia today. Every year, 70–80,000 raiding attacks take place in Russia and up to 5,000 succeed (TsPT 2008: 40). This is enough to create a real threat to the dominant position of the majority of big insiders and compels them to take precautions. According to the Investigations Committee attached to the General Attorney's Office, in 2008–10 alone, the damage caused by criminal raiding amounted to 4 billion roubles (BFM.ru 2010). Pleskatchevski argues that today 'not a single JSC is guaranteed against an adversarial takeover' (Kondratyeva 2006).

The modern Russian state's role in the violent redistribution of 'property rights' should be noted. Mikhail Grishankov, chairman of the State Duma Committee on the Prevention of Corruption, maintains that 'not a single raider would dare to take over an enterprise, if not propped up by the corruption ties both in the law enforcing agencies and other structures' (ibid.). A court official confessed in his interview that 'last year' he participated in at least ten takeovers; that is, he was bribed to transfer $10,000 to his superiors after each transaction (ibid.).

While the number of raiding incidents has diminished compared with the early 1990s, the mid-2000s still saw the expansion of the so-called 'Kremlin group', that is, bankers and businesspeople who had close ties to the Kremlin and who exploited those connections (Menshikov 2006). Property redistribution extended far beyond the company YUKOS. The year 2007 saw the formation of the state corporations ZhKKh Reform Assistance Fund, Rosatom, Rostekhnologii, Rosnanotekh and Olimpstroy, which brought together substantial assets. Some researchers have termed this process 'quasi-nationalisation', because it essentially resulted in the nationalisation of costs and the privatisation of profits (Ustyuzhanina et al. 2010: 77). State corporations are characterised by exemption from the established practices of control by law enforcement agencies, along with opaque financial flows, networks of affiliated structures, and enormously inflated production costs. State corporations that emerge from government control are notable for their financial activities' opacity, and for their secretive asset handling. In practice, they feature the same model of insider control found in big business. This is quasi-nationalisation since it conceals private appropriation (insider rent) carried out on the basis of state property.

3.4.2 The Mechanisms of Corporate Raiding

The nature of corporate raiding is clarified if one takes into account the methods by which property rights are redistributed today in Russia. Raiding – the hostile takeover of enterprises – has become an industry in contemporary Russia. The mechanism of this process was examined by the journal *Kompanya*, which investigated the Russian economy's corporate sector (Vorobyev 2005). The journal's findings suggest that there is a fully grown market providing services of this sort, with established firms and prices. Vorobyev identifies five major stages of the typical takeover as follows:

1. Assets evaluation – First, raiders study the company in an attempt to discover its real financial performance (which usually differs significantly from the official report), and estimate the value of its territory, constructions and equipment. The fee for such research: $5,000–20,000.

2. Security assessment – At the next step, raiders study the security system created by the dominant owners. They are particularly interested in the owners' internal security systems and connections – including informal ones – with private security enterprises and state law-enforcment agencies. If, for example, insiders are associated with an important state official, then typically, the whole operation's price increases. The fee of this service: $3,000–10,000.

3. Planning for the takeover – Raiders make a distinction between friendly and hostile acquisition methods. Friendly acquisition methods are applied when dealing with 'weak' dominant owners, who have only nominal security structures and lack any serious connections. Hostile acquisition methods are used if the company has an efficient security system and 'strong' informal positions. Hostile takeover plans include: gaining access to the shareholders' register and initiating necessary changes, neutralising (that is, bribing) the local judiciary, militia and authorities; shouldering out the current management from the enterprise's territory, and, if necessary, organising a corresponding mass media campaign and other measures. The price of the service: $10,000–30,000.

4. Organising the takeover – The takeover is organised according to the plan developed. The cost of the action usually amounts to three times the sum of the aforementioned expenditures.

5. Measures facilitating the takeover: Measures may include setting up a criminal case against the owner (involving, for example, drugs, sexual abuse, espionage, and so on): $50,000 in Moscow and $20,000 in the provinces; resolving the criminal case: $30,000–1,500,000 (Moscow), $450,000–200,000 (provinces); mobile phone tapping without court authorisation: – $1,500 per day; abduction and imprisonment of the owner and/or their relatives: from $20,000; having a question raised in the State Duma: $5,000–8,000; influencing a government decision: from $500,000; appearing on a television programme (90 seconds–2 minutes): $5,000–30,000.

The research shows that the hostile takeover is based on evaluation of the infrastructure of control. Raiders carefully study the external and internal protection of the company's 'property rights', as created by the big insiders. They are particularly interested in the informal positions of the dominant owners in the law-enforcement agencies and in government circles. As mentioned, the price largely depends on such connections. The whole takeover's plan depends on the structure and development of the infrastructure of control. The research testifies that companies with underdeveloped protection systems are vulnerable and more susceptible to a hostile takeover. Numerous publications recount the violent actions which have taken place in the course of such 'corporate wars'. For instance, in Ekaterinburg (Sverdlovskiy Region), there was an attempt to capture a big market complex by force (Nikolski 2006). In the press and on television, organisers advertised vacancies in the security profession, then hired 200 young unemployed men and dressed them in a special force militia uniforms. They rushed into the market's building complex and began to eject personnel, even throwing the market's security service chief out the window. When the genuine militia arrived, their counterfeits refused to yield and continued to resist until they were forcibly defeated. This particular raid's organisers were sued in court and accused of instigating mass riots (ibid.).

Popova noted that if previously raiders had predominantly relied on intimidation and rough physical force, they now frequently resort to intricate legal schemes (Novikova 2006). Owing to corporate law developments during the later 1990s, relationships in the sphere of property rights became more stable, and takeover struggles formally shifted to the law courts, although corruption still underlies this process. Numerous quasi-legal methods are employed (Radygin 2001: 28). Through the following four main procedures, former big insiders can be deprived of their 'property rights' (Deryabina 2001: 2–9, Dolgopyatova 2002: 45, Radygin 2001: 26–45):

- Additional issue of shares, with their distribution via closed subscription among the successful big insiders and the organisations controlled by them;
- Restructuring of the joint-stock company, stripping the rights of the losers. The company's assets and liabilities are redistributed

in such a way that the assets accrue to the successful big insiders, and the liabilities left with the losing (former) big insiders;

- Consolidation of shares, when the large portion of equities is converted to a lower amount. Moving to a single share is a particular type of consolidation. In such case, the losing big insiders, possessing small amounts of shares insufficient for such transformation, are offered monetary compensation. As a result, they became just ordinary creditors;
- False bankruptcy, as a result of which, the enterprise finds itself under the mastery of an external manager, who represents the winners. The losers are deprived of the control over the financial flows.

Sometimes more than one of these schemes are applied simultaneously. For instance, restructuring can take place, while simultaneously assets are transferred and shares consolidation takes place. It is important to note in this connection that the big insiders deprived of control usually do not obtain any compensation comparable with lost income. They may count only on a modest remuneration for the shares extracted.

Radygin notes the paradoxical situation existing in the Russian economy where sound and relatively efficient enterprises are involved in bankruptcy procedures. This is done to benefit a takeover from an opportunity on the part of rivals. At the same time, hopeless enterprises avoid such a procedure, because no one is eager to take them over. The chances of obtaining debt compensations in the course of bankruptcy are usually not high (2001: 32–3). One may conclude that bankruptcies actually became a low-cost version of a hostile takeover (see Juravskaya and Sonin 2004). The National Anticorruption Committee, founded in 1999, is a Russian non-governmental organisation investigating ways to eliminate the conditions that facilitate corruption; the committee reported that, in the aftermath of the 2008–09 crisis, bank raiding became predominant in Russia (Kabanov 2012). The increase in enterprises' borrowing in the course of their troubles placed Russian banks in a strong position to take over enterprises. A bank, represented by its top-tier management or direct beneficiaries, can be an initiator of a raid, or its executor. The mechanism of a bank's hostile takeover is based on corruption and illegal methods, including the fabrication of criminal cases, illegal arrests, forced deals and pressure to give up assets in favour of third parties. Sometimes quite robust and viable enterprises are forced to take loans which are used as a vehicle to stage artificial bankruptcies and violent takeovers (ibid.).

Meanwhile raiding is a very profitable business. It has been reported that raiders can obtain 20–25 per cent of the captured assets' value (Chernigovski 2005). According to experts' estimates, profit rate in the raiding business is about 1,000 per cent (Ukhov 2006). This is supported by research conducted by the Centre of Political Technologies, which estimates raiding profitability in modern Russia as ranging between 200 and 1000 per cent (TsPT 2008: 40). The enormous scale of this phenomenon can be seen from the fact that, according to specialists' estimations, this 'industry's' annual turnover in the mid-2000s amounted to $30 billion (Mayetnaya and Shypitsina 2004).

We cannot say that Russian authorities do not recognise the problem. Rashid Nurgaliyev, the then Minister of Domestic Affairs, has called violent takeovers 'the most dangerous type of economic crimes' (Nikolski 2006). An Interrogation Committee attached to the MIA has begun to study and publicise the practice of hostile mergers and acquisitions, but up to the present, it has done little to change the situation. The then Minister of Economy German Greff admitted that the state is unable to provide economic agents with protection against such 'acts of robbery' as hostile takeovers (Somov 2006).

It is necessary to note here that the very essence of the Russian pattern of ownership and control discussed above hinders the legal protection of the big insiders' position. As was mentioned, informal institutions play the crucial role in the infrastructure of insider control, but their illegal or semi-legal character means that they cannot be recognised and protected by the law. Hence, the current Russian corporate governance model is essentially unstable. We may conclude from the above that arbitrary redistribution of property rights is institutional-ised in the Russian economy and has become a persistent feature of the national corporate governance model. This explains the crucial role of the highly developed infrastructure of control, which should diminish the probability of losing business. This persistent threat of hostile takeover means that control over the assets on the part of big insiders remains fundamentally unstable; this has enormous consequences for the behaviour of economic agents in the Russian economy.

3.5 Conclusions

The genesis of modern Russian corporate governance can be traced to private income appropriation, resulting from informal and criminal activities under the surface of the Soviet state economy. The current form of ownership and control of Russian enterprises was shaped by privatisation beginning in the early 1990s. From the start, Russian reformers ignored other countries' privatisation programmes, which had been focused on improving the performance of former state enterprises. In contrast, Russian reformers pursued the objective of creating a new business elite as quickly as possible, whatever the costs, in order to guarantee that the dismantled Soviet system would never be revived. This perfectly suited the interests of both the triumphant Russian pro-capitalist coalition and its western supporters. The privatisation process in Russia created widespread opportunities for abuse of the legal system by state bureaucrats and criminals and enabled them to gain control over the most profitable enterprises. Characterised by the large-scale undervaluation of former state enterprises, privatisation led to an increasing concentration of production and capital and the emergence of the corporate sector in the Russian economy.

The initial stage of the corporate sector's emergence in Russia was characterised by the predominance of insider ownership. Later, equities redistribution took place in favour of those owners who had taken over companies from the outside, that is, they were not previously working for the company as managers, directors, and so on, who became big insiders dominating many Russian enterprises. A number of studies have established that the lack of law enforcement in modern Russia means that formal ownership rights cannot be exercised if they are not backed by control over the enterprises. Big insiders create an infrastructure of control – a network of formal and informal institutions enabling them to manage both the firm's internal and external environments. Ties of corruption with the state and criminal coercion are important ingredients of this infrastructure. Thus, the modern pattern of the Russian corporate governance is characterised by the inseparability of ownership and control.

The Russian economy regularly experiences waves of property redistribution among rival groups of big insiders. The overwhelming majority of such takeovers are hostile in character and enforced by criminal coercion. Corporate raiding became a separate sector of the Russian economy with its own market for services and with a large annual turnover. First of all, hostile takeovers threaten big insiders who fail to create an infrastructure of control strong enough to protect their dominant positions. This means that Russian business is characterised by a fundamental instability of ownership and control.

4

Rent Withdrawal, Social Conflict and Accumulation

4.1 Introduction

This chapter examines the nature of insider rent and the implications which its extraction has for social relations in Russian enterprises and for their investment behaviour. The central notion on which the whole analysis in this treatise hinges is introduced – insider rent as the major form of income appropriation by the dominant owners of Russian corporations. This is the income of the dominant individuals, expropriated as a result of their control over the firm's financial flows. Further, it is shown that in modern Russia insider rent extraction produces a number of intra-corporate social conflicts. These are conflicts over the distribution of income created by a firm. They lead to struggle between the dominant owners-big insiders on the one side, and workers, minority shareholders and rank-and-file managers on the other. This affects investment behaviour of Russian firms greatly.

Corporate conflicts compel dominant groups to spend more time and resources on the infrastructures of control, diverting funds from investment in directly productive assets. At the same time, these conflicts have a negative effect on profits. Hence, corporate conflicts increase the costs of obtaining internal funds. Secondly, under the influence of rent extraction, Russian big insiders, on the one hand, tend to reduce the total amount of funds available for investment, whilst, on the other, they largely ignore long-term projects. As a result, profitable investment opportunities are missed even when sufficient funds are apparently available. Insider rent maximisation makes the dominant group screen-out investment projects which would only become profitable beyond the short-term time horizon. The same kind of rent-seeking behaviour reduces the availability of funds for investments. Thus, intra-firm conflicts affect the time horizon of Russian corporations. They undermine the stability of ownership and control, increasing the probability of a hostile takeover. Apart from this situation, corporate conflicts prevent implicit contracts from appearing and operating, thus reinforcing big insiders' short-termism.

To summarise, Section 4.2 introduces a pivotal notion for this book on insider rent. Section 4.3 examines the essence and consequences of the major corporate conflicts taking place as a result of insider rent extraction. The adverse effects on investments caused by frictions with minority shareholders, opportunistic behaviour by employees and worker unrest are explored. Section 4.4 is focused on effects on the supply of, and the demand for, investment funds which are a consequence of rent extraction and corporate conflicts. Section 4.5 examines the effect of corporate conflicts on the time horizon of the big insiders and explains the implications for investment behaviour of firms having a short-term perspective. General conclusions drawn from the above are presented in Section 4.6.

4.2   Insider Rent as the Income of Dominant Groups

The previous chapter provided some important conclusions which will be now used to identify the particular kind of income extracted by big insiders from controlled assets.

4.2.1   Income Derived from the Control of Financial Flows

The most important result of the fundamental instability of insider control over the assets is the short-term business orientation of dominant owners. Under permanent threat of 'expropriation' by some rival group, big insiders are discouraged from making large investments, profits from which – even when significant in amount – will be available only in the long run. Indeed, facing the fundamental instability of their 'property rights' and control, insiders cannot be sure that they will enjoy any future gains themselves. As previously mentioned, existing legislation is unable to protect the rights of big insiders because their real powers greatly exceed their formal position. For the same reason, it is difficult to transfer control of financial flows to children as a right of inheritance. For big insiders' heirs, it will be not enough to prove their legal rights, winning the struggle with their rivals would be necessary for them to benefit from their assets. All this contributes to the short-term business orientation of the Russian dominant owners.

Another important condition is the undervaluation of assets during the course of privatisation, as previously discussed. As was mentioned in Section 3.2, the majority of the dominant owners in big business acquired their enterprises for prices much lower than their true market values. This difference between the cost of privatising state enterprises and their real market value became the 'windfall' benefit, 'donated' to the new private owners by the Russian government at the rest of society's expense. The big insiders' short-term time horizon and the inefficient running of these businesses, although ruinous in the long run, can be acceptable for the dominant owners for a short time. It is important to note that such cheap appropriation of assets is not a thing of the past. As previously mentioned, raiders can still secure takeovers for their clients for only 20–25 per cent of the asset's market value. This means that new owners of acquired enterprises can enjoy the same 'premium' as their predecessors at the time of privatisation.

This essential feature of the modern Russian economy – the fundamental instability of control over undervalued enterprises – determine the type of income which big insiders extract from their assets. A number of studies maintain that the individuals dominating Russian enterprises extract their incomes from their control over the businesses' financial flows (Dolgopyatova 2005, Papper 2002b, Dorofeev 2001, Desai and Goldberg 2000, Radygin 2000 and others). Thus, Papper (2002b) argues that inseparability of ownership and control has many consequences, recognised as unacceptable by the standards of advanced market economies. The first consequence is the non-transparency of the financial flows and distribution schemes, which enable owner-managers to appropriate income in 'non-dividend form'[1] (ibid.: 87). Dolgopyatova (2005: 4) argued that according to the Russian corporate governance model that appeared in the 1990s, owners have been able to obtain revenue only if they enjoyed 'control over the cash-flows of an enterprise'. Avdasheva and Dolgopyatova (2010: 25) speak of 'premium derived from control', under which term, the extra price of shares of the dominant shareholders in comparison with equities of other stakeholders is meant. Dorofeev (2001: 8–9) argues that for the big insiders, 'mastery of the financial flows of the controlled firms is a non-market (non-tradable) asset'. The essence of corporate control in modern Russia is real control over financial flows: 'As it is known, the most "delicate" sphere of activity of the modern Russian corporation is diversion of the financial resources from paying: taxes, debt obligations to the creditors and dividends to the "alien" shareholders' (Radygin and Sydorov 2000). The main struggle for corporate control usually takes place here in the sphere of corporate finances, which is hidden from outsiders. Due to the specific organisational character of Russian corporate finances, this struggle necessarily assumes a certain tint of criminality.

The World Bank experts Desai and Goldberg argue that ever since privatisation, manager-owners have significantly degraded their enterprises' assets. 'Instead of increasing a firm's value through reinvestment', they

> ... have typically extracted income streams from these firms at the expense of minority shareholders. The managers have diverted cash flows to offshore accounts and shell corporations, concentrating losses among subsidiaries held by outsiders (rather than evenly distributing them between insider-owned holding company and subsidiary), and by delaying the payment of dividends. Since dividends are taxable and have to be shared with other shareholders, manager-owners are more inclined to withdraw cash flows from their enterprises through fictitious expenses or theft. (Desai and Goldberg 2000: 8–9)

This important conclusion was supported in interviews I conducted with experienced Russian business managers. One of them – Irina Smirnova – at the date of interview was the chief accountant of the Trade House 'Altair'. She maintained that the owners 'extract their income not as a result of the efficient running of their businesses, as due to control over the financial flows of the enterprises. Simply speaking they withdraw money from the turnover' (Smirnova 2002). Another expert, Vladimir Popov, at the time of his interview in July 2004 was an adviser to the chairman of the Board of Directors of NGK ITERA – a big Russian natural gas production company. Under Gorbachev, Popov was a member of the State Commission on economic reforms attached to the USSR's Council of Ministers, and in the 1990s, he was department head of the Russian Federation's State Tax Collecting Agency. He explains that when he was with the State Tax Collecting Agency, he was well-placed to study closely Russian big owners' business methods (Popov 2004). The agency had created an electronic database of business reports, that had been provided to the taxation bodies. The database helped to identify sizeable, well-performing companies, which allegedly 'could not' pay taxes. The agency would send in their controllers, who would work out the full scheme of the firms' offshore structures and shadow operations, which enabled the owners to avoid taxes. This activity revealed to Popov the actual connections in Russian business. He found that the big owners, whether they were members of the Board of Directors or not, systematically interfered in the current activities of the managerial apparatus: 'This interference has only one aim – to secure extraction in their own favour of as large a share of financial resources as possible.' The origins of such behaviour lie in the pattern of privatisation: 'This will continue as long as the owners obtain revenues due to their control over the enterprises' financial flows' (ibid.).

Empirical studies support the experts' proposition that big insiders benefit from control over their enterprises' financial flows. In fact, dominant owners receive their incomes mainly in 'non-dividend forms' (Dolgopyatova 2005: 9). Only in recent years have some large companies started paying dividends, but this happens only in such organisations which had consolidated ownership and practically eliminated minority shareholders: 'In this case dividends serve as a legal source of high incomes of the company's owners and can be openly used for acquisition of the new assets.' Companies with significant state shares are sometimes compelled to pay dividends due to government pressure, but 'the majority of public companies fail to pay dividends or do it irregularly' (ibid.). According to a survey of 304 public companies, 60 per cent of those questioned did not pay any dividends at all in 2000–02. Only one-fourth of the companies paid dividends every year and one-fourth did it twice in the same period (Golikova et al. 2003). Another survey of 882 joint stock companies revealed that 61 per cent did not pay anything to their shareholders in 2001–03 (Dolgopyatova 2005: 9).

The character of big insiders' control over financial flows will be clearer from the following exposition provided by Popov (2004). Concerning the sources of the rapid accumulation of bank capital in the 1990s, he argues that one principal source was the banks' takeover of industrial enterprises. Banks did not introduce competent and efficient management to these companies, they just imposed their control. Inkombank,[2] for instance, controlled around 70 big enterprises. The banks appointed their own people to these companies' top managerial positions and 'sucked out' all the revenues, that is, tapped the turnover capital. These enterprises were then bankrupted and sold for nothing. The bank would impose an intermediary firm upon the controlled enterprise, which was established by the same bank through a chain of puppet structures. All the sales were organised through these intermediaries. After accumulating profits, these fly-by-night firms disappeared. No one initiated lawsuits against them. Some banks formed groups of enterprises, relying on which they tried to establish efficient business, but this relates only to a small group of highly profitable organisations, created in Soviet times and operating in the economy's export sector (for example, oil, metallurgy, and so on).

The banking activity itself, argues Popov, was organised incompetently but brought great benefit to the owners. For instance, loans were provided to their own enterprises at token interest rates, and to themselves and their relatives for an indefinite time period. High inflation rates in the 1990s depreciated these debts. Another money-making method was to deposit relatively modest sums of money into their own personal accounts, but the interest paid was incredible – 1,500, and even 10–20,000 per cent (!) annually. These banks' *actual* owners were the offshore companies, established by dominant owners. Popov observes that in 1998 many banks failed, but none of their owners suffered. They had already managed to withdraw their capital and move it to the West, while their property assets were registered with other organisations. Later, these same people appeared at the head of the industrial enterprises. Their main task remains the same – to secure control over financial flows.

We may conclude from the previously mentioned situation that *insider rent is a kind of private income which is extracted from enterprises due to control over their financial flows and appropriated by individuals or groups dominating those organisations.* A more detailed discussion of big insiders' major income-extracting methods is useful for a better understanding of the mechanisms of insider control. The most widespread are discussed below.

4.2.2 Methods of Rent Extraction

Cash Scheme   The cash scheme is the most primitive form of income appropriation by big insiders (Yakovlev 2002). Its essence lies in transferring some portions of the controlled organisations' income streams from non-cash into cash forms. For instance, an enterprise can issue a payment order on a certain sum in favour of a particular firm. The latter provides a fictitious invoice on allegedly undertaken work. Afterward, a particular bank or individuals, who established the previously mentioned firm, pays the cash to an insider or their representative (subtracting, of course, their commission). Insiders can also ask the buyers of the controlled enterprise's production to transfer payments to their own firm. In total, the specialists recorded eleven basic forms of the cash scheme. They differ by the risk–return relationship and correspondingly by the amount of interest paid to mediators. Research on tax avoidance provides us with the following typical cash scheme.[3] Figure 4.1 is based on Yakovlev 2002. A big insider signs a fictitious contract with a one-day firm for providing some services – for instance, for equipment repair work. The big insider then transfers to the firm's account 10 million roubles in non-cash form for these services allegedly provided. The point is that non-cash payments can be traced, according to bank records. Formally, these transactions were legal; the illegal appropriation of money, on the contrary, is easier to execute in cash form. In making another oral agreement – that the firm will return 9,850,000 roubles in cash to the big insider, they obtain the difference (1.5 per cent of the initial sum) as remuneration for all intermediary services. The one-day firm makes advances (10 million roubles) to a financial company to purchase bonds. This kind of bond is called a 'junk bond' and is sold for 1–2 per cent of their nominal price. On placing the preliminary order, the bank provides to a financial company 9,870,000 roubles in cash to make the deal; 987,000 roubles are paid to the bank for this transaction and 31,300 roubles accrue to the financial company as its remuneration for the operation. The financial company will use 20,000 roubles of its cash money to buy the bonds with the nominal price of 10 million roubles.[4] This operation will not be reflected in its accounts. At the same time of accounting for the firms providing the 'junk bonds', this situation will show that the latter were bought by particular individuals. Afterward, fictitious contracts will be signed by the financial company with the same individuals for the purchase of the bonds with the nominal price of 10 million roubles for 9,870,000 roubles. At the last crucial stage of the process, 9,850,000 roubles in cash will be delivered to the big insider. This cash does not officially exist, because it was allegedly transferred to individuals in exchange for the bonds. Actually this money is part of an enterprise's income which has been appropriated by the big insider, who will not pay any taxes on it, because officially (according to the firm's accounting), it is paid for services and hence constitutes part of production costs.

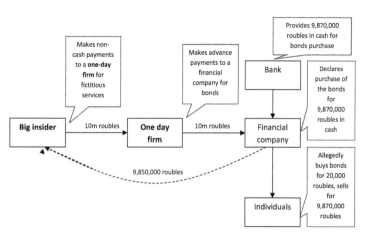

Figure 4.1 The cash scheme of rent extraction

Theoretically, individuals taking part in these transactions should pay taxes on their income, but rarely do taxation bodies see these taxes in reality. To register their dealings, the financial company may use stolen passports, or documents of deceased people, or give a bottle of vodka to some marginalised person for a loan of their passport (Yakovlev 2002). A crucial role in all these operations belongs to the one-day firms. They are established for a short time period – a few months or even weeks – to provide services which are certainly legally dubious. After playing their role, these firms disappear. Usually such firms are organised by financial companies (FCs) or investment funds. FCs advertise their services and find clients; a single financial company may run half a dozen one-day firms simultaneously. Such firms' transactions should not exceed a few tens of millions of roubles, in order to evade the attention of taxation bodies. The actual number of one-day firms is determined by the demand of the big insiders served by the particular financial company (ibid.). The FC never belongs to the organisation's formal founders. Usually a one-day firm is registered by a fake identity or using someone's lost identification documents. For example, Yury Vladimirovitch Gerasymchik, who lived in a small village, Pokrovskaya Sloboda, in the Moscow district, was reported in the press as the founder of about 1,200 firms (Latynyna 2002). The executive director and the chief accountant in this bogus firm were also dummy positions, who just signed the necessary documents. According to experts, such firms could be established for only US$300 and the salaries of such false directors and accountants do not exceed US$100 per month. The most significant costs of running a one-day firm are payments to the criminal structures 'covering' these activities. On average, a financial company spends $5,000–10,000 per quarter on financing one-day firms. The scale of the problem can be seen from the following: according to the Agency of the Russian Federation's Attorney-General, in 2000, the number of firms registered with lost identity documents amounted to 27,000 in Moscow alone (*Noviye Izvestiya* 2000). Experts argue that all these organisations should be considered as fraudulent (ibid.)

Cash schemes are widespread predominantly in small and medium-sized businesses. They are used by large organisations with less frequency because it is difficult to extract large amounts of rent in such a manner. However, such schemes can be used by sizeable businesses if a dominant group needs money in cash for some operations or for personal expenditures.

Penalty Scheme Sometimes penalties for the failure to fulfil deliveries are used to withdraw rent. In such a case, a company makes a commitment to deliver its products to another company but deliberately fails to do so. Subsequently, the former company assiduously pays penalties. These finances are transferred further to accounts controlled by big insiders. Some outstanding examples of such transactions have been reported in the press.

We have already considered the intertwined ownership chains of the prominent Russian banks: Mejprombank. According to *Novaya Gazeta* – one of the most informed liberal newspapers in Russia – 'such a network of firms is usually used for money laundering and tax evasion' (Latynyna 2002). For example, Mejprombank took on a commitment to provide 300 million roubles to the Concern Uteck with ownership capital of only 15 million roubles. Moreover, the contract's conditions were very stringent – if Mejprombank failed to provide the loan, it would have to pay Concern Uteck 15 million roubles in penalties. At first glance, the situation is absurd: one of the biggest Russian banks providing a tiny organisation with enormous credit on very unfavourable terms. However, as is already known, Concern Uteck actually belonged to the same Mejprombank which was in danger of incurring severe penalties. If Mejprombank failed to fulfil its commitments, then 'according to accounting it would appear that these 15 million roubles are Mejprombank's losses, but actually this money would be transferred to accounts of the firm headed by a member of Mejprombank's Board of Directors. Most of all, it resembles a bonus to a top manager not susceptible to taxation' (ibid.).

False Delivery Scheme Financial resources are withdrawn from businesses with the help of fictitious deals on conditions of advanced payments. Company A transfers to Company B payments for some deliveries but in reality no deliveries take place. Company B was established by Company A insiders in order to extract money from the latter (Katasonov 2002: ch. 7).

Loan Scheme Company A can provide a loan to Firm B, actually not expecting to be repaid. Applying this and the previous false delivery scheme, Company A accumulates bad debt. Usually such manipulations are used by very short-term-oriented big insiders, who are eager to withdraw the major part of finances from their businesses (ibid.).

Transfer Pricing Scheme   In stable corporations, big insiders extract rent by predominantly relying on administered (transfer) prices. The latter enable the dominant groups to depreciate income and appreciate expenditures of their controlled business. Big insiders initiate contracts between their organisations and specially established trading firms. The latter play the role of profit centres. They accumulate the difference between the transfer and actual market prices, which is nothing but the rent of the big insiders. Profit centres are often established in Russian and foreign offshore zones, and allow insiders to minimise their rent's tax leakages.

We can consider some aspects of Gasprom's operation to study an example of such activity. As is well-known, this state-owned company is one of the most significant natural gas producers in the world and an obvious monopoly in the Russian market. In 1997, Gasprom created its affiliated trade company Mejregiongas to sell natural gas and acquire local gas supply networks. Financial flows commanded by the new structure were estimated as amounting to $6–8 billion annually. In a few years, Mejregiongas gained control over 30 regional gas companies and 128 gas-distributing organisations. The scandal happened in 2001 when the Gasprom's new CEO, Alexey Miller, initiated a revision of his 'daughter company's' activity. It was revealed that much of Gasrpom's financial flows had been illegally appropriated by Mejregiongas's top managers (Krasavin and Makeev 2006). They had used their monopolistic position in the natural gas market when consumers – that is, industrial enterprises – needed fuel in addition to their contracted limit: 'For decisions in their favour, consumers, apart from direct gas payments, transferred additional money sums to the firms affiliated to Mejregiongas's top management' (ibid.). According to some press reports, many business directors privately maintained that these operations were 'only slightly disguised forms of bribes' (Latynyna 2003). In 2002, gas mediators affiliated to Mejregiongas inflicted heavy losses, just on energy-producing companies, amounting to more than 500 million roubles (Reznik 2002). In 2001, another fraud was revealed. To run the supply companies' acquired assets, a new organisation, Regiongasholding, was established. On later investigation, it was found that only 20 per cent of its shares belonged to Mejregiongas (and thus to Gasprom itself); the other assets were in the ownership of companies established by Mejregiongas top management (Krasavin and Makeev 2006).

Other structures established by Gasprom were also very profitable, because, according to some reports, one needed to pay $5–20 million to be appointed head of one of Gasprom's affiliated companies, depending on its profitability (Davydova and Romanova 2003). Profitability is measured here, of course, not in terms of return on investments in productive assets, but in terms of potential insider rent extraction. In 2003, after another scandalous revelation, Mejregiongas's financial flows, amounting now to $10 billion annually, were shifted to 'Gasprom itself. It means that now the 'opportunity to receive "kickbacks"[5] from industrial consumers, interested in additional cheap gas deliveries, moved to the top managers of the central holding company' (Krasavin and Makeev 2006).

The most widespread form of rent extraction is through the offshore concentration of a portion of the sales revenue. This is undertaken by many exporting corporations. In such cases, transfer prices are set at levels close to, but not lower, than current production costs, which means that they are significantly lower than the market level. Making too strong a price deduction in the export contract would increase the possibility of sanctions from Russian tax-collecting bodies. Sales are usually organised through the foreign offshore zones, but not only in case of foreign trade. Commodities produced for domestic market consumption may also go through offshore companies, which resell these goods to other offshore companies with a mark-up, determining the scale of insider rent. The latter companies, in their turn, make deliveries in Russia without mark-ups. According to Russian legislation, the latter companies do not pay any taxes on profit (Katasonov 2002: 59–60).

Offshore companies, which buy their products from Russian enterprises, are not able to resell commodities in Russia directly if their big insiders are seeking to evade taxes. Clause 10 of the Federal Law, 'About the profit taxes of enterprises and organisations' N 2116-1 in its version of 31 March 1999, states that the foreign organisations are obliged to pay taxes on income received from Russian sources. The obligation to obtain and transfer taxes in the state budget is incumbent on Russian organisations paying incomes to non-residents. According to the law, an enterprising resident must reserve 20 per cent from an offshore company's profits to pay taxes. If the non-resident organisation fails to provide documents proving its costs incurred in the purchase/production of commodities, the fiscal authorities are obliged to calculate profit assuming a 25 per cent profit rate.

We can study such kinds of insiders' income extraction with the example of one of the largest Russian metallurgical companies, Evrazholding, whose structure is illustrated in Figure 4.2 (Khrennikov 2003). Evrazholding was established in the second half of the 1990s by the EAM Group which was controlled by Alexander Abramov. It runs three metallurgical enterprises: Nijnetagilsky (Sverdlovsky district), Zapadno-Sybirsky (Kemerovsky district) and Kuznetsky (Kemerovsky district), which in total produce more than 13 million tons of metal annually (about one-fifth of the national production). This holding

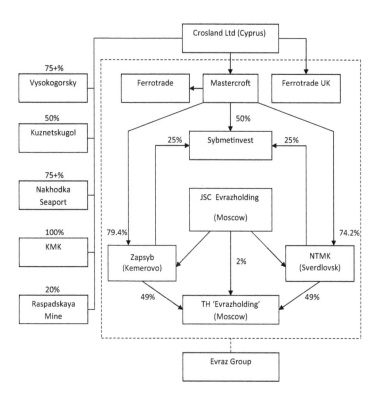

Figure 4.2 Ownership and control of Evrazholding

also incorporates a number of coal and ore suppliers, and the port of Nakhodkinsky (Khrennikov 2003, Ponomarev 2003).

After restructuring in 2002, the Cypriot company Crosland Ltd became Evrazholding's owner. On 1 September 2003, Crosland Ltd controlled the coal and ore suppliers, and the port of Nakhodkinsky through which the holding exported its production. Crosland Ltd owns another Cypriot company – Mastercroft. The latter controls the Evraz Group, including the Nijnetagilsky and Zapadno-Sibyrsky metallurgical business conglomerates. Ferrotrade Gibraltar became the unitary Evraz Group trader in the foreign markets, while the trading company Evrazholding concentrated on the domestic market. Both trading companies also belong to Mastercroft. Evrazholding is one of the most closed companies in Russia and information about the Mastercroft owners is not public knowledge, but Nicolas Ivanov, analyst with the consulting company IK Prospect, argued in 2003 that Alexander Abramov and Oleg Boyko were among the beneficiaries (ibid.). This complicated structure of ownership and control provided big insiders with favourable opportunities for extraction of funds, which can be seen from the reported data. According to an investment memorandum of the second Eurobond issue EvrazSecurities SA, in 2003, Mastercroft revenue increased by 52.5 per cent, amounting to $2.9 billion, while its net profit rose by 2.2 times, reaching $527 million. However, the net profit of all three metallurgical groups was only $180 million, which is roughly 25 per cent of the corresponding figure for the entire holding. At least half of the overall Mastercroft return, and more than 75 per cent of its net profit, was earned by the trading companies involved: Ferrotrade UK (return $1.47 billion, net profit $352.5 million), and Ferrotrade Gibraltar (correspondingly $101.4 million and $45.9 million) (Fedorinova 2004). The concentration of profits in the trading companies is a tax-avoidance scheme. One senior manager maintained that 'if Ferrotrade is a profit centre it can pay incomes in the form of dividends to its mother company registered in Cyprus. As a result the tax rate equals zero. If this mother company was Russian the tax rate on dividends would be 15 per cent' (ibid.). Experts think that this means that the real profitability of metallurgical enterprises belonging to the group was actually higher than was announced. Accounts are distorted by this transfer pricing.

This is confirmed by the findings of the Russian Federation's Financial Control Chamber, which checked the holding metallurgical groups' activities for 2004 and the first nine months of 2005. According to the Chamber's auditor, Vladimir Panskov (Fedorinova 2006), in that period, exports through the groups' Gibraltar trader, helped the enterprises to diminish their export returns by 9.9 billion roubles and tax payments by 2.37 billion roubles. This happened because 'prices on exported products were lower than the average world market prices', believes Panskov. Ferrotrade Gibraltar had a certificate valid to 2010 fixing its annual taxes at the level of $415 (ibid.). Thus, in the case of Evrazholding, one has a classic example of the offshore profit centre accumulating insiders' income through transfer payments.

Expenditure Schemes The essence of these schemes for insider rent withdrawals is the 'padding' of certain kinds of the controlled company's expenditures. Big insiders establish a firm whose sole task is to disguise the expropriation of insider rents. These firms I will call 'rent' or 'profit centres'; they organise deliveries and provide services to the controlled enterprise. The price of such deliveries and services is higher than the market level. This mark-up determines the scale of insider rent extraction. Such transactions have an additional advantage in that they help to boost the company's costs and, hence, avoid taxes. Later, these profit centres transfer accumulated rent to the private accounts of the big insiders. Such schemes are numerous. Profit centres can be used to deliver to the controlled firm appreciated raw materials; provide loans at artificially high interest rates; rent assets for inflated payments, and so on. Appreciated interest payments on credit are sometimes transferred to banks which in turn transfer them to the private accounts of the big insiders. Companies are also able to sign contracts for purchasing these services, the costs and actual providing of which it is difficult to control. Usually marketing research, consulting activities, auditing and some other activities are used for such purposes. A significant portion of payments on such contracts can be connected with insider rent withdrawal. 'Tolling schemes' simultaneously allowed the price of delivered raw materials to increase and the price of produced commodities to decrease. The difference in these prices is often minimal and does not correspond to the real value added in the production process.

In order to preserve their positive image and to alleviate the risk of encroachments on their rents by the state, some big companies create systems, comprising two or more levels of profit centres. In such cases, two organisations controlled by big insiders are established, which are not affiliated with the main corporation. The first firm operates in some respectable European country, for example, Britain. Another company is established in another jurisdiction with lower taxes, which has an agreement with Britain about avoiding double taxation, for example, Montenegro, Hungary, or Spain. The second firm gives an order to the first to make deals, with the finance appearing in the first company's accounts being transferred to the second. Remuneration of the company established in Britain usually amounts to only a small portion of the whole profit (say, 5 per cent). All the other sums go, for instance, to Montenegro where the profit tax rate is only 2.5 per cent. The British-registered company provides the official records, while the second firm leaves no traces. It is virtually impossible to control such organisations' actual profits (Shokhina 2002: 62–3). In large corporations, the schemes as explained are often jointly implemented and are more sophisticated than these basic variants illustrated above. Insider rent is distributed among many organisations, the variety of which allows for both the exploitation of the different countries' legislative advantages and for risk diversification. (For more details regarding offshore businesses, see Gorbunov 1997, Katasonov 2002: 58–66, Fedorov 2011.)

To summarise the arguments suggested above: (a) the essence of the Russian corporate governance model is control over enterprises' financial flows; (b) income extraction from this control is semi- or wholly illegal; and (c) money withdrawal is undertaken at the expense of the enterprises and to their detriment. The latter reflects the dominance of short-termism among big insiders. However, the short-term nature of big insiders' income-generation techniques is not its only important characteristic.

4.2.3   The Nature of Insider Rent

Insider rent plays the pivotal role in the model of Russian capitalism presented in this book. We arrived at this notion after studying the historical genesis of modern Russian capitalism (see Chapter 2) and its institutional nature (see Chapter 3). In the following parts of this book, social relations, capital accumulation, price structure and economic growth in Russia are all treated from the perspective of insider rent, which is why we focus more on this phenomenon here and discuss its meaning.

Essentially, insider rent differs from the ordinary entrepreneurial profit accrued in the accounting sense. First, this income is a 'return' on non-invested capital, that is, it was not invested by those who accrue its yields. Secondly, insider income is partly sourced by under-payments of dividends, taxes, investments, borrowed money and other contractual commitments. As will be shown later, to this list should be added funds obtained at the expense of employees' wages and salaries. This means that the origins of Russian big insiders' income are from a much wider range than entrepreneurial profit in the sense of ordinary accounting practices. Among the sources of such income, there are some articles which belong to production costs rather than to the residual income. We may conclude that while the normal entrepreneurial profit's size depends on the difference between costs and returns, big insiders' income depends in part on the size of the enterprise's financial flows.

All this means that insider rent is a product of unpaid labour. Indeed, every above-mentioned source can be traced to the latter. As such, insider rent represents a form of surplus value. It is a rather abstract category pointing to the foundations of the capitalist mode of production. As was mentioned above (see the Introduction), this book attempts to apply to the modern Russian economy the Marxian methodology of the ascent from the abstract to the concrete. It sees the major task of economic analysis to be the examination of how capitalism's basic, abstract notions are transformed into their concrete forms, which are located at the surface of an economy. We can see this from the Marxian treatment of concrete forms of surplus value: 'Up to the present, political economy ... has never separated surplus-value from profit, and never even considered profit in its pure form as distinct from its different, independent components, such as industrial profit, commercial profit, interest, and ground rent' (Marx [1894] 1959: 146). Elsewhere, Marx adds taxes to this list of components (see, for instance, ibid.: 32).

At the heart of the present model of Russian capitalism lies the notion of insider rent as a concrete form of surplus value. In this context, an important issue is insider rent's position in the hierarchy of other transformed forms of surplus value.[6] Indeed, in the above quotation from Marx, surplus value first becomes profit in its pure form. Without doubt, the results of the transformation of labour values into prices of production are meant here. Indeed, it is in the course of this process, that surplus values, produced according to labour, are redistributed according to a uniform rate of profit. It is a transformation of the first order. Then profit in its pure form, in turn, splits into industrial profit, commercial (trade) profit, interest and ground (land) rent. Again this happens in the course of redistribution of incomes created by labour. It is a transformation of the second order. Now where is the position of insider rent: above, between, or among these phenomena? All transformed forms of surplus value discussed by Marx can become sources of big insiders' short-term income. All transformations discussed by Marx take place in the sphere of distribution and exchange. Insider rent appears in the course of further redistribution of these kinds of incomes. This gives us reason to think that we are talking about the transformation of surplus value of a third order. Such an approach helps to define the socio-economic nature of the current Russian society with more precision.

As already mentioned, insider rent is quite a concrete phenomenon lying at the surface of the economic system. That is why it is affected by a wider range of factors than the forms of surplus value of the lower orders. More concrete economic relations possess more complex inner structures. As was previously mentioned, insider rent demonstrates the synthetic features of the entrepreneurial income and the feudal rent. Its relative dependence on the difference between costs and returns expresses connection with the former, while dependence on infrastructure of control – with the latter. Russian capitalism belongs to the periphery (more precisely to the semi-periphery) of world capitalism (Krasilshchikov 2008). In such societies, the elements of the different modes of production do not just coexist, but permeate each other, creating numerous transitive, synthetic forms. Insider rent is probably one of these forms. The redistribution of surplus value in such an economy necessarily assumes a specific form, distinguishing it from the 'classical' versions pertaining to the developed economies of the capitalist world-system's core.

Chapter 2 discussed the dual genesis of modern Russian capitalism, which emanated from the degeneration of the Soviet bureaucracy and the impact of global capitalism. These historical preconditions are reflected in the phenomenon of insider rent, which also displays dual features. On the one hand, it has certain properties of an entrepreneurial profit since part of it comes from productive investments. On the other hand, it has much in common with feudal rent as was previously demonstrated. The dual nature of insider rent reflects a dialectical approach to modern Russian capitalism, viewed as a result of the historical evolution of Soviet society in a given world-system context.

As was shown in Chapter 1, violence is an indispensable element of current Russian business culture, which is not something completely alien to capitalism, and this does not represent only the Stalinist legacy. On the contrary, it provides the common ground for both aspects of insider rent. The role of violence puts the modern Russian economy in the perspective of the Veblenian 'predatory capitalist' approach, previously discussed. As was demonstrated, coercion always belonged to formative features of capitalism and is particularly pertinent to its modern, globalised version. It is only natural that this dark side of capitalism facilitated its embrace of the remnants of Stalinism in a harmonious unity.

It is the infrastructure of control which provides the common ground for this unity. Here there is a certain similarity of this study with the Kaleckian degree-of-monopoly theory of distribution.

According to the latter, the size of mark-up, which a firm sets as its unit costs, reflects a number of institutional factors such as concentration of production, promotion efforts of the firm, the level of labour organisation, the size of indirect costs and other factors (Kalecki 1971). The infrastructure of big insiders' control over their firms (see Section 3.3.6) strengthens the market power of Russian enterprises as well. Indeed, for the firms, the infrastructure's external elements secure favourable legislation, taxation, restraints on rivals entering markets, and so on; while the internal elements of infrastructure help to control employees. Another important factor enhancing Russian firms' market power is unique to those in export-oriented industries. Since currently there is no foreign competition in their domestic market, firms belonging to this sector are able to increase their foreign deliveries, thus limiting domestic supply of their products and putting upward pressure on domestic prices (Uzyakov 2000: 103–4, Alexandrovitch 2001: 8, and see below). Big insiders' income depends on the particular factors of the degree of monopoly, characteristic of the modern Russian firm. Mair and Laramie (2002) complement the list of the degree-of-monopoly factors with the lobbyist's 'collective organisations' of capitalists. This is very similar to the functions of the elements of infrastructure of control, which are called here 'external protection of property rights'. Mair and Laramie argue that in relating the corporate income to the market power of the firm, Kalecki provides an alternative understanding of rent-seeking behaviour. This aspect of modern Russian capitalism raised doubts concerning the nature of the nascent social system in Russia.

Kotz (2001) studied the income sources of Russian big businesses in different economic sectors, such as:

1) oil and gas export,
2) ownership/control of urban land and buildings,
3) money-lending to the state,
4) trade,
5) speculation,
6) skimming revenue from enterprises,
7) theft of public funds, and
8) extortion.

He finds that only a minor share of income from (1) is created by present-day labour, while the major portion is the result of labour of previous Soviet generations and of workers from other countries; (2) gives land rent rather than profits; (3) transfers budget incomes and to an extent externally borrowed funds into private hands; (4) is a source of merchant profits; (5) is based on purchasing assets cheaply and selling them dearly and, hence, is again a kind of merchant profit; (6) is conducted through selling products to a trade house at prices lower than the market level and accumulating profits after reselling them at market prices. It is only another form of merchant profit; (8) is extorted from enterprises by criminal gangs, which has nothing to do with entrepreneurship at all:

The point is not that capitalist profit-making is completely absent in Russia. Some enterprises do manage to make a profit from their employees' labor, despite the severe depression and social chaos. The point is that capitalist profit-making does not form a major part of the incomes of Russia's new class of wealthy property owners. Instead, their incomes flow predominantly from non-capitalist relations. (Kotz 2001: 171)

This made Kotz conclude that the new social system in Russia is not capitalist at all, but is a sort of predatory/extortionist model of society (ibid.). This analysis was based on the experience of the 1990s and was inspired by the extremes of that tumultuous time. In the 2000s, the Russian economy experienced some relative economic recovery as a result of unprecedentedly favourable conditions in the world market of energy resources; elements partially improved and the system became closer to a rational entrepreneurship (Pirani 2010). Within these new conditions, Kotz recognised that the new Russian society is a capitalist one (Kotz and Weir 2007).

Despite the profound changes in Russia in the 2000s, much of Kotz's argument discussed above still holds today. At the heart of his position lies the idea of non-capitalist forms of income mixed with entrepreneurial profit derived from the exploitation of hired labour. This is a real problem which was only mitigated, but not eliminated, by recovery in the 2000s. As was previously stated, one of the major advantages of the insider rent concept is its double nature, reflecting the double nature of current Russian capitalism. This helps us to discuss the place of Kotz's classification of Russian big business's income in the context of capitalism. Revenues from 'oil and gas export' (1) created by the actual labour of Russian and predominantly foreign workers is industrial profit. (The revenues derived from the labour of previous generations of the Soviet people resemble the embezzlement of depreciation funds, which is discussed below.) The 'ownership/control of urban land and buildings' (2) yields land rent. 'Money-lending money to the state' (3) obviously yields a kind of interest. The merchant profit explains the following sources of income for Russian big businesses: (4) trade, (5) speculation and (6) skimming revenue from enterprises. Sources (1)–(6) are all derived from pure profit and belong to the transformation of the second order. 'Theft of public funds' (7) means theft of public income by avoiding taxes, which are identified by Marx as a component of profit (see above). Source (7) and 'extortion' (8) do not fit the traditional surplus-value approach. However, these kinds of income result from further redistribution of components of profit through non-economic coercion, which relates them to the 'feudal' side of insider rent. It seems reasonable to conclude that it is a transformation of the surplus value of the third order.

An alternative vision of the same problem is demonstrated by Aslund (1999). He relates the rent-seeking behaviour of the Russian elite to the slow implementation of market reforms in a mineral-rich country. He argues that the hybrid coexistence of central planning and market systems allows bureaucracy to divert resources to its own benefits. Aslund refers to the experience of the late 1980s, when the directors of state enterprises set up private firms and transferred profits from the former to the latter. Later, these proceeds were deposited in offshore companies for private appropriation. Aslund believes that these fraudulent operations would be impossible if there was liberalisation of both prices and interest rates.

From the standpoint of this book, this essentially neoclassical reasoning fails to grasp the nature of events taking place in Russia. It takes into account only 'business takeover' on the part of the state and ignores powerful movements in the opposite direction. Meanwhile, 'after only a decade of transition, the fear of the *leviathan state* has been replaced by a new concern about powerful *oligarchs* who manipulate politicians, shape institutions, and control the media to advance and protect their own empires at the expense of the social interest' (Hellman et al., 2000: 2, original emphasis). As this work tried to demonstrate in Section 3.2, there is no discontinuity between private-income appropriations under central planning and under the market economy in Russia. Insider rent is only a more developed form of the same kind of income appropriation which was discussed by Aslund. Privatisation in Russia was unprecedented in its scale and rapidity, but it not only failed to prevent dominant groups from diverting the funds of their controlled enterprises to their benefit, but greatly enhanced this process. The abundance of mineral resources, although providing an additional source for corruption, is not its prime cause. As was demonstrated by Auty (2001), resource-poor CIS countries have similar or even higher corruption rates than Russia and other oil-rich countries of the Caspian region. Price liberalisation only strengthened the position of big insiders in the fuel-producing industries in Russia (Dzarasov and Novojenov 2005: 124–46).

Among the Russian specialists, the concept of insider rent capitalism attracted favourable attention, but also aroused many critical remarks made in the course of defending my doctoral thesis at Moscow State University in 2010 (Dzarasov 2010) and in private communication. Their major critical remarks and extensions are summarised and analysed below.

A number of colleagues observed that not every source of insider rent, previously mentioned, could be traced to surplus value. For instance, appropriation of a portion of the wage fund can be treated as an encroachment on the necessary product of labour when real wages sink below the workforce value. Meanwhile, the Marxian approach assumes that exploitation is 'honest', that is, the workforce is sold for an equivalent of its value. I think that the decline of Russian workers' real wages corresponds to decline of the workforce's value. The latter is the result of the relative power of capital and labour. Owing to the dissolution of the transitory Soviet system, its socialist elements were dismantled. This decisively changed the balance of forces to the workers' detriment, which naturally resulted in the decline of the value of their workforce. Hence, capitalists still buy the latter for a 'fair' price, corresponding to the conditions of a triumphant capitalism.

It is more difficult to integrate the appropriation of the depreciation fund by big insiders into the concept of surplus value. Indeed, this source of insider rent constitutes a part of the past, already embodied, labour contained in the consumed elements of capital. Meanwhile, surplus value, as it is known, is produced by live labour. However correct this idea is, it is also not an insurmountable problem for the concept in question. C^7 as a part of commodity value represents the surplus value accumulated in the past. Appropriating the depreciation fund, big insiders just add the surplus value created by the past labour to s, created by live labour. Of course this source of insider rent can be used only in the short term, but this does not change anything with regard for the concept in question.

The two facets of insider rent fit the Marxian duality of surplus value split into absolute and relative forms perfectly. As is known, only the former assumes an introduction of technical progress, while the latter assumes it away, emanating from brutal exploitation of labour. Obviously, insider rent, especially in its short-term variant, is close to absolute surplus value, while its medium-term version is associated with the relative one.

Represented as a synthesis of the capitalist and non-capitalist modes of production, insider rent provides an important link between the core and the periphery of the capitalist world-system. Indeed, as was previously shown, the motives of rent withdrawal include savings abroad and conspicuous consumption of imported luxury goods. It was mentioned that Russia is widely seen by its business elite only as a source of rapid enrichment, while the West is regarded as the place to live. This corresponds to Andre Gunder Frank's notion of the 'lumpen-bourgeoisie' in Latin America, meaning comprador capitalists unable to carry out development of their countries (Frank 1972). Thus, insider rent reflects the place of contemporary Russia at the periphery of the capitalist world-system.

It is only natural that under the impact of non-commodity, extra-economic relations of violence and coercion that the transformed phenomena of the first and second-order experience undergo further transformation. Thus, extension of the system of categories through adding the notion of insider rent allows us to grasp the specific nature of current Russian capitalism. Intensive development of this idea will help to explain some important characteristics of this economy (see below).

If the treatment of insider rent as a concrete form of surplus value is dropped, than we should admit that the Russian economy is not capitalist at all. This theoretical possibility cannot be excluded off-handedly. However, it raises another question: what kind of society emerged in Russia and what system of ideas explains it? This book argues that understanding insider rent as transformed surplus value provides a vital clue to a non-contradictory analysis of the current state and dynamics of the Russian economy, and Russian society as a whole.

4.3   Income Distribution and Corporate Conflicts

We have already examined how the struggle between the different groups of big insiders for business mastery leads to fundamental problems of instability. As will be shown in this section, both actual and potential private-income appropriation by big insiders in the form of rent creates a number of corporate, or intra-firm, conflicts. While the conflicts between the different groups of big insiders are waged within the business elite itself, the conflicts described below reflect a struggle between dominant individuals and suppressed social groups. Intra-firm conflicts greatly affect a firm's ability to modernise and expand its productive capacities. Hence the analysis developed in this section is necessary to better understand the mechanism of capital accumulation in modern Russia.

4.3.1   Conflict between Big Insiders and Minority Shareholders

Initially, privatisation in Russia provided a large share of firms' equities to the firms' current employees, who often initially constituted the overwhelming majority of shareholders, as was discussed in Section 3.2. However, as we observed in Chapter 3, without informal control over the enterprises, these formal property rights were frequently useless to shareholders, including those who had bought shares on the open market. Their inability to exercise real control over the enterprises is reflected in Russian corporations paying negligible dividends, or none at all. According to Avdasheva and Dolgopyatova's research (2010: 32), only 40.6 per cent of Russian joint stock companies with foreign partnership and only 23.9 per cent of other companies regularly pay dividends in Russia (see Section 3.3.1 for more details). In 2001, specialists in the international financial services agency Standard & Poor's studied 42 Russian companies whose aggregate capitalisation amounted to 98 per cent of the country's securities market (Alekseyev 2001). Available data was examined on the companies' ownership structure, production and financial-economic performance, relations with investors, actions of headquarters, and so on. On average, Russian corporations provided investors with only 34 per cent of the data necessary to make sound decisions regarding share purchases. Compare this with the 40–85 per cent of information disclosed by the leading companies in the Asian-Pacific region and developing Asian countries. In terms of transparency, Russian companies generally occupy a position at the same level as those in Latin American countries. It is interesting to note that the most difficult information to obtain in Russia covers top managers' remuneration and the membership of companies' Board of Directors (ibid.), information which may be directly connected to the enrichment of big insiders.

Due to the lack of information, and unsatisfactory law enforcement referred to in Section 3.3.1, minority shareholders have very little influence on companies' behaviour. As a consequence, shares are generally undervalued in Russian companies. Dorofeyev (2001) argues that the market value of Russian corporations' securities depends on the readiness of the dominant individuals to share 'their' surplus finance – which they perceive as their private income – with minority shareholders. Since dividend rates in Russia are usually lower than inflation rates, and Russian firms have low investment rates in new assets, minority shareholders find themselves with low returns; as a result, financial investors value Russian corporate shares at a very low level compared to similar institutions in other countries. This is one reason for the under-capitalisation of the majority of Russian corporations. As Dorofeyev explains, investors simply decrease the share prices sought by companies at an estimated value of insider rent accruing to the dominant groups. He compared the leading Russian and foreign companies operating in oil and gas industries, which are the most profitable industries in Russia. He concluded that the differences in their capitalisation were greater than the differences in their financial flows and levels of output justified (ibid.: 34). A number of specialists (ibid.; Kapelushnikov 1999) believe that this cannot be explained by high political and criminal risks alone and the explanation should be complemented by reference to the domination of big insiders.

In terms of the current concern, the main effect of the systematic undervaluation of sizeable Russian companies' shares is the failure of the securities market to be an important source for external investment funds. According to Dorofeyev (2001: 8–9), big insiders estimate the value of their shares in their controlled enterprises to be higher than the market prices. They are not interested in participation in market operations. On the one hand, they are reluctant to increase their holdings if they already possess a controlling share. On the other hand, selling shares may jeopardise their dominant position (ibid.). As a result, for instance, the capitalisation of JSC Gasprom in 2002 was slightly more than $15 billion. But if one compares this company with its counterparts in the West, capitalisation should have amounted to between $200 billion and 1 trillion (Fadeyev 2002: 25). The same situation is characteristic for the oil-extraction and oil-processing industries: 'Comparative analysis of the leading Russian and foreign companies of the oil-gas sector of the economy testifies that the difference in their capitalisation ... is by a few times greater' than the difference between their financial flows and physical quantities of the extracted mineral resources (Dorofeyev 2001: 34). This study shows the undervaluation of such large Russian companies as RAO UES (Unified Energy System of Russia), JSC Kamaz and JSC Aeroflot (*Expert* 2002: 152). Papper (2002b: 84) argues that the majority of significant Russian companies do not trade their shares at all, and that those who do trade only a minor portion of the amount issued: 'In such conditions the securities market has failed to become a significant source of accumulation of capital in Russian business' (Dorofeyev 2001: 31).

4.3.2 Conflict Between Big Insiders and Managers

Novojenov (2003b) argues that the income of managers of Russian corporations who do not belong to the dominant group are less than they would be without rent extraction by big insiders. Timofeyev (2003) maintains that dominant owners of Russian corporations rarely apply personnel motivation schemes, such as relating salaries to corporate performance. Potentially, insider rent extraction is at the expense of spending that would have enhanced the position of the rank-and-file and mid-level managers. This situation explains the career prospects of Russian managers: 'management is hired not on the basis of expertise, but relying on personal loyalty' (ibid.). The so-called 'adventurous career', when certain individuals are rapidly promoted, is a common phenomenon among Russian managers. According to Timofeyev (2000) those banks and industrial companies with a proportion of 'adventurous careerist' managers exceeding one-third were more likely to go bankrupt during the 1998 crisis: 'Providing jobs through connections and bribes is the major method of hiring personnel by Russian companies ... One of the reasons for this is that insider control demands loyalty' (Timofeyev 2003). This is indirectly confirmed by the results of Abe and Iwasaki (2010). As was previously mentioned, they find that the presence of a dominant shareholder in a

Russian company significantly increases the probability of managerial staff turnover, while foreign owners tend to change only CEOs. Managers' loyalty should be treated as a part of the infrastructure of control imposed by the dominant group on enterprises.

Such conditions lead to widespread opportunistic behaviour by managers. According to Yakovlev et al. (2010: 137): 'The owners do not have adequate information about the condition of their businesses, and it is difficult to prevent managers from engaging in opportunistic behaviour.' The latter, according to Novojenov (2003a: 61–7), can assume a number of forms. The most primitive type of illegal income appropriation by manager-opportunists is the theft of technical resources and end-products, and using the firm's equipment for their own benefit. Usually theft is applied to highly tradable materials: fuel, precious and non-precious metals, spare parts, and so forth. Middle-level managers can inflict more serious damage on a firm. They establish their own firms, which make deals with their employer's company on conditions unfavourable to the latter. Traditionally, departments in charge of selling end-products and purchasing raw materials and equipment are the elements of the managerial hierarchy that are the most susceptible to opportunism. Manager-opportunists from these services provide allowances to purchasers of the firm's products, or buy inputs at prices higher than market level. In both cases, they divert finances from their employer's firm and obtain part of them as bribes paid to them by the firm's suppliers (Novojenov 2003b). Sometimes, such machinations may even lead to firms losing control over their sales networks. According to Novojenov (ibid.), investment by Russian firms suffers more from managers' opportunistic behaviour than does production. The reason is that every investment project is a unique combination of purchases, installation works, construction, and so on. Unlike current production, it contains less routine operations and procedures, and is hence much more difficult to monitor and control. Manager-opportunists try to take under their own control as large a portion of investment finances as possible (Novojenov 2003a: 64). Using their advantages over the dominant group in terms of information and expertise, they appropriate part of these financial flows as their own private income, in addition to their salaries.

The goal of all these numerous opportunistic practices is to obtain control over part of the firm's financial flows in order to extract one's own illegal private income. Essentially, these activities are very similar to the ways by which big insiders enrich themselves. Indeed, this income is obtained due to the largely informal control over part of a firm's finances. It is even possible to say that such managers create elements of their own infrastructure of control, for example, establishing informal relationships with the firm's business partners, colluding with colleagues, and so on. Therefore, it seems relevant to treat income accruing to the manager-opportunists as a kind of insider rent. Unlike the members of the dominant group, manager-opportunists are typically 'small insiders'. Given their system of remuneration, their interests are contrary to the interests of big insiders. The more rent that is extracted by small insiders, the less rent is likely to be available to the dominant group and the less funds can be directed to investment. According to Novojenov (2003a: 66), the 'victory' of big insiders over small insiders is 'a lesser evil for the corporation', because only the former are ready to reinvest part of their income in the business. Apart from that, the small insiders' behaviour damages companies more than the amount of the actual funds withdrawn by them.

4.3.3 Conflict Between Big Insiders and Workers

The entrenching of big insiders in Russian corporations is frequently accompanied by a drastic deterioration in workers' conditions. According to Menshikov (2004: 256), labourers' share amounted to 40.5 per cent of GDP in 1990, while in the post-reform period, it dropped to just 26 per cent. This is a characteristic even of the economy's privileged exporting sector. For instance, at the beginning of the 2000s, wages constituted only 10 per cent of unit costs in metallurgy (both ferrous and non-ferrous) in Russia, while in Japan it was 23, in Germany 25, and in the US 27.7 per cent (Shalayev 2002: 115).

Klimantova and Mukhetdinova (2001) maintain that, during the radical market reforms, the real incomes of the Russian population decreased by more than a half. Real wages declined by more than 60 per cent during the same period (Kokoritch 2004). While per-hour productivity in Russian metallurgy was about half of that in developed economies, its per-hour real wage amounted to only one-26th of that in Germany, and to one-22nd in Sweden (Shalayev 2002: 115). In addition, the post-reform period witnessed a drastic deterioration in the *regularity* of wage payments. Delays in wage payments became widespread practice in the 1990s. In 1998, about two-thirds of surveyed workers complained of significant wage-payment delays, which amounted to 4.8 months on average (Erl and Sabyrianova 2001: 107). By postponing wage payments, big insiders obtain interest-free loans. Meanwhile, in the course of such operations, real wages declined due to inflation. In 1992–98, these delays led to a savings on total wages of Russian enterprises amounting to 1–5 per cent in real terms (Kapelushnikov 1998). Even in 2001, during the economic recovery, 25 per cent of workers reported wage delays of one to three months or even more (Maximov 2002: 29).

In the 1990s, wages were often paid in kind, creating additional opportunities for big insiders to reduce the remuneration of workers in real terms. For instance, miners in Vorkuta were paid in foodstuffs, but at prices 20–40 per cent higher than the market level (Ilyin 1998: ch. 6). Workers' wages may also be undermined by 'grey' wage-payment schemes (in cash and off the books), which help to avoid taxation. On average, 21–8 per cent of the wage fund in Russia is paid on such a basis (Menshikov 2004: 237). Since there is no legal obligation to pay this part of workers' remuneration, such practice helps big insiders control employees. One of the most startling paradoxes in Russian market reforms is that they not only decreased the level of real wages, but also greatly increased the egalitarian nature of worker remuneration compared to Soviet times (Timofeyev 2003). This was due to the elimination of managerial departments which were in charge of developing output-related pay schemes and the methodology for measuring and assessing individual workers' contributions to production. At the beginning of the 1990s, these were often considered by big insiders, desperately struggling for control over the former state enterprises, as excessive and too costly and only a minority of Russian companies now do this (ibid.). Investment in developing productivity-related pay systems is thought only to be self-funding over a time period beyond the big insiders' short-term time horizon. This curtailment of wages has reciprocal connections with Russian corporations' investment strategies. In addition to the workers' direct exploitation previously described, big insiders introduce indirect exploitation mechanisms through lowering investment, which leads to productivity decline and contributes to reductions in wages (see Section 6.3). These downward pressures on wages have as their origin rent extraction by big insiders.

To this situation, we might counter that during the 2000s an influx of petrodollars brought increased incomes to all of Russia's population. Indeed, in the course of recovery in the 2000s, wages grew significantly and, according to official estimates, their GDP share reached 36.1 per cent in 2010 (Rosstat 2011: 402). Still, this is lower than in pre-reform times and very low according to global standards.[8] Official figures show that the share of overall money income received by 80 per cent (!) of the Russian population steadily declined between 2002 and 2009. Only for the richest one-fifth did it increase (Rosstat 2008b: 132; 2010: 131). Consequently, the average figures for living standards mask growing social inequality. Research confirms this conclusion. In the fourth quarter of 2010, the Russian government set the monthly subsistence minimum income at a Russia-wide figure of 5,902 roubles per head of population. For the employable population, the figure was 6,367 roubles (US$210–15); for pensioners 4,683 roubles; and for children 5,709 roubles:

> Two wages are barely enough to cover the essential four subsistence minimums. In thirty-six regions, the sum per family does not exceed 10,000 roubles [US$330–350]. This is despite the fact that the subsistence minimum in our country is a paltry amount that only by a great stretch of the imagination corresponds to the biological requirements for survival. (RIA-Analitika, 2011)

The results of this situation include a reduction in the domestic market's volume, since in modern society the basis for this market is provided by demand exercised by hired workers. This means that if Russian capitalism were to shift from maximising insider rent to maximising entrepreneurial income, the demand for good-quality labour power would induce capitalists to raise wages, and the volume of the internal market would increase.

The many-faceted deterioration in working conditions engendered numerous conflicts between the workers and big insiders. Currently, these conflicts rarely assume the form of collective worker unrest. Sociological research (Gordon 1995: 51–2) suggests reasons for this. In the mid-1990s, 30–40 per cent of respondents to a survey were individualist workers, disappointed in trade unions and eager to 'sell their own labour under the most favourable conditions'. Approximately the same percentage of workers followed a paternalistic strategy, craving a 'good master' who would be fair and pay decent wages. Only 20–30 per cent of workers expressed loyalty to a trade union ideology and believed in taking common action to defend their rights (ibid.). This means that the majority of workers do not rely on unions in their relations with their employers.

These results are confirmed by recent research. Vinogradova and Kozina (2011: 32–3) had shown in a survey that the idea of acting for the benefit of workers' common interests at Russian enterprises were shared by only 18 per cent of workers and 24 per cent of managers. Forty per cent of workers and 49 per cent of managers recognise a partial overlap of workers' and administration's interests, while 41 per cent of workers and 27 per cent of managers believed that 'the superiors pursue their own interests, while personnel is only a mean to achieve their goals' (ibid.). They conclude that the general picture is one of a fragile equilibrium between the confrontational and 'pluralist' attitudes of Russian enterprises' hired personnel.

In response to impingements on their interests, Russian workers have developed their own types of opportunistic behaviour. One such practice is 'alternative production' (Kleman 2003: 68–9). This means that some production is organised using the firm's equipment but the workers are privately paid for their work. Such an example was studied at the Samara engineering plant (ibid.). Timofeyev (2003) interviewed a metalworker at a large power station, who explained that he worked for the company only half a day and during the other half he produced privately some products for the local market. But with every delay in wage payments, theft by workers increases (ibid.). An extreme form of workers' opportunistic behaviour is their participation in organised criminal communities (OCC). In some cases, such structures, created by workers, were able to crowd out small insiders and even challenge large insiders, for example, in the timber and coal industries in Vorkuta (see Ilyin 1998: ch. 3).

Although inflicting reductions on the dominant group's incomes, opportunism is unable to change workers' general conditions for the better. Potentially the greatest danger for big insiders is collective action by employees. The most famous example of this was events at the JSC Vyborgski Cellulosno-Bumajni Kombinat (VCBK). At the start of market reforms in the early 1990s, this modern-equipped enterprise had the highest output in Europe and third in the world in terms of cellulose-paper products (Maximov 2001: 46). During privatisation, offshore companies representing different dominant groups struggled fiercely with each other for control over the company (Rudyk et al. 2000: 11). They applied the typical schemes of insider rent extraction through intermediaries: selling products at prices lower than market level, purchasing raw materials at prices higher than market level, blocking investments, and so on. Finally, with significant violations of the law, the enterprise was taken over by an offshore company Alsem, representing St Petersburg-based criminal interests (ibid.: 12–14). An outbreak of worker riots occurred in January 1998, after the dominant owners' new plan was revealed, namely: to make half the workforce redundant, stop cellulose-paper production, sell the equipment, and start a new business on the premises. A new trade union organisation, embracing all employees, refused to recognise the new owner, referring to the illegal character of their acquiring property rights. Since wages had not been paid at all since 1996, the trade union declared that the employees were the enterprise's prime creditors and they became its only legitimate owners. Under workers' control, order was restored: new, efficient managers were recruited, the large paper-producing machine resumed operation for the first time since 1996, connections with suppliers and buyers were established, and so on. Despite the Office of the Public Prosecutor refusing to recognise the offshore company's property rights (thus indirectly supporting workers), the local authorities supported Alsem (ibid.: 16–17). Law enforcement agencies and Alsem's security department made a few attempts to storm the enterprise; using firearms, they wounded some defenders, but eventually were kicked out by the workers. The violence caused public outrage and the authorities changed their tactics. As a result of a railway blockade, deliveries were stopped; penalties started to mount up and the trade union was compelled to surrender. But this time Alsem got the message: the company denounced its former plans, signed a new collective agreement with favourable conditions for workers, and so on (ibid.: 18). Open conflict between workers and big insiders, accompanied by violent struggle also occurred elsewhere, for example, at Leningradski Metallicheski Zavod, Kombinat Tsvetnoy Pechaty in St Peterburg, Yasnogorski Machinostritelni Zavod and other large industrial enterprises (ibid.).

Pirani notes that the relative recovery of the 2000s had an ambiguous impact on the Russian workers' movement; on the one hand, the number of strikes declined, while on the other, the number of independent trade unions increased (Pirani 2010: 163). He observes that the new stance of the labour movement appeared on the basis of independent trade unions established at foreign factories, most notably at the Ford factories, with workers from GM-Avtovaz and the Nokian tyre factory following suit. Remarkably, the strikes at the Ford factories in Vsevolzhsk and at Avtovaz in Togliatti in 2007–08 revealed a new model of workers' resistance, changing from the hunger strikes of the 1990s, to the struggle for the redistribution of profits (ibid.: 168–72). These facts assume that the new generation of Russian workers are demonstrating more militancy in the struggle for their rights. Still they face strong resistance from the dominant owners.

Big insiders typically do all they can to suppress organised labour and gain full control over their employees. Official trade unions are often used by dominant owners to prevent workers' collective actions or to attack independent labour organisations (Kozina 2001: 53–5). In the course of a prolonged conflict with its workers, managers of Gorno-Metallurgicheski Kompaniya Norilski Nikel prepared an unofficial document instructing managers how to deal with organised labour. The memo recommended instigating conflicts between the independent unions' leaders, so discrediting them, as well as providing additional remuneration to workers who did not support the new structures, and so forth (Varfolomeyev 2003). Organisations created by the big insiders to suppress labour should be treated as an important part of the infrastructure of control.

The nature of the current argument assumes that the larger the portion of finance withdrawn by big insiders as their private income, the more intensive is the conflict between the former and their workers. To suppress employees, the dominant group needs to spend more on the corresponding elements of the infrastructure of control.

This means deduction from financial flows, which otherwise could be used for investment. Thus, conflict between big insiders and workers reduces the available supply of internally generated investment funds.

4.4 Corporate Conflicts and Accumulation

Rent withdrawal and corporate conflicts affect greatly both the supply of and the demand for investment funds of Russian firms. Apart from this situation, both phenomena have defined an impact on the pricing of Russian big business. This situation leads to an increasingly short-term time horizon of large insiders.

4.4.1 Insider Rent Effects

Fund withdrawal by big insiders produced external and internal effects affecting both the supply of and the demand for investment funds of Russian companies. Unfavorable changes in the macroeconomic environment which are caused not by any individual dominant group, but by big insiders taken as a social class, we call *external* insider rent effect. For a firm, the consequences of rent extraction undertaken by particular big insiders taken as an individual dominant group we call *internal* insider rent effect. Let us consider their influence on the supply of funds for Russian corporations.

Conflicts between big insiders on the one side and minority shareholders, managers and workers on the other, have two major consequences for the accumulation of investment funds. First, finances available for investment are decreased. Minority shareholders do not favour the shares of Russian corporations. Manager-opportunists worsen the firm's performance and divert part of its funds. Conflict with workers incurs reduced productivity, theft and unrest. Costs increase, thus reducing the margin. Secondly, to supress small insiders and worker unrest, the dominant group centralises the decision-making process, introduces complex control procedures, expands the firm's security department, and so forth. All these are costly but necessary elements of establishing and maintaining an infrastructure of control. Thus, to the extent that big insiders seek to address the above problems by investing in the infrastructure of control, big insiders are using funds that otherwise would be available for investment or rent extraction. It should be emphasised that an alternative way to alleviate intra-firm conflicts would be by increasing wages and salaries, and paying sound dividends. Thus, there is a certain trade-off between expenditures necessary to suppress intra-firm conflicts and expenditures eliminating the sources of conflicts. However, the latter would mean that the dominant group's members would stop seeking rent extraction and, hence, stop being big insiders.

In aggregate, insider rent extraction from Russian corporations as a whole affects the distribution of the national income, resulting in greater inequality (Rimashevskaya 2006). As a consequence, the Russian domestic market shrinks, depressing profits. This diminishes incentives to invest in productive capacities. Thus, the *external* insider rent effect decreases both the supply of, and the demand for, investments in the Russian corporate sector.

The *internal* insider rent effect includes a number of effects on the internal generation of investment funds by Russian companies. First, a reduction in profits, inflicted on a firm by intra-firm conflicts, should be treated as the cost of these conflicts (and hence of insider rent withdrawal), especially as there must be some expenditure on the infrastructure of internal control, which enables the big insiders to suppress opportunistic behaviour and worker unrest. At the same time, strengthening the internal elements of the infrastructure is likely to increase centralisation. According to Novojenov (2003a, 2003b) over-centralisation, in turn, may damage managerial efficiency and inflict additional reductions on the firm's profits. Secondly, financial institutions charge an additional risk premium based on their estimated potential of rent withdrawal. The effect of insider rent diminishes the supply of funds from Russian corporations.

The effect of insider rent on the demand for Russian corporations' investment funds is not less prominent. Since, as previously mentioned, the *external* insider rent effect leads to a decline in expected profits, the demand for investment funds in such conditions becomes relatively low (see Chapter 6). Reduced market opportunities and decreased internal rate of return (IRR) of investments lead to rejection of otherwise profitable projects and induce firms to choose the shorter-term and usually less efficient, although often less expensive, projects. These phenomena affect corporate investments portfolios as a whole. Apart from this situation, short-term orientation and the reluctance to sacrifice their potential current income induce the dominant groups to decline investments with long pay-back periods and significant costs (in present-value terms). For these reasons, in practice, only relatively inexpensive projects are funded, which only maintain or insignificantly expand production (see Chapter 6). It is possible to single out two principal mechanisms by which a dominant group reduces a corporation's investment portfolio. First, by comparing the different methods of implementing particular projects, big insiders prefer the short-term, small-scale variants to large and long-term ones. Secondly, big insiders set the length of the pay-back period and the maximum size of the projects allowed. Investments which do not correspond to these restrictions are not realised.[9] Thus, the *internal* insider rent effect is connected to the decline of the internal rate of return, and the scale and quantity of investment projects undertaken by firms.

The current type of income distribution at Russian corporations and the ensuing corporate conflicts are reflected in the price structure of these institutions.

4.4.2 Russian Corporations' Price Structure

Figure 4.3 shows the price structure of the final product of a firm controlled by big insiders, where *a*) assumes the intra-firm conflicts and opportunism, while *b*) and *c*) reflect the situation with a significant role for the small insiders. *b*) is the case of the small insiders selling their firm's final product at a price lower than the market level. *c*) is the case of the small insiders purchasing spare parts and raw materials at a price higher than the market level.

Figure 4.3 is drawn to show that insider rent is generated through the mark-up on unit costs. In reality, it is possible for the large insiders to enrich themselves by increasing the company's debts to suppliers, contractors, hired labour, tax agencies, through direct theft of the long-term credits and the use of depreciation funds. In these cases, part of the expenditure regarded as production costs is appropriated by big insiders as their rent as well. Since this is the particular case of a very short-sighted big insider and for the sake of simplicity, we do not consider it here. In Figure 4.3, *a*) shows that in a firm without intra-firm conflicts and opportunistic behaviour, the share of the small insiders in the mark-up is zero. At the same time, firms where such tensions are

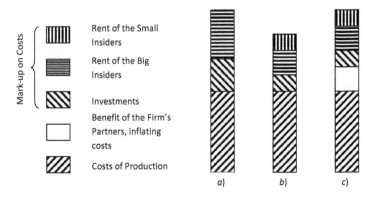

Figure 4.3 Price structure and rent distribution among the large and small insiders

persistent exhibit two kinds of rent distribution between the big and the small insiders. In case *b*), the small insiders provide discounts to the buyers of the firm's products, obtaining a portion of this as bribes. In case *c*), they inflate costs, providing the diagram's white portion of the unit price to the firm's partners, and again obtaining a portion of the fee as bribes. In both situations, this small insiders' income is their rent. In both cases, the company's financial flows are extracted, reducing the big insiders' share, as well as investments. According to Novojenov (2003a: 66) as was mentioned above, the 'victory' of big insiders over small ones is 'a lesser evil for the corporation', because only the former are ready to reinvest part of their income in the business. Apart from this situation, as can be seen in Figure 4.3, the small insiders' behaviour damages companies more than the amount of the actual funds withdrawn by them.

Thus, the price structure of Russian corporations reflects the damage of insider rent extraction inflicted upon accumulation of funds.

4.4.3   The Time Horizon of Big Insiders

The discussion of the consequences of income distribution for investment in Russian corporations would be incomplete without relating these problems to the time horizon of big insiders. This issue was already addressed in Section 3.4, where Russian big business's short-termism was explained by the fundamental instability of informal control over the enterprises. The time horizon adopted by

Russian big insiders strengthens their preference for short-term income appropriation in the form of insider rent. This section will emphasise that the latter in turn strengthens their short-term time orientation. Thus, the whole process becomes self-perpetuating.

First, an important conclusion from the discussion about rent-seeking behaviour in conditions of the instability of informal control is that the threat of a hostile takeover on the part of the short-term-oriented big insiders compels more medium-term-oriented big insiders to become more short-term as well. Indeed, it is assumed in this book that the more profitable projects are more capital-intensive and more time-consuming. Hence, longer-term projects tend to be more profitable and create better opportunities for future insider rent extraction. This is exactly the factor which induces the rival dominant group to challenge the established group's position. As previously noted in Section 3.3.4, big insiders can avert this threat by developing the external elements of the infrastructure of control. However, these are costly and adversely affect a firm's profit margin. The probability of a hostile takeover and the additional costs associated with defending the firm from such an event increase the rate at which future income is discounted by Russian big insiders. Without any probability of them losing control over the firm, the big insiders discount future income just as ordinary investors. The probability of a hostile takeover increases disproportionately with an extension of the pay-back period (PBP). This means that there is a value of the PBP with a prohibitive, associated level of discount rate which sets a limit on the time horizon of big insiders. Since short-termism is defined as the 'excess discounting of long-term cash flows relative to short-term cash flows' (Miles 1995: 1224), this contributes to the short-sightedness of Russian corporations with regard to investment.

Secondly, there is another aspect of how hostile takeovers are related to short-termism. According to some studies (Pugh 1998), hostile takeovers in western economies, notably in the UK and the US, lead to short-termism of the companies' time horizons, rather than prevent managers' opportunistic behaviour. This result arises due to undermining business relationships based on trust; Pugh means such relational contracts which are not fixed in legal contracts: 'Rather, they are implicit rules of behaviour enforced by the value to all parties of the continuing relationship' (ibid.: 12). Such informal contracts mean that a firm provides some important advantages to other stakeholders, for example, do not reduce the workforce during temporary fluctuations of demand; do not shift to lower-cost suppliers from its established partners; maintains its reputation among retailers and customers providing only high-quality products, and so forth. In exchange, the other parties in the relationship stay loyal to a firm and provide it with high-quality services, supplies do not shift to new partners suggesting better conditions, and so on. These tacit obligations are important, because they underlie long-term recurring business relationships. The prevalence of these implicit contracts creates the possibility of a trade-off between long-term business performance and short-term opportunistic profit increase (ibid.).

Hostile takeovers are often undertaken using borrowed money and are 'thus likely to be under pressure to generate immediate cash flow to service their debt' (ibid.). Often there is only one way to do this. Kay (1993: 60) argues that due to the nature of relational contracts, which are not fixed by any legal commitments, it is possible to draw short-term financial gains by breaking these relational contracts. For instance, a firm can make part of its workforce redundant in times of cyclic decline of demand; move to a new lower-cost supplier; mislead a retailer into stocking goods which are difficult to sell; reduce a product's quality without decreasing its price, and so on (ibid.). This will permit increasing short-term profits, but only at the expense of long-term performance (Pugh 1998: 13). Kay argues (1993: 60) that if such practices frequently occur, then 'the business partners become less willing to form relational contracts. This suggests the formation of "negative externality" of hostile takeovers' (ibid.).

All this is very relevant to modern Russia. As previously mentioned, hostile takeovers in Russia lead to Russian corporations maximising insider rent as the short-term income of the dominant group. An important consequence of insider rent extraction is that it has an effect on Russian enterprises very similar to the effect of short-term profit taking at the expense of long-run performance which often happens after hostile takeovers in the West. Intra-firm conflicts, which are a result of rent extraction by big insiders, make implicit contracts impossible between the dominant group and the other stakeholders. Paying negligible dividends, big insiders increase their current income, but deprive their organisations of an important source of capital by making it more difficult to access the external capital market. How big insiders eliminated managerial departments which were in charge of developing output-related pay schemes has been shown. This is nothing other than a short-term profit increase at the expense of the implicit obligation to remunerate better-quality work. This is further aggravated by the curtailment of firm-based workforce training. As a result, in the longer term, Russian industry suffers from a huge shortage of well-qualified workers. According to a survey by Gimpelson (2004: 82), in Russian industry, 'one observes the nearly total deficit of human capital, i.e. scarcity of people, demonstrating the necessary knowledge, qualification and skills.' Another example of the violation of implicit contracts by Russian big insiders is the position of managers, who are promoted not on the basis of their merits, but on the basis of association with the dominant group. Over time, these weaknesses in qualification and skills will reinforce the constraints faced by companies in the form of the fixed capital stock's limitations. Thus, insider rent extraction, by preventing implicit contracts from being concluded and observed, undermine trusting relationships between the stakeholders and further strengthen the big insiders' short-term orientation.

The major conclusion from the previously mentioned situation is that the *short-termism of Russian corporations, predicated on insider control, leads both to a decline in size and to lowering the quality of their investment in productive capacities.*

4.5 Conclusion

This chapter introduced the main concept of this book – insider rent. This term connotes the dominant groups' income derived from control over the firms' financial flows. The ability to appropriate these funds is conditioned by the infrastructure of insider control over the company's assets. Essentially, insider rent is a form of surplus value, since it is appropriated at the expense of cutting wage funds, investments, depreciation funds and other sources ultimately reducible to unpaid-for labour product. Withdrawal of funds from enterprises to enrich big insiders has numerous repercussions for the economy and society at large.

We may identify and distinguish between the internal and external effects of the dominant groups' activities. The domestic market shrinks as a result of the greater income inequality produced by insider rent extraction. The former is connected with the decline of investment by particular companies as a result of the withdrawal of funds by their dominant groups. Insider rent extraction undermines the income of minority shareholders, that is, managers who do not belong to either the dominant group or the workers. This leads to numerous corporate conflicts, increased opportunistic behaviour by employees and worker unrest. As a result, the dominant group is compelled to increase its investment in the infrastructure of control. This situation undermines any investment in enhancing a firm's capacity and product development. Insider control therefore curtails the supply of funds to Russian corporations. Due to its external and internal effects, the interest rates of the internal generation and borrowing of funds are high in comparison with a firm with a longer-term time horizon. The effect of internal insider rent is connected to the increasing costs of internal accumulation of funds. Insider control undermines the demand for investment by Russian corporations as well. Due to its external effect, the internal rate of return and the investment rate are low. The effect of internal insider rent is also connected with these variables' decline, as well as with corporations' rejection of large projects with long pay-back periods. As a result, the firm's long-term business prospects deteriorate sharply. Rent extraction and the short-termism of Russian big insiders are strengthened further by the probability of hostile takeover, which rises with longer-term investment. This reinforces big insiders' preference in favour of current income appropriation. At the same time, insider rent extraction leading to corporate conflicts precludes adhering to implicit contracts. Without observing the latter, it is impossible to extend the time horizon of a firm into the long term.

5

Insider Rent and Conditions of Growth in the Russian Economy

5.1   Introduction

Previously we have examined how dominant groups appropriated businesses through control over the firms' financial flows. Different types of intra-firm conflicts over the distribution of the firms' income have been discussed. It was maintained that rent withdrawal and the ensuing conflicts undermine capital accumulation by Russian corporations. Thus, we have looked at the institutional foundations of economic growth in Russia. Now the effect of the type of income distribution, peculiar to the Russian corporate sector, on the country's economic development should be analysed. This will be another step up the ladder from the abstract to the concrete. Treating the notion of insider rent as a concrete form of surplus value allowed us to model the pricing of Russian corporations (see Section 4.4.2). As a result, it is possible to explain the price structure of the national economy as a whole. This demands modification of the idea of insider rent to make it fit conditions in different sectors of the Russian economy. Such a modification will shed light on the established price proportions.

Section 5.2 briefly reviews the essence of the value and technological conditions of growth. Both are examined from the standpoint of Marxian transformation of labour values in prices of production. Section 5.3 takes up the issue of violation of the value and technological conditions of growth in the modern Russian economy carried out under the influence of the whole number of internal and external circumstances. A further extension of the insider rent concept is provided in Section 5.4. Section 5.5 is focused on some conclusions from the above.

5.2   The Value and Technological Conditions of Growth

In examining the abovementioned problems, this book departs from the Marxian logic of the transformation of labour values in prices of production. As is known, the latter depends on two key factors: the so-called 'organic composition of capital' (the capital-labour ratio) and the formation of an average rate of profit as a result of the inter-industrial flow of capital. Consequently, the difference appears between the amount of value, created in a given industry, and the sum of its prices of production (that is, costs plus profit corresponding to the average rate). The difference arises because the surplus value is created according to labour, but appropriated according to the power of capital. This divergence between the values of goods and their prices of production has engendered a huge body of literature on the so-called 'contradiction between the first and the third volumes of *Das Kapital*'. However, this is not the place for examining this discussion. For the present work, the difference between the two value sets is crucial in explaining the price structure of the modern Russian economy.

Analysis is carried out through comparison of the technological structure of the economy and the distribution of the sectorial mark-ups on unit costs. This approach helps to identify the distribution of financial flows among Russian industries, creating different external conditions for the accumulation of capital in different industries. To follow this research path, one should incorporate in their analysis a few theoretical models which view growth through the lenses of pricing and technological structures.

When examining the macroeconomic aspects of corporate investments, Alfred Eichner used Piero Sraffa's seminal work *Production of Commodities by Means of Commodities*, and complemented it with von Neimann's similar approach of (Eichner 1991: 338). This synthesis is quite plausible, since both works belong to the 'classical' understanding of value and distribution (Kurz and Neri 2001: 161). In particular, according to Vernengo (2001: 343), the Sraffian approach (just as that of J. Keynes) radically departs from marginalism

176

and manifests a return to the surplus-value approach of the classical political economy.

Dropping the mathematical exposition of these models, I will just move to the Eichnerian formulation of the 'value condition of growth in the national economy, which means a group of prices covering both the current costs of production and the costs of expansion of productive capacities at the level of full employment' (ibid.). The two sides of the value condition correspond to two functions of the Sraffian relative prices – conditioning reproduction and distribution of the net product – and to the two factors of Marxian transformation process – the organic composition of capital and the inter-industrial flows of value.

It is important to emphasise that the value condition of growth is determined for any given economy, since it is met not by a random group of prices, but only by the one providing full employment. It was a precept of Soviet planning that the full employment of resources is reached only under the condition of their proportional allocation among industries.[1] Consequently, the value condition of growth can be interpreted as a group of prices which secure economic balance. This understanding corresponds to the Sraffian theory of value and the legacy of the classical school of political economy.

The group of industrial prices reflecting the value condition of growth redistributes financial flows among the economic sectors at the level of full employment and allows individual corporations to accumulate capital necessary to obtain the highest expansion rates. Hence, the value condition makes it possible to unite micro- and macroeconomic processes.

As was mentioned above, the Sraffian model and, hence, the Eichnerian value condition of growth, implies that prices correspond not only to technical conditions, but to social relations of production as well. Full employment growth assumes that all the produced output is realised. This demands a market of corresponding scale, which primarily depends on demand of the wage labour. Hence, the balanced growth demands that increase in aggregate investments is met by the corresponding increment of the wage fund. From this follows that significant inequality in national income distribution is incompatible with balanced growth and, hence, violates the value condition.

The capitalist class, seeking wealth increase, has an ambiguous attitude to full employment. This was discussed as early as 1943 by Kalecki in his well-known work 'Political Business Cycle' (Kalecki 1971). Capitalists are allegedly interested in maximising output as a condition for augmenting profits. This can really be observed in periods of under-employment. However, as full employment is approached, the control of capital over labour weakens. This happens because labour obtains stronger leverage in the struggle for a wage increase. This decreases the monopoly power of capitalists and cuts into their profit margins. Thus, full employment increases the absolute *level* of expected profits, but diminishes their *share* in the national income. Kalecki concludes that eventually such a policy will face strong opposition on the part of big business, because workers will seek greater rights and this will prompt the 'captains of industry' to teach the workers a lesson (Kalecki 1971: 144). He notes that in such conditions a powerful big business bloc will probably emerge and many economists eager to substantiate a policy against full employment will be at their service. This is exactly what happened with the revenge of the neoconservatives, at the turn of the 1980s. From that time onward, neoclassical mainstream economics prioritised an anti-inflationary policy over the policy of full employment (Michie 1995: xxii).

Macroeconomic balance can be upset not only by the policy of the ruling class as a whole, but by price strategies of particular big corporations or by their oligopolistic unions. Mark-ups on unit costs reflect corporations' power (the Kaleckian 'degree of monopoly'). This is why any given set of oligopolistic prices reflects the relative power of corporations rather than objective proportions of an economic system. Left to its own internal impulses, the corporate economy will not necessarily tend to equilibrium, as is assumed by neoclassical mainstream. Indeed, if mark-ups are distributed across the economy in a chaotic manner, then the volumes of accumulated capital in industries can only randomly match the value condition of growth. Under violation of the value condition, long-term deviations from the full employment growth path inevitably occur due to excessive and insufficient investments in different sectors. Such a factor of the 'degree of monopoly' as the collective activities of capitalists in favour of their vested interests can be particularly perilous for full employment. Entrepreneurial unions often practice rent-seeking behaviour in an attempt to increase their share of national income. These activities impair technical progress and efficient reallocation of resources, resulting in decreasing growth rates (Mair and Laramie 2002: 578). This means that full employment is sacrificed to the interests of capitalists.

The value condition of growth implies its technological condition. Indeed, its component – covering costs of the current production – depends on technologies. As was already mentioned above, the same is reflected by Sraffa (providing conditions for renewal of production) and Marx (the organic composition of capital). In terms of Leontief's 'input-output model', this is represented by the matrix of 'technical coefficients'. They reflect shares in which different industries contribute their output as input in a unit of a given industry's production. All these ideas are only different dimensions of proportions of various industries to each other. These proportions are based on technologies. Thus, to grasp the effect of any particular price structure on accumulation in the national economy, one needs to analyse it in the context of the distribution of technologies among industries.

For the purposes of further analysis, it is convenient to use the framework of the 'qualitative non-homogeneity of resources' approach, which was developed by the Soviet economist Yuri Yaremenko (1935–96).[2] He departed from the obvious observation that any economy applies resources of different quality: 'In its immediate form, the qualitative cohort of resources is determined by the technological level of the means of production and by the qualification of the workforce used for reproduction of those resources' (Yaremenko 1997: 29). In other words, the factors of production differ according to the degree of technical progress embodied in them. From this standpoint, the two opposite poles of the concept in question are: high-quality resources and their mass-produced counterparts. These are relative, historically changing categories, because what corresponds to the latest technological achievements today may well become obsolete tomorrow. The actual factors of production usually fall somewhere in between the two above-mentioned poles, but to simplify the discussion, Yaremenko used the notions of high-quality resources and mass-produced resources.

One and the same level of output can be secured by a lesser quantity of the former and greater quantity of the latter. The real process of economic growth witnesses the continuous interplay of different-quality resources. Yaremenko singled out two types of such interactions: 'compensation' for the shortages of high-quality resources by their mass-produced counterparts, and 'substitution' of the former for the latter. It is the distribution of resources of different quality over national economy that defines that economy's technological structure. Naturally, the economy dominated by the substitution effect is technologically more advanced, achieves higher productivity and greater competitiveness at the world market.

Departing from the theory of the 'qualitative non-homogeneity of resources', one can define *the technological condition of growth, meaning such a combination of compensation and substitution effects, which under the current price system secures full employment and maximum growth rates.* The technological condition of growth allows considering the value condition as a group of prices, which not only covers the current production costs and costs of expansion, but reinforces technological equilibrium as well.

Changes in the proportions of high-quality and mass-produced resources in any significant sector of the economy will engender a chain of compensation and substitution corrections across the whole national economy. Suppose that, in a given industry in a balanced economy, high-quality resources were substituted for their mass-produced counterparts. This means that under the previous distribution of compensation and substitution effects among industries, a surplus of mass-produced resources appeared and the economy deviated from full employment. To return to the balanced-development path, it is necessary to redistribute resources. This demands price correction. Whether growth depends primarily on high-quality or mass-produced resources, they both should be available at prices allowing enterprises/consumers to obtain their necessary quantities. This being the case, the price of mass-produced resources should be lower than of high-quality resources. Now, under any given technological economic structure, there is only one group of prices corresponding to full employment. The connection between the value condition and the technological condition of growth is that *prices, covering current production costs and costs of expansion, should correspond to the proportion of industries (reflecting the relation of compensation and substitution effects) securing full employment.*

The spontaneous interplay of supply and demand only occasionally coincides with technological advances and the corresponding changes in technological proportions. This periodically leads to divergences between prices and technological structure. The subsequent violation of the value and technological conditions of growth diverts the economy from its full employment path and engenders the failure of investors' expectations regarding part of their return. An even more complicated situation arises in the corporate economy, since the pricing of big business reflect its power over markets (that is, the degree of monopoly). This expresses the imperative of distribution according to the power of capital peculiar to capitalism. As was already mentioned, the unique price system formed in such an economy can only randomly coincide with the value condition of growth. Hence, it is difficult to meet simultaneously the value and the technological conditions of growth. Even if originally, the economy met these conditions, technical progress and corporate price strategies most likely will cause it to deviate from the trajectory of full employment.

5.3 Price Disparity in the Russian Economy

On the eve of market reforms in Russia, it was widely believed that price liberalisation would provide business with a universal mechanism for efficient resources allocation. It was expected that price signals produced by a free market would convey invaluable information about real market demands, enabling businesspeople to correctly estimate their expected future profits, and thus secure a flow of private investments into the industries whose products were most valued by consumers. Progressive structural changes would inevitably follow, allowing for adjusting production to people's needs. It was assumed as obvious that technical progress would be automatically introduced by market forces to meet consumers' quality demands, that the economy's modernisation would increase productivity and international competitiveness, and Russian people, at last, would be able to attain the high consumer standards enjoyed in the West.

This optimistic approach, based on the principles of the Washington Consensus, failed to take into account many real-life circumstances in Russia (see Section 2.5). Among other problems with this agenda, some well-qualified Soviet economists tried to draw public attention to incompatibility of the Russian economy's technological structure and the free pricing system. For instance, academician Yuri Yaremenko substantiated his critique of the impending price reform with the results of a unique mathematic model analysing the Russian economy's technological structure. Over many years, he studied the allocation of different-quality technological resources across the Soviet economy. In a number of his works (1997 being the most prominent),[3] Yaremenko had shown that in the Soviet economy the bulk of high-quality resources were concentrated in military production. As a result, the civil sector was left to develop on the basis of mainly mass-produced, low-quality resources. In such conditions, sustained growth could be achieved only through increased application of mass-produced resources: low-quality labour, energy resources, metals, and so forth. In this type of economy, equilibrium is reinforced by some industries fulfilling 'maintenance functions' (Yaremenko 1997), that is, they supply mass-produced resources at sufficiently low prices and in growing quantities. This role was played in the Soviet economy by the energy-producing and metallurgy sectors, as well as many sub-sectors of civil engineering, construction, transport and others. Prices for their products were significantly lower than world market levels, due to low wages (according to western standards), the availability of large reserves of easily extractable raw materials, and significant economies-of-scale effects secured by Soviet planning. Sources of growth based on labour-intensive technologies were largely exhausted by the beginning of the 1980s, making the need for reforms urgent (ibid.).

Thus, the Soviet economy with its heavy bias in favour of military production had been 'technologically non-homogeneous', in Yaremenko's terms. This fact in itself severely limited the possibilities of operation for the market mechanism. If prices of the 'maintenance'-sector products started growing to world market levels, argued Yaremenko, then the civil industries could not adjust. In fact, they would just collapse. (Free marketeers expected that under the pressures of free pricing and competition, Russian manufacturing would carry out large-scale modernisation with the introduction of energy and labour-saving technologies.) In order to benefit from market competition, argued Yaremenko, an economy should be more or less technologically homogeneous (ibid.). In the Soviet-type economy with its concentration of high-quality resources confined to military production, the civil sector had no domestic suppliers for modern investment goods, while purchasing any meaningful quantities of these goods at world market prices was impossible due to lack of funds. To this, one may add environmental (that is, a cold climate) and geographical (long distances) factors, which historically conditioned the wide application of mass-produced resources in the Russian economy.

Thus, radical market transformation in such a technologically non-homogeneous economy, implying sudden price liberalisation, inevitably produces price shock. This is manifested in an impetuous and uncontrolled change of the established value proportions which impairs conditions of growth. As a result of the 'maintenance' sector abandoning its functions, a large proportion of resources become idle, production slumps, and the national economy diverges from the full employment path. This means that technological changes, renovation of civil engineering being the principal step, should pre-date price liberalisation. If this precondition is ignored, then price liberalisation produces only price shock followed by production slump, collapse of investments and subsequently the economy's technological degeneration. This is the essence of price shock in technologically non-homogeneous economies. The post-reform Russian experience fully vindicated Yaremenko's position.

Despite the naïve expectations of the free-market proponents, price proportions in the Russian economy, while changing significantly as a result of liberalisation, failed to come closer to equilibrium (Bessonov 1999). A new price structure in the Russian economy was formed during the period of hyperinflation in the first four years of reforms (1992–95). In this period, the fuel, energy and transportation costs grew 2–3 times faster than the average price level in the economy (Volkonsky and Kuzovkin 2002: 22–3). Prices in the engineering, light industry and agricultural sector grew at only half the overall inflation rate. Relative prices remained more stable over the next five years (1996–2000), as the government tried to limit gas, electricity and transport price increases, as well as curtailing the depreciation of the rouble in order to suppress inflation (ibid.). Price indices across different sectors of Russian economy in 1990–2003 are provided in Figure 5.1.

The thick horizontal line indicates the average growth of prices in the economy as a whole. The data show that industries can be

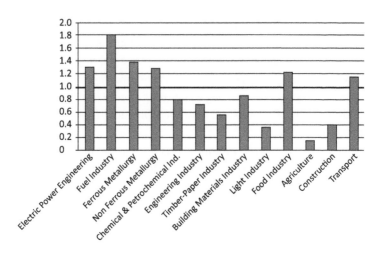

Figure 5.1   Price indices for Russian industries, 1990–2003

Calculation is based on Rosstat 2004a: 385, 387, 389; Goskomstat 2001: 593, 595, 597, 598.

divided into two unequal groups: those whose prices grew relatively faster or slower than the average. The first comprises the fuel-energy complex, ferrous and non-ferrous metallurgy, foodstuff production and transport; the second includes all the others. The first group of industries belongs to those which fulfilled maintenance functions under the planning system. Due to the advantages mentioned above, they enjoy relatively lower costs than their competitors in the world market. For instance, in the mid-1990s, production costs for a ton of nickel by the Russian JSC Norilski Nickel were $3,250, while the same figure for their major western competitors was much higher: $3,850 for the JSC INCO, $3,850 for the JSC Western Mining, and $4,450 for the JSC Falconbridge (Andrianov 1999: 274). In 2003, the same costs of production of the Russian enterprise were $4,595, while the average figure on the world market was $5,000 (Nornikel 2003: 65). Using their cost advantages, the fuel-producing complex, ferrous and non-ferrous metallurgy, some transportation elements, chemical enterprises and some other companies started to benefit from exporting their products. During this whole period, these enterprises' domestic-market prices did not reach the world market level; as a result, big insiders of these enterprises obtained an additional advantage. Facing no foreign competition in the domestic market, they grasped the opportunity to limit the supply of their production to the Russian market and sell instead to foreign buyers. This became a source of their power over the domestic market: 'The world market and its price structure became the prime and most powerful factor driving price changes in the domestic market, especially for large-scale exporters and importers' (Uzyakov 2000: 103–4).

Fuel prices provide a good example of this situation. In western Europe, the proportion of prices – that is, money paid to generate a given amount of energy from different fuels – for natural gas, coal and crude oil (to be refined into conventional fuel) is as follows: 1:0.625:1.06. In Russia it shifted from 1:0.8:1.3 in 1990 to 1:1.54:4 in 2000 (Alexandrovitch 2001: 8). This change reflects the relatively stronger positions of large insiders in the private oil industry, in comparison to the state-owned Gazprom. For instance, in the summer of 1999, the export share of the total production of automobile petrol suddenly grew from 14 to 41 per cent, and of crude oil – from 45 to 81 per cent (Vodyanov et al. 2000: 11). This created a shortage of these products in the domestic market, which led to their price increase during the next year by 2.04 and 2.26 times correspondingly (ibid.). The increasing profitability of their internationally traded cargo enabled railways to increase their domestic tariffs (Mysharin et al. 2001: 90). One may conclude that the profits generated from their relative advantage in the world market provided big insiders in these sectors with the opportunity to strengthen their infrastructure of control. Thus, the advantages of the world market were converted by the big insiders of the former maintenance industries into an increase in their power over the domestic market.

Unfortunately, it is impossible to continue the data series on the diagram from Figure 5.1, since Rosstat stopped publishing these industrial statistics. However, it is possible to observe the same tendencies through data on the types of economic activities in Table 5.1.

The data show that price increases of energy resources and of transportation tariffs in 2003–10 steadily exceeded the same indicator for manufacturing and agriculture. Thus, in this period, the average annual price increase of energy-producing materials grew faster than the same figure for manufacturing as a whole by nearly 10 per cent, machinery and equipment by 11.5 per cent and agriculture by 8.5 per cent. The inferior state of machinery and equipment manufacture is particularly indicative, since this sector determines the technological level of the whole national economy and prospects for competitiveness in the world market.

Table 5.1   Producer price indices by kinds of economic activities
(December to December; percentage)

	2003	2004	2005	2006	2007	2008	2009	2010	Average
Mining and quarrying of energy-producing materials	101.8	164.7	131.0	101.6	152.3	61.6	149.2	117.1	122.4
Cargo transport	123.5	109.3	116.6	115.8	106.8	132.3	97.5	133.1	116.9
Manufacturing	115.8	121.5	108.1	113.3	117.9	101.9	105.9	116.9	112.7
Manufacture of machinery and equipment	109.8	114.4	110.4	110.5	113.9	118.5	103.7	105.5	110.9
Agriculture	124.7	117.7	103.0	110.4	130.2	102.5	98.2	123.6	113.8

Sources: Rosstat 2004b: 389; Rosstat 2010a: 506, 507, 510, 513; Rosstat 2011b: 529, 530, 533, 536.

Without any significant changes in the Russian economy's technological structure, price increases in the 'maintenance' sector have inflated manufacturing costs: 'In the majority of Russian industries in the mid-1990s, the unit costs of production were higher than in Japan by 2.8 times, the US 2.7, France, Germany and Italy 2.3, and Great Britain 2 times. Compared to the developed countries, industrial production in Russia is more material and labour intensive' (Adrianov 1999: 273). These data allow one to think that the relative difference in price indices is the main factor upon which the differences in the industrial rate of profitability depend. Let us consider Figure 5.2.

Figure 5.2 shows that fuel and energy production, and ferrous and non-ferrous metallurgy are the Russian economy's most profitable sectors. As already mentioned, these industries benefited from advantageous changes in their products' relative prices. It is worthy to note that before price liberalisation in Russia, the differences in profitability among these sectors of the economy were insignificant. Thus, in 1992, the profitability of industry and agriculture was 38.3 per cent and 37.5 per cent respectively (Goskomstat 2001: 551). In the new economic conditions, many businesses found themselves in

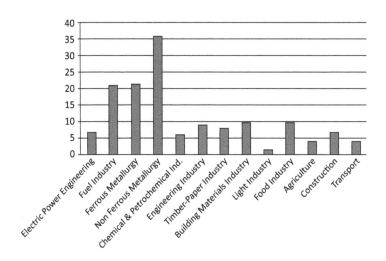

Figure 5.2 Profitability of industries' output in 2003

Calculation is based on the following sources: Rosstat 2004b (Moscow: Goskomstat): 336–8.

a difficult position, when their costs exceeded the market prices of their products, which led to widespread losses. Thus, in 1998, losses were characteristic for 53.2 per cent of Russian enterprises. That year, the share of businesses failing to gain any profits amounted to 47.2 per cent in engineering, 61 per cent in light industry and 84 per cent in agriculture. With economic recovery beginning in the 2000s, this situation began to improve. In 2003, 'only' 41.3 per cent of Russian enterprises were reporting losses (Rosstat 2004b: 333). In 2010, 27.8 per cent of Russian firms were still reporting an unprofitable performance (Rosstat 2011c: 446). Industries, disadvantaged due to price disparity, found themselves trapped in a vicious circle: low or negative profitability leading to lack of investments (both internal and external), resulting in lack of modernisation. Unfortunately, the data represented in Figure 5.2 cannot be extended to the following years, because Rosstat changed methods of their calculation. In fact, Rosstat moved from estimating profitability by industries to estimation of this indicator by kinds of economic activities. However, these new data reflected the same tendency with no less vividness. Let us consider Figure 5.3.

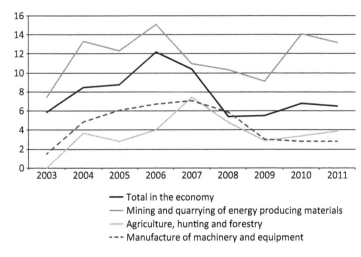

- Total in the economy
- Mining and quarrying of energy producing materials
- Agriculture, hunting and forestry
- Manufacture of machinery and equipment

Figure 5.3 Profitability of organisations' assets, by kinds of economic activities (percentage)

Sources: Rosstat 2006: 343–4; Rosstat 2008a: 382–4; Rosstat 2009: 399–401; Rosstat 2010a: 425–7; Rosstat 2011c: 449–51.

Figure 5.3 clearly demonstrates that in the 2000s, the profitability of assets of mining and quarrying of energy-producing materials was significantly greater, while the same indicator for agriculture and for the manufacture of machinery and equipment was significantly lower than the average for the total economy.

Such great differences in industries' profitability are not an occasional phenomenon of the transition period. Manufacturing efficiency is severely undermined by the greater market power of large insiders in the export sector. They appropriate additional insider rent at the expanse of domestically oriented manufacturing. Such conditions became institutionally fixed and obtained permanent character, which has ruined industries which potentially could play an important role in increasing Russia's competitiveness in the world market.

Hence, the essence of the value proportions established in the Russian economy as a result of radical market reforms is the one-sided reallocation of capital from domestically oriented sectors of economy to the exporting industries. In particular, this manifested itself in the drastic curtailment of maintainence functions, carried out by industries generating mass-produced products. As a result, the majority of

Russian enterprises have experienced great shortages or simply lack of investments, and have failed to adjust to new market conditions. The Russian economy's structure has drastically changed in favour of the extracting industries: 'The orientation of production towards raw materials extraction means, first, economic stagnation, a low ceiling of development, and narrow limitations to economic growth; next, the disintegration of the national economy, its enclavisation, as some parts of the national economy are integrated into the global economy as auxiliary elements of the core economies. The raw materials extraction sector severely narrows the investment process, makes redundant all the engineering industries. The only industries that manage to survive are those oriented towards the world market' (Yaremenko 2001: 11).

5.4   Modification of the Insider Rent Concept

Examination of the two major sectors of the Russian economy – that is, the privileged sector and the sector which is the victim of price disparity – makes the idea of homogeneous insider rent insufficient. Large insiders of the two above-mentioned sectors of the economy appropriate incomes very different in their amount and character. To express this discrepancy in different firms' position in the hierarchy of Russian businesses, one needs to distinguish between different forms of insider rent. In moving from discussion of the typical Russian firm to the firms' behaviour at the aggregate level, one passes from an abstract to a more concrete stage of analysis. This demands modification of the original concept of insider rent.

As previously defined, insider rent is the short-term income of the dominant group, appropriated due to control over the firm's financial flows. Even when an enterprise is unprofitable, but still creates some financial flows, it can enrich its owner. (It may sound absurd, but the reader should remember from Chapter 3 that many Russian businesspeople obtained their assets for prices many times below their market levels through privatisation and criminal raiding.) An extremely short-term-oriented large insider would invest nothing in their controlled business, but would just 'milk' the business dry, eventually levelling it. On the other hand, a medium-term-oriented large insider will invest in maintaining the business, for example, partially renovating equipment in order to secure current profits, and some future profits as well. This latter dominant individual (or group) will more closely resemble a rational entrepreneur aiming to maximise long-term growth. Still, they will remain a large insider, because they need to invest in an infrastructure of control, which is costly and undermines investment in the business's productive capacities and limits the large insider's time horizon. In fact, it is only by creating a sophisticated means of informal control over enterprises – and thus securing domination over them – is it possible to move from a short to medium-term strategy under Russian conditions.

Obviously, it is necessary to distinguish between the two types of rent pertinent to different investment strategies and time horizons. The first (short-term) type of rent only presupposes control over the business's assets and not investment; whereas the second (medium-term) implies investment maintenance and the partial development of productive capacities. The former type of income is close to the Marxian notion of absolute surplus value, based on exploitation without productivity growth (and without technical progress). The latter type of income is close to the Marxian relative surplus value, assuming productivity growth.[4] I have previously referred to the two types of insider rent as absolute and differential, following the Ricardian-Marxian treatment of agricultural rent under capitalism (distinguishing further between the differential insider rents I and II, the former being acquired in profitable industries without investment on the part of large insiders, and the latter as a result of investments) (Dzarasov and Novojenov 2005: ch. 3). Since the two types of income in question are based on two types of surplus value, it may be more consistent to call them 'absolute' and 'relative' insider rent.

The issue of so-called 'intangible assets' or 'goodwill' was discussed in Chapter 1. It was mentioned that Veblen saw these assets as reflecting the power of corporations over the market. He argued that a company which did not possess intangible assets at the time of its origination should create them, otherwise it would fail in competition. This approach was incorporated in the Keleckian degree-of-monopoly theory. Now it is time to apply this framework to interpret price disparity in modern Russia.

Infrastructure of control is the most important intangible asset in contemporary big business in Russia, indispensable if one intends to preserve control over their company. This infrastructure of control embodies the power of the dominant groups over the market and over controlled enterprises. As was demonstrated above, export-oriented companies have an additional factor of this kind of power: access to the world market. This secures their privileged position in the price disparity hierarchy. Facilitating the redistribution of financial flows in favour of large exporters helps to strengthen and expand the infrastructure of control. This degree-of-monopoly factor plays such an important role in Russia today that it merits greater consideration.

Let me pose a question: why is access to the world market granted in Russia only to some extracting industries and to the production of commodities with low levels of processing, such as pig iron and fertilisers, but not to manufacturing? This changes the relation between the two sectors in this country. In developed capitalist countries, it is the latter sector which creates greater added value and dominates the former. In the Kaleckian framework, manufacturing oligopolies constitute the capitalist economy's core, enjoying mark-up-determined pricing, while prime commodity production is only peripheral, with much less stable demand-determined prices (Kalecki 1971). In Russia, it is the other way round. Russian oil and gas companies manage to appropriate surplus value created by foreign and Russian workers in the manufacturing sector. This apparent paradox can be solved only by considering the wider framework of modern global capitalism. One way to do this is to apply the Global Commodity Chain (GCC) approach.

As was discussed in Chapter 1, the literature on this topic originates from the world-systems approach (Bair 2009), which understands the market not as an atomised competitive structure, but as a network of global chains of commodity production. These chains running from the production of prime commodities to the sale of the final, manufactured products, link together the core and the periphery of the world-system. Such networks are governed in such a way that the core concentrates the chains with high value-added production, while the periphery is compelled to limit itself with labour-intensive, low-value-added stages of production. In fact, these value-chains demonstrate the empirical validity of the Marxian transformation of labour values in prices of production. Labour-intensive chains at the periphery produce the bulk of surplus value, which is appropriated at the capital-intensive chains of the core. Veblenian intangible assets provide monopoly power to the core's corporations, securing their favourable position in the GCCs.

This fits the Kaleckian framework of the oligopolistic 'mark-up determined' versus 'demand determined' pricing. The same can be interpreted in terms of Yaremenko's qualitative non-homogeneity of resources approach. The periphery of the world-system relies on compensation, while the core relies on substitution effects. Cheap labour is the prime mass resource of the periphery. This is true not only for staple commodities production, but also for manufacturing moved from the core to the periphery countries. The latter compete with each other by suppressing their workers' wages, that is, they compete in the scale in which the compensation effect is applied.

Integration in the world market, which was among the first priorities for the Russian reformers, meant joining the low value-added chains of global production networks. Despite the significant decline of real wages in post-reform Russia, due to the Soviet legacy, wages are on average still higher than in many periphery countries. This is why Russia cannot compete with poorer nations as a manufacturing products supplier. Demand-driven energy resources are the prime items with which Russia can jump onto the lowest rungs of the GCCs.

Hence, distribution of power among the dominant groups in the Russian corporate sector is predicated on the core–periphery relations pertinent to the modern capitalist world-system. The ability of the fuel-energy production industry and some others to form the lowest chains in the GCC hierarchy became the prime intangible asset, the decisive degree-of-monopoly factor, which secures for the large insiders of this sector their dominant position in Russian big business. Due to this, they appropriate the differential or relative insider rent, in addition to its absolute form. This greatly affects the price structure of the Russian economy. Let us consider Figure 5.4.

Figure 5.4 summarises the results of the above discussion. It depicts the price structure of a typical corporation belonging to the Russian economy's privileged export sector (a) and of the industries put in disadvantage by price disparity (b). The (a) diagram is taller than (b), indicating the higher relative prices of the products of the former industries than of the latter. Note that unit production costs of (b) are depicted as being greater than those of (a). This reflects the fact that

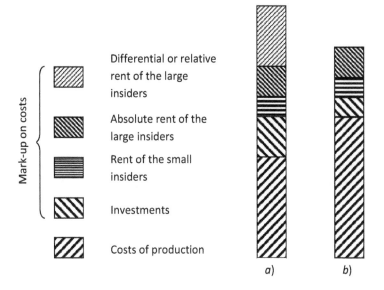

Figure 5.4 Price structure and rent distribution among the large insiders of a) the privileged sector and b) the industries disadvantaged by price disparity

manufacturing firms' costs are inflated by the price increases of the former 'maintenance' sector. Due to this, the rent of large insiders of (a) includes the differential or relative portion in addition to the absolute one and in total is greater than the rent of their counterparts from (b). Enjoying much greater discretional financial flows, large insiders of (a) undertake more investments than their rivals. The diagrams assume medium-term-oriented large insiders in both sectors of the economy. In the case of absolutely short-term focused dominant groups, there will be no investments at all.

One may conclude that *price disparity reflects the peripheral, or rather semi-peripheral, position occupied by Russia in the capitalist world-system.*

Now we have a range of concrete forms of surplus value ranging from the absolutely short-term type at one end of the spectrum to the long-term entrepreneurial profit at the other (where rent disappears). The majority of the real, as opposed to theoretical, large insiders fall somewhere in between these extremes. After distinguishing between the different types of income, we are in a position to move from a static to a dynamic model of modern Russian capitalism, thus grasping its historical development.

5.5   Conclusion

From the above, one can draw the following conclusions.

Departing from his model of a typical corporation, Eichner formulated the *value condition of growth, meaning existence of such group of industries' prices which covers both costs of current production and costs of expansion at the level of full employment.* The value condition of growth is determined for any given economy, since it is met not by a random set of prices, but only by one providing full employment. From the experience of Soviet planning, it is known that the full employment of economic resources is achieved only under their proportional allocation among industries. Hence, the value condition of growth can be interpreted as the price vector securing balanced national economy. At the same time, the group of prices in question redistributes financial flows among industries, which allows individual corporations to accumulate funds necessary to maximise their growth.

The ability of prices to cover current costs of production and costs of expansion, and hence the value condition of growth itself, depends not only on redistribution of financial flows, but on technologies applied as well. In this connection and based on the theory of qualitative non-homogeneity of resources, one may formulate the *technological condition of growth. It consists in the combination of effects of compensation and substitution which under a given price structure secure full employment and maximum growth rate.* The link between the value and the technological conditions of growth is provided by the fact that prices, covering current costs and costs of expansion, should correspond to the technological structure (that is, the distribution of compensation and substitution among industries) of economy, allowing for the full employment of resources.

The essence of price disparity in the Russian economy is in the existence of the two unequal groups of industries: with prices growing relatively faster and relatively slower than the average. The first group includes the fuel-energy complex, ferrous and non-ferrous metallurgy, foodstuff production, and transport, while the second includes everything else. The privileged sector companies enjoy the opportunity to limit their products' domestic supply, reserving them for export. This power over the market (an additional factor of their degree of monopoly) is manifested in their price increase in the domestic market. This results in an uncontrolled costs surge in manufacturing and the transfer of capital from this sector to the raw-materials extraction industries.

The Russian economy's price structure shows that large insiders of the privileged sector and of the industries disadvantaged by price disparity appropriate incomes widely different in both amount and character.

6

The Accumulation of Capital by Russian Corporations: Some Empirical Evidence

6.1   Introduction

This chapter provides some empirical evidence in support of the reasoning derived in previous chapters. Unfortunately, official data on the accumulation of capital in Russia are unreliable. According to a number of studies (Khanin and Fomin 2007, Voskoboynikov 2004, and others), calculations made by Rosstat (Federal State Statistics Service – the highest body of official statistics in Russia) of the crucial variables in this area are flawed. These flaws include incorrect assessment of the dynamics of the fixed assets stock, coefficients of withdrawal of capital and of its replacement, the size of depreciation and investment funds, and so on. Besides being unreliable, the official data are also incomplete for the purposes of our study. There are no official statistics at all on such crucial issues as the amount of insider rent withdrawn from enterprises, investment in the different elements of infrastructure of control, activities of small insiders, and so forth. Taking into account these deficiencies, it is impossible to test these hypotheses with the help of an econometric model, based on the official statistics. That is why one is compelled to rely on other kinds of empirical evidence, such as enterprise surveys and case studies.

Based on the previous chapters of this book, one may derive the following main ideas for empirical research:

1. *Informal control is associated with the inseparability of ownership and management. There are at least two observationally equivalent hypotheses of the causation link: (a) the former causes the latter; (b) the reverse.* In the original model of a 'managerial firm', typical for the 'Golden Age Capitalism' of the late 1940s to the early 1970s, management and ownership are distinctly different (see Chapter 1). It was demonstrated in Chapter 1 that in the ensuing age of financialisation, the shareholder revolution overcame this separation of ownership and control. In Chapter 3, the specific Russian model of corporate governance was discussed. In particular, the inseparability of ownership and control as a salient feature of Russian corporations was emphasised. This chapter provides three case studies, where particular groups of big insiders will be identified. The informal character of their control over the enterprises will be discussed.

2. *The fundamental instability of insider control leads to the short-term time horizon of large insiders. One of the most important aspects of this instability is the possibility of a hostile takeover. Other things being equal, the greater the threat of a hostile takeover the more short-term the time horizon of big insiders should be.* The case study of the 'Chimprom' company will show how an acute struggle between rival groups of big insiders for control over an enterprise led to its short-term time horizon.

3. *The shorter the time horizon of big insiders, the greater the share of the firm's funds extracted as rent.* As is demonstrated in Chapter 4, this leads to Russian corporations preferring short-term investment projects and ignoring potentially profitable investment opportunities with long pay-back periods (PBPs). I will compare two companies with unstable control (Chimprom and Volgakabel) and the other with entrenched big insiders (Petchoraneft). The time horizon in the latter case is medium-term, while in the former cases, it is short-term.

4. *The greater the portion of the firm's financial flows appropriated by large insiders, the greater is the potential for corporate conflicts.* In case of Chimprom, where the rent extraction is particularly high, I will show that highly developed opportunistic practices are common.

5. *The greater the potential for corporate conflicts, the more developed is the infrastructure of control.* In the case study of Volgacabel, I will show how the development of infrastructure of control stopped the previous disruptive and criminal activities of small insiders.

6. *Increased intra-firm conflicts increase the probability of a hostile takeover.* I will give a few examples of how rival groups of big insiders use intra-firm conflicts to undermine the position of the established dominant owners.

7. *The shorter the time horizon of large insiders and the greater the portion of funds extracted by rent are, the lower will be the size and quality of the firm's investment. This suggests that:*

 (a) *The greater the potential for rent extraction at a borrowing firm estimated by the lender, the higher will be the risk premium charged by the former, and consequently the interest rate will be higher;*

 (b) *Russian large insiders prefer shorter-term PBPs;*

 (c) *A large proportion of investment by Russian firms is in second-hand equipment;*

 (d) *Large insiders generally undertake small investment projects in terms of the present values of their costs.*

This will be shown in all three case studies. In addition, I will use results from the regular surveys of Russian enterprises, undertaken by the Institute of Forecasting of the Russian Academy of Sciences.

Section 6.2 provides some general evidence on Russian corporations' investments, contrasting independent experts' findings with official statistics, and using the results of some surveys. Sections 6.3–5 discuss case studies, examining the activities and investment strategies of enterprises with short-sighted, medium-term-oriented and actively struggling large insiders correspondingly. Section 6.6 focuses on conclusions from the abovementioned.

6.2 The Behaviour of Fixed Capital Stock

The results of Russian corporations' investment strategies, taken as a whole, are embedded in accumulated fixed capital stock. The size and properties of the nation's productive capacities reflect in material form the social interests dominating among the property-owning class of society. I begin discussing investment strategies of Russian corporations with examining the current state of the fixed capital stock as a generalised form of accumulation by big business.

According to official statistics, both investment and GDP in Russia declined enormously during the years of the radical market reforms. Let us consider Figure 6.1, which shows that in 1998, investment in fixed capital in the national economy amounted only to one-fifth of its 1990 level. Even after 1998, in the 'recovery' years, the growth of investment in fixed capital has not compensated for the enormous fall in the 1990s. In 2010, this indicator had reached only 58.9 per cent of its 1990 level in real terms (Rosstat 2011a: 43).

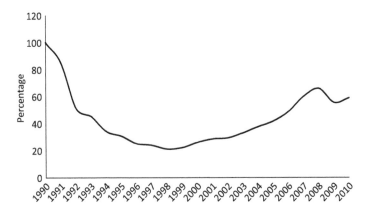

Figure 6.1 Private and public investments in fixed capital in Russia, 1990–2010 (percentage, in real terms)

Source: Rosstat 2011a: 42–3.

The analyses by Valtukh (2000), Voskoboynikov (2004) and Khanin and Fomin (2007) reveal that the accumulation of capital is insufficient to maintain the current fixed capital stock and avoid its growing obsolescence (see below). In contrast with this, Rosstat's official data suggest that during the years of recovery, the fixed capital stock of Russia was increasing. This understanding is substantiated by such important variables as gross investment and scrapped fixed capital as proportions of the total capital stock. Note that depreciation takes in more than scrapping, as it includes machinery which is still in operation but has reduced in value from the previous year. In 2005–11, in manufacturing, gross investment as a proportion of total capital stock[1] fluctuated between 12.6–14.9 per cent, while scrapped capital stock as a proportion of the total capital stock,[2] was between 0.8–1.2 per cent (Rosstat 2012a: 121–2). These data mean that new investment in Russian industry allegedly consistently exceeded the capital scrapped. The indices of investment in fixed capital in Russian industry also testify the same. In 2005–08, these indices ranged from 112.1 to 116.6 per cent for manufacturing, falling to 79.4 per cent only in the crisis year of 2009 (ibid.: 122). With the exception of the year 2009, when the world crisis engulfed Russia, Rosstat's statistics report a robust growth of investments in fixed capital. This conclusion about the expansion of production capacity is further reinforced by the calculation of its value, shown in Table 6.1.

Table 6.1 Dynamics of the value of fixed capital in industry (in current prices)

	2000	2001	2002	2003	2004	2005*	2006	2007	2008	2009
1. Fixed capital stock, $billion	137.2	143.1	198.3	223.1	257.8	308.7 −265.1	375.8	478.0	469.5	554.2
2. Investments, $billion	15.9	19.3	20.6	27.0	34.2	46.5	65.5	97.0	105.8	96.8
3. Depreciation, $billion	3.8	4.0	5.6	6.3	7.2	8.6 −7.4	10.5	13.4	13.1	15.5
4. Net investment, $billion	12.1	15.3	15.1	20.7	27.0	37.9	55.0	83.6	92.7	81.3
5. Increase of the value of fixed capital in %	8.8	10.7	7.6	9.3	10.5	12.3	14.6	17.5	19.7	14.7

Source: Rows 1 and 2 are taken from Rosstat 2005c: 119, 128; and calculated upon the data from Rosstat 2010: 107, 120. Data on fixed capital and investments for 2005–09 are obtained through summing up indicators for the different types of economic activities. The figures are converted from roubles into US$ using the values of official exchange rates at the end of December for the corresponding years.

* There are conflicting data for 2005 in Rosstat, 2005c and Rosstat 2010 due to Rosstat's change in their methodology of statistical inference starting from that year. Therefore, the figures from Rosstat 2005c for the year 2005 are presented in brackets.

There is no exact data on the size of depreciation in Russian industry, but the best survey in this field for the economy as a whole took place in the mid-1990s (Khanin and Fomin 2007: 27). In 1998, the ratio of the yearly level of depreciation to the balance sheet value of fixed capital was calculated as 2.8 per cent and this is the best available measure of this variable, even in the 2000s (ibid.). Applying this figure to the industrial sector, one obtains Row 3 of Table 6.1. If the amount in Row 3 is subtracted from Row 2, one sees a significant increase in the value of the fixed capital of Russian industry, approximately at the rate of 8–20 per cent annually (Rows 4 and 5).

The official picture of the robust investment growth in Russia is consistent with the results of Izyumov and Vahaly (2008), who try to assess the ratio of the old capital (fixed assets) to the new in the fixed capital stock of the CIS countries. They subtract from the capital stock inherited from the Soviet times about 30 per cent of what they consider as 'market unworthy' capital, allocated to such sectors of the economy as military production, unprofitable trade with Cuba and the like. After adjusting the capital stock to market conditions, Izyumov and Vahaly estimate the new capital based on official data on investments. The authors arrive at the conclusion that the new share of capital stock of Russia is 46 per cent. This optimistic conclusion means that Russia is relatively successful in creating a new, efficient market economy. However, there are a few considerations which prevent us from sharing this optimism.

First, as has already been mentioned, Soviet military production concentrated the best human and technological resources of the country to produce high-tech weaponry, matched only by the US's military-industrial complex (MIC). Today, while the Russian MIC is greatly reduced, weapons exports are still among the prime sources of Russian currency revenues, and hence, still market worthy. According to an estimate by a very credible source, the Soviet military-industrial complex needed to replace about 20 per cent of its productive capacities to become a source of high-quality equipment for Russian civil production.[3] This could be achieved in ten years[4] of investments financed from internal Russian savings (Yaremenko 1997: 25). If these estimations are correct, the assumption is that about 80 per cent of the capital used in military production was market worthy at the starting-point of the reforms. The inability of the highly short-sighted Russian capitalism to put these potentially (and very often actually) profitable resources to good use underscores its own inefficiency. Izyumov and Vahaly (2008: 95) compare the

THE CONUNDRUM OF RUSSIAN CAPITALISM

capital-stock accumulation in Russia with the same variable in some South American countries, but we learn nothing about whether they subtracted the value of military productive capacities from the latter's capital stock. In any case, simple subtraction without any reservations of the best part of the capital stock inherited by Russia from the Soviet times looks unreasonable.

Secondly, treating the capital used to produce goods for Cuba as market unworthy, because this trade was unprofitable, also seems dubious. The Soviet Union supplied Cuba with many badly needed products, such as weapons, energy resources, refrigerators, cars, and so on. This trade was unprofitable because it was actually a form of aid to an important ally. This does not mean that the products themselves were not in demand. Of course, Soviet cars – unlike Soviet tanks – were inferior to their western counterparts, but they were sold for profit in the markets of the Third World countries and even in western markets at corresponding prices. This means that, in their own market niches, these products were quite competitive.

Next, in total, the destruction of capital in Russia in the aftermath of the market reforms was enormous, but one hardly can see it as 'constructive', because, as I have tried to demonstrate here, Russian capitalism itself is very backward, short-term-oriented and economically inefficient. In the majority of cases, it is simply unable to send the right signals to the market agents about the true needs of society. Indeed, given the short-term time horizon of Russian business, the prime victims of this destruction were the most advanced industries in the technological sense (not only in the military sector), upon which the technological level and competitiveness of the whole economy depends. And this poses the major issue concerning this book.

Fourth, even if we take the calculation of new capital, as suggested by Izyumov and Vahaly, at face value, the major problem of its quality still remains. As illustrated in this chapter, even at the height of economic recovery in the 2000s, the majority of enterprises undertook investment capable of securing only partial improvements or only to maintain their productive capacities. Even more than that, the majority of Russian corporations invest in machinery and equipment that they themselves consider to be of inferior quality. They still make such investments because they are seen as cheap methods to obtain capital.

Last not least, the official data on investment and fixed capital stock in Russia, upon which Izyumov and Vahaly based their research, are highly unreliable, as I will attempt to demonstrate further here. Despite the wide usage of the official data by Russian authorities to substantiate the economy's current expansion, these figures raised many questions among independent analysts (see, for example, Valtukh 2000; Voskoboynikov 2004; Khanin and Fomin 2007). Even some official statistics cast doubts upon the reality of fixed capital growth.

As mentioned above, the ratio of depreciation to the fixed capital stock is estimated at about 2.8 per cent, while the proportion of scrapped capital stock in manufacturing in the late 2000s fluctuates between 0.8 and –1.2 per cent (see above), meaning that the ratio of depreciation is 2–3 times higher. Of course, as was mentioned above, these are two different variables, but some correlation between them should exist. This may mean that the rate of scrapping of equipment in Russian industry is under-estimated. Indeed, the value of this variable would suggest that the average longevity of equipment in Russian industry tends to be 66–100 years. Rosstat's data (2005c: 128) show that in the first half of the 2000s, the proportion of new equipment (that is, aged up to 5 years) in the industrial sector has not reached the level of the mid-1990s. The categories of equipment with the uncompleted lifespan of 6–10 years and of 11–15 years have sharply decreased. At the same time, the shares of equipment in the range of 16–20 years and of more than 20 years greatly increased, with the latter reaching the enormous level of 51.5 per cent. As a result, the average longevity of industrial equipment exceeded 21.2 years (ibid.).

However, for 2006–11, Rosstat gives much more optimistic figures estimating the average longevity of Russian industrial equipment as ranging from 14.4–13 years (Rosstat 2012a: 129). This raises serious doubts about the reliability of the official statistics concerning fixed capital in Russia. In two years only (from 2004 to 2006), such an enormous stock of fixed capital as was accumulated in Russian industry simply could not experience such a dramatic change from an average longevity of 21.2 years to 14.4 years. It is characteristic that, starting with its 2008 handbook on Russian industry statistics, Rosstat ceased publication of its series on the longevity structure of fixed capital. This makes us conjecture about the change in Rosstat's accounting methodology.

Independent experts do not take at face value the official data on the longevity of fixed capital; indeed, they provide very different values. Thus, Aganbegyan (2008: 138) argues that the average lifespan of industrial equipment in the Russian economy taken as a whole amounts to 18–19 years, instead of the usual maximum of 7–8 years. According to Kornev and Lavrenev (2011: 67), the current average longevity of machines and equipment of Russian industrial assets amounts to 21 years, while in 1990 (in the last, but not the best, year of the Soviet Union), it was only 10.8 years. (The normative period of equipment renovation in the USSR was twelve years.) The share of equipment with a longevity of less than five years in the production apparatus of the machine-tool construction comprises 3.5 per cent of the total stock, and in engineering as a whole 14.5 per cent, while the share of equipment of less than ten years' longevity is 5.2 and 18.5 per cent respectively (Borisov and Pochukayeva 2011: 59). We may conclude that according to independent experts, the average lifespan of equipment in Russian industry remains at 21 years in the 2000s.

First, these data suggest that the values of gross investment as a proportion of total capital stock shown in Table 6.1 are too low. Secondly, the rate of expansion of fixed capital stock in Russian industry is at least insufficient to overcome the growing obsolescence of its production equipment. These considerations are further reinforced by the distribution of the industrial organisations according to the period of purchasing the major part of their machinery and equipment, which is shown in Figure 6.2.

Figure 6.2 shows that the majority of Russian industrial enterprises primarily use equipment installed before the start of market reforms. Such a conclusion is reinforced by further studies. (We take the data, published before Rosstat's change of accounting methodology as the most reliable.) Grishankov (2004) examined the 400 best-performing Russian companies. Only 6 per cent of their total revenues were generated by companies which were not privatised former state enterprises and, hence, did not own some productive capacities created in the Soviet times. They operated mainly in the fields of telecommunications, IT technologies and retail trade, that is, these companies produced services and not goods (ibid.). The fact that the majority of Russian companies still largely rely upon equipment dating back to Soviet times, confirms the opinion that the significant part of

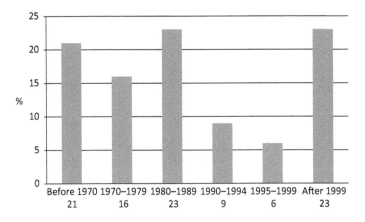

Figure 6.2 Distribution of the industrial organisations, according to the period of purchases of machinery and equipment

Source: Rosstat, 2005a, p. 123.

depreciated equipment in Russian industry has not been scrapped at all (Valtukh 2000: 3). This contradicts the official conclusion that the Russian industrial sector regularly replaces its consumed capital and expands its fixed capital stock by a significant percentage annually. Some international comparisons also question the validity of this official optimistic picture. In 2008, the per capita investment in Russia amounted only to 33 per cent of the same variable in the US, while in France this figure was 88 per cent, Germany 78, Italy 90, Britain 70, Japan 91, the Czech Republic 60, Slovenia 93, Estonia 63 per cent, and so on (Rosstat 2011a: 296–7). It is not clear how Russia, falling so much behind not only the advanced market economies but also some other transition countries, manages not only to maintain but even to expand its fixed capital stock. One's doubts are further reinforced by some contradictions in the official calculations of particular aspects of capital accumulation. Thus, the share of gross investment in fixed capital in Gross National Expenditure was 14.5 per cent in 1999 and 18.0 per cent in 2002 (Rosstat 2004: 73). These figures were obtained on the basis of the national currency. Calculation of the same ratio using accounting procedures common in the West and on the basis of the Purchasing Power Parity (PPP) produces very different results: 9.4 per cent for 1999 and 10.1 per cent for 2002 (Rosstat 2005b: 24,

36). Both values are provided by Rosstat; these contradictions largely reflect the particular methods of calculation applied by Rosstat.

According to the methodological commentaries provided by Rosstat (2010a: 448), 'the full book value and the residual balance sheet value of fixed assets is calculated, as a rule, in mixed prices' (authors translation). This means that a part of the stock is appraised in prices at the date of the last reassessment of productive capacities, while the other part in the purchase prices of investment goods (ibid.). Meanwhile the current (purchase) prices for equipment are overvalued in Russia. According to Khanin and Fomin (2007: 29), this overvaluation occurs because there is a sharp decline in the supply of Russian-produced investment goods when there is a certain growth in demand for them by the economy's privileged export-sector businesses. Another important fact is that in 1998 the Russian government abolished the requirement to regularly re-estimate the value of enterprises' fixed capital, which effectively brought re-estimation to a halt (ibid.: 31). Hence, the older portion of the enterprises' productive capacities is reflected in the balance sheets according to their renovation prices as of the mid-1990s, while the newer portion is calculated in current purchase prices. Taking into account inflation in the prices of investment goods, this means that the balance-sheet value of production equipment is greatly distorted. As a result, gross investment and scrapped fixed capital as proportions of total capital stock, as well as the values of depreciation and investment are not directly comparable. Indeed, the above means that the scrapped productive capacities are undervalued, being appraised at historical prices, while the newly installed equipment is overvalued, being appraised at current, inflated prices.

According to the alternative estimations provided by Valtukh (2000: 8), in reality, the proportion of scrapped capital exceeded gross investment as a proportion of total fixed capital stock in 1995 by 5 times. At the same time, only 56 per cent of the depreciation funds were used for financing investment, while the rest was diverted to other purposes. In order to replace all fixed capital consumed that year, Russia would have needed to increase the GDP share of its investment to 46 per cent (ibid.), while in reality it was only 18.7 per cent in 1995 (Rosstat 2005a: 11). According to Khanin and Fomin (2007: 46), in reality, scrapped fixed capital as a proportion of the total capital stock exceeds gross investment as a proportion of total capital stock by a factor of 2.24. Every year, the residual balance-sheet value of fixed capital measured by its replacement value[5] decreases by 2.75 per cent. Just to maintain its fixed capital stock at its present level, Russia would need to increase the share of investment in production capacities to 46.8 per cent of GDP (ibid.), while according to official data, this ratio ranged in 2000–08 from 15.9 to 21.3 per cent (Rosstat 2011a: 11). In 2010, the GDP share of investment in fixed capital amounted only to 20.4 per cent (ibid.: 11), or to 21.4 per cent (ibid.: 186). (Another contradiction in data was provided by the same source in the same year.) Other calculations suggest that the size of the effective fixed capital (that is, the fixed capital used for producing goods) decreased by the year 2002 by 2.6–2.7 times, in comparison with the pre-reform year 1990. In the same period, the proportion of the fixed capital fit for operating declined by 1.2–1.6 times (Voskoboynikov: 2004: 3).

As can be seen above the independent scholars' alternative calculations of the dynamics of the fixed capital stock in modern Russia suggest an enormous decrease and degeneration in production capacities, which at least was not offset in the years of recovery of the national economy. This is empirical evidence that the Russian corporate sector's investments taken as a whole are of inferior character. The same conclusion can be drawn from empirical data on the dominant types of investment strategies.

6.3 Corporate Investment Strategies: General Evidence

While official sources of data on investment in Russia are unreliable, the direct data on the informal control of large insiders and their rent extraction are not available at all. As a result, it is impossible to develop any formal econometric model to test the hypotheses posed in Section 6.1. Hence, empirical support for the main hypotheses advanced above is obtained by providing general evidence on investment strategies, based on the results of the surveys of enterprises provided by Kuvalin and Moiseyev (2011a and b). These surveys embraced 170–190 enterprises from 55–60 regions of Russia that have been conducted regularly since the late 1990s. About 35–40 per cent of the respondents are small- and medium-sized firms with up to 500 employees, hence there is a bias in favour of big business, which is consistent with the focus of this book. The sample's distribution across different industries approximately reflects national distribution. However, some important industries are not represented, for instance the oil, gas and coal-extracting sector. The survey questions were answered by the enterprises' managers.[6] Despite certain drawbacks of the sample, Kuvalin's results are relevant for this book because they are focused on Russian firms' long-term activities. Apart from that, to the best of my knowledge, no other Russian survey has achieved such a broad representation across the businesses' size, industry and regional location. In addition, it is important to note that Kuvalin's surveys are conducted on a regular basis and ask the same questions over a number of years. The data presented below reflect the period of the Russian economy's recovery. In addition, case studies are provided, which demonstrate links between insider rent extraction and investment strategies. The enterprises examined represent three exemplary cases of the investment strategies implemented by Russian big insiders operating in different conditions. The corresponding data are obtained through publications in the press and through personal cooperation with analysts, studying the enterprises in question.

The current discussion will start from Hypothesis 7, that is, 'The shorter the time horizon of large insiders and the greater the portion of funds extracted by rent, the lower will be the size and quality of the firm's investment.' In the previous section (6.2), it was shown that the findings of independent studies contradict the official statement about the steady growth of fixed capital stock in Russia. The official data may be checked by examining the results provided by Kuvalin and Moiseyev (2011a: 145).

Figure 6.3 shows that among the survey participants, the share of enterprises undertaking investment varied in the 2000s approximately between 45 and 79 per cent. Although the share of enterprises not undertaking any investment at one point declined to 20.98 per cent (in January–February 2002), it is remarkable that in 2011, that is, in the twelfth year of the Russian recovery and a year after the global financial crisis, nearly half of the businesses surveyed (48.11 per cent) abstained from any projects at all. The trend over time is obvious. Besides, in March–April 2011 only 45.65 per cent of respondents were sure that they would undertake any investments in the coming 1–2 years, while 17.94 per cent had no such intention and the remaining 36.41 pre cent did not know (ibid.: 146). According to Kornev (2005: 67), the aggregate decline of demand for machinery in the period of

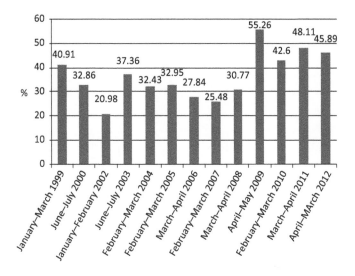

Figure 6.3 The share of enterprises abstaining from any investments

Source: Kuvalin and Moiseyev 2011a: 145.

the radical market reforms led to a fall of 80 per cent in the purchase and production of machinery and equipment.

The age structure of fixed capital is another important dimension of accumulation of capital by Russian corporations. In March–April 2011, business managers were asked 'In your company, how great is your current need of production modernisation and techno-logical innovation?' (Kuvalin and Moiseyev 2011a, p. 149). Of the respondents, 22.04 per cent answered that they did not need any special modernisation and that they would introduce innovations as the need arises; 56.45 per cent believed that they needed partial modernisation, such as renovation of some of their equipment, communications, and some technologies, while 21.51 per cent acknowledged that radical modernisation was needed urgently. This survey's findings mean that the overwhelming majority of Russian enterprises was not satisfied with their current technologies and felt the need to modernise their production capacities. However, the scale of actual investment was insufficient. Let us consider Figure 6.4.

It can be seen from Figure 6.4 that the share of respondents whose investments meet their perception of that required for modernisation

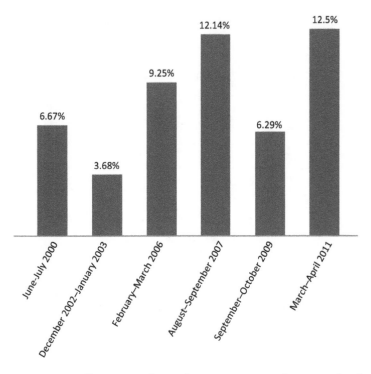

Figure 6.4 Affirmative replies to the question 'Does the current level of investment in your enterprise secure necessary modernisation?'*

*'Necessary modernisation' means replacement of scrapped machinery, technology upgrades and expansion of productive capacity to meet current demand.
Source: Kuvalin and Moiseyev 2011a: 149–50.

fluctuates between 3.68 and 12.5 per cent. At the same time, investment of nearly 90 per cent or more of enterprises is insufficient even for maintaining their current production level, capable of securing only partial improvements, or only maintaining their production capacities.

Another survey conducted at the beginning of 2006 focused on investment processes and covered 179 enterprises from 58 regions of Russia (Kuvalin and Moiseyev 2006). The share of enterprises needing complete modernisation of their production capacities reached 26.4 per cent of all those participating, which was the highest value for the last three years. At the same time, the share of businesses having no need for any significant modernisation has fallen to its lowest rate for the same period – to 11.2 per cent (ibid.: 112). These findings suggest that the overwhelming majority of Russian firms undertake insufficient capital formation even in a period of allegedly robust economic recovery, indicating that these businesses are capacity constrained. In order to understand the reasons for this situation, let us consider Figure 6.5.

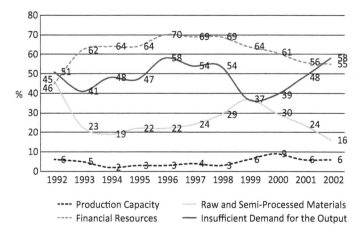

Figure 6.5 Factors limiting production (% of respondents referring to a given factor*)

* The sum of answers is more than 100 per cent because respondents were able to cite up to three factors.
Source: Aukutsionek 2003: 126.

The insufficient demand for Russian firms' products, indicated in Figure 6.5, may mean that the aggregate demand is a significant constraint and/or that the individual firms are not competitive. This gives rise to three different possible explanations:

(a) Uncompetitiveness of Russian firms.
(b) Insufficiency of aggregate demand.
(c) Reallocation of the national income (*external* insider rent effect, see Section 4.4.1).

Beginning with explanation (a): being uncompetitive, Russian firms have low prospects of sufficient returns on their investments and thus there is a low demand for investment funds. As a result, big insiders have excessive funds which they prefer to withhold for their private enrichment rather than 'waste' on inefficient production capacities. In this case, insider rent is extracted because investment is low rather than vice versa. Although the evidence of Russian enterprises' low competitiveness is provided, this reasoning is unconvincing. Indeed, the demand for investment funds is not based on current, but expected, profit, which means that some enterprises operating with obsolete and worn equipment should be eager to obtain modern and efficient machinery to increase their future returns, if nothing else prevents them from doing so.

Explanation (b) suggests that aggregate demand declined due to the external shock caused by the transitional crisis. Chapter 4 provided some evidence that leaves no doubt that aggregate demand declined in Russia in the early 1990s. The external shock engendered by the transition crisis was also significant. Blokhin (2002) argues that this was partially a result of the state withdrawing from its role as the monopoly intermediary which would establish connections between enterprises. The sudden liberalisation of prices was another external shock, with enormous consequences for the Russian economy and especially for its manufacturing sector (see Section 5.3). Other aspects of the shock inflicted by transition can be identified, such as economic agents' lack of market experience, foreign competition, and so on. Thus, this explanation has some justification. Nevertheless, one cannot ascribe prime significance to it, because even the most powerful of these shocks are of only temporary nature, and an economy should eventually adjust to them. For instance, as the Russian economy developed a new sector of market intermediaries (ibid.), investment in modern production capacities should enable Russian enterprises to adjust to the new pricing system, and economic agents to gradually accumulate market experience, and so forth. Despite all this, the evidence suggests that even in the years of recovery, aggregate demand is still insufficient to sustain previous employment levels. Such continuing problems indicate a more persistent cause. As was demonstrated in Chapter 4 (see Section 4.4.1), the cause is income redistribution, and the associated increased income inequality. This redistribution was dramatic and profound and has not been alleviated significantly, even given the prolonged recovery. This is why explanation (c) is considered to be the most likely explanation for this result.

This survey of Russian enterprises suggests that neither in the slump nor in the recovery was the shortage of productive capacity seen as the main constraint on production. The shortage of funds available to finance wages and the purchase of raw materials, and insufficient demand for Russian enterprises' products were perceived as much more important. Apparently, these data contradict the previous reasoning suggested above about the inadequacy of investment in the majority of Russian enterprises. In order to resolve this apparent contradiction, one needs to examine the quality of investment undertaken by Russian enterprises. First, one should consider the type of demand for investment goods of Russian corporations.

According to a Rosstat survey (Rosstat 2012: 23): 'the main aim of investing in 2011, just as in the previous years, was replacement of worn machines and equipment', an answer given by 69 per cent of those business respondents (56 per cent in 2000 and 67 per cent in 2010). This suggests that in the 2000s, in the overall Russian economy, physical wear and tear was the prime reason for scrapping equipment, with inefficient but still functioning machinery not being systematically replaced. This is indirect evidence of the short-term time horizon of Russian corporations, which neglect the long-term consequences of preserving inefficient production capacities. This observation is further reinforced by the data on the origin of investment goods purchased by Russian corporations. Let us consider Table 6.2.

The data show that the overwhelming majority of Russian corporations buy Russian equipment in both the category of new and that of second-hand machinery.

Table 6.2 Origin of the machinery and equipment purchased by Russian firms (in percentage, answers total to more than 100%)

Origin of equipment	2000	2005	2008	2009	2010
New Russian	80	87	85	87	88
New imported	47	65	60	37	35
Second-hand Russian	21	22	24	17	22
Second-hand imported	4	6	10	4	7
Leased	4	22	24	17	15
Repaired and modernised	N.A.	69	60	49	50
No purchase	9	7	7	11	10

Source: Rosstat 2011a: 134.

However, in Figure 6.6 the study demonstrates that these kinds of equipment are considered by Russian enterprises to be of inferior quality. Another interesting observation is the importance of repairing and modernisation of old equipment. Evidence of these decisions by Russian companies is confirmed by unofficial surveys (Kuvalin and Moiseyev 2010: 128–9).

The data (Kuvalin and Moiseyev 2012: 140) indicate that Russian enterprises primarily rely on new and second-hand machinery and equipment produced in Russia and other CIS countries; however, the portion of western second-hand equipment is also significant; in some industries, it amounts to half of all machinery purchases (Borisov 1999: 69). Overall, these figures suggest that many Russian corporations are unwilling or unable to purchase equipment, which, as demonstrated below, they view as being of superior quality. These results are confirmed by the breakdown of the types of investment goods purchased by Russian industry. Russian statistics of fixed capital stock in industry distinguishes between different kinds of equipment, that is, major industrial plant, auxiliary equipment and calibration/measurement instruments (Kornev 2005: 63). The share of the first category amounts to 54–88 per cent of the whole stock in different industries. In the mid-2000s, 80 per cent of major machinery was produced in Russia and the rest was imported. More than 60 per cent of the second and third kinds of equipment are of foreign origin, with the latter share highest for the controlling/measuring calibration equipment (ibid.). To better understand the essence of such an investment strategy, one should take into account the differences in the quality of these types of equipment. This is reflected in Figure 6.6.

As can be seen from Figure 6.6, few respondents believe that Russian machinery is of similar quality to imported products. For the overwhelming majority of the surveyed enterprises, competitive Russian-produced machinery is either rare or non-existent. Even more than that, the same survey shows that in 2010 only 15.72 per cent of the participants thought that the difference in quality between Russian and western equipment was diminishing, while the others believed that it either remained the same or even was increasing. More than a third of the surveyed enterprises have seen no improvement in Russian equipment in comparison with global standards, while nearly a half thought that it had deteriorated (ibid.). The situation worsened

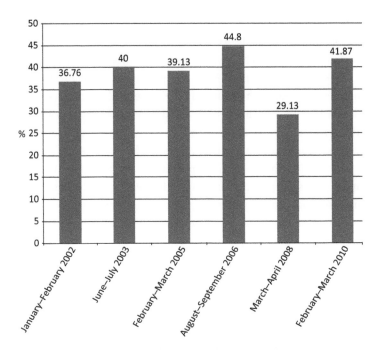

Figure 6.6　Negative responses to the question 'Is there available Russian-produced machinery, necessary for your enterprise, which is not inferior to their imported counterparts?' (in %)

Source: Kuvalin and Moiseyev 2010: 130.

in the year of the global financial crisis and its aftermath. In 2008–10, the share of respondents thinking that the quality of Russian-produced machinery and equipment had 'on the whole significantly deteriorated' increased from 7.14 to 21.25 per cent. Correspondingly, the share of positive appraisals had dropped from 49.21 to 42.50 per cent in the same period (ibid.: 129).

Relating this to the data presented in Table 6.2, one can conclude that the majority of Russian corporations invest in machinery and equipment that they themselves consider to be of inferior quality. According to Kornev (2005), a reduction in quality is one of the major ways Russian engineering adjusts to the decline in demand for investment goods on the part of Russian industry. Engineering enterprises cut their production costs by simplifying the machinery produced, moving from better-quality technologies to inferior counterparts, resulting in cheaper and less efficient models, and so on. Sometimes the quality of engineering production declines because the equipment is simply physically worn out (ibid.: 68). According to Borisov (2000), in the 1990s, the production structure of civil engineering changed drastically: as the share of the technologically advanced equipment diminished, the proportion of technologically inferior machinery increased. This meant that Russian enterprises often purchased equipment that in the West would be viewed as obsolete.

The reason why Russian corporations largely choose inferior capital goods is that they are much cheaper. Some Russian firms purchase best-quality pieces of imported machinery for crucial production processes, and combine them with some Russian new or second-hand equipment, or simply prolong the life-span of existing counterparts. This usually occurs in the old Soviet-era factories, which were idle due to the 1990s recession. According to Gladyshevsky et al. (2002: 16), such 'cheap' strategies usually require two or three times less investment per capital item than the strategies requiring new construction or expansion of existing enterprises. The average annual costs of newly installed production capacities in the ferrous metallurgy industries were in 1991–2000 around 45 per cent of the 1986–90 costs (ibid.: 19). A similar situation is observed in engineering where the cost of increasing production fell by up to half in the same periods (ibid.: 21). Investment in inferior capital goods explains why many Russian enterprises feel the need to expand and modernise their productive capacities and at the same time are not concerned about the shortage of the latter. Big insiders solve this problem by purchasing inferior but cheap equipment. According to Novojenov (Dzarasov and Novojenov 2005: 425), 'the general decrease in wages compensates for the high current costs of production based on cheap but low quality equipment. As a result of this investment in such equipment labour is partly substituted for capital', which puts additional downward pressures on wages (author's translation). As a result of such inferior investment strategies, Russian enterprises experience increasing pressure from foreign competitors. Let us consider Figure 6.7.

The data show that, prior to the global financial crisis, foreign competition was generally becoming more widespread and significant. In such conditions, the investment strategy described above was leading to Russian corporations increasingly concentrating production

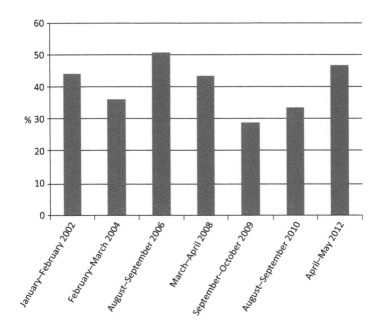

Figure 6.7 The share of enterprises which management thinks that competition from non-CIS producers in their markets is increasing, in %

Source: Kuvalin and Moiseyev 2011b: 155.

in labour-intensive and energy-intensive sectors of economy in the long run. The position of Russian big business somehow improved in the crisis years of 2008–09. This, probably, reflects foreign capital fleeing from emerging markets. However, in 2010, foreign competition again began to increase.

Figure 6.8 illustrates that, in terms of innovative activities, the overwhelming majority of Russian companies fall far behind their foreign counterparts. This assumes the decline of Russian big businesses' competitiveness in the global market. These results are consistent with official data on innovations. At the brink of the global financial crisis or at the height of the Russian recovery in 2007, only 9.4 per cent of Russian enterprises undertook any innovations, while the share of innovative goods and services in their delivered products amounted to a meager 5.5 per cent (Rosstat et al. 2009: 10).

The above material is consistent with the hypotheses about the decline in the size of, and poor quality of, Russian corporations'

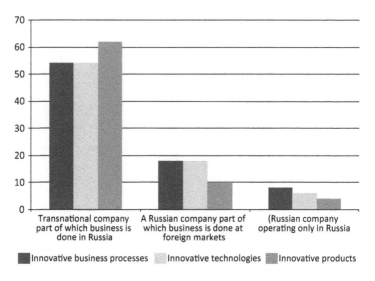

Figure 6.8 The share of companies introducing globally innovative business practices, technologies and products

Source: NES et al. 2010: 16.

investments and the short-term time horizon of their investment strategies.

Now we can consider the financing of investment in Russia. The following survey shows the term structure of the bank credits provided for financing investment by Russian enterprises. Let us consider Figure 6.9. In 2003, the share of enterprises provided with investment loans reached the level of 28 per cent and has been roughly constant from that time. From this, one may conclude that in the Russian economy, 'an enclave of enterprises was formed amounting to 25–30 per cent of the total, which had access to long-term loans' (Kuvalin and Moiseyev 2007: 160, author's translation). As can be seen from Figure 6.9, during the global financial crisis of 2009, the number of enterprises obtaining investment loans declined, only to be restored in 2010. However, of 24.86 per cent of these firms, 10.64 per cent had access to 1–2 year loans, while credits for 3–5 and more years were available only for 15.96 per cent (Kuvalin and Moiseyev 2011: 144).

Kuvalin and Moiseyev studied what Russian enterprises view as the major obstacles to their external borrowing (2006: 116). Their findings suggest that high interest rates are considered by Russian enterprises

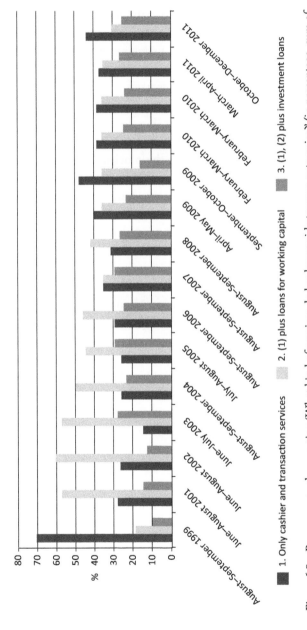

Figure 6.9 Responses to the question 'What kind of services do banks provide to your enterprise?' (in percentage, sum of the answers 100 per cent)

■ 1. Only cashier and transaction services   ■ 2. (1) plus loans for working capital   ■ 3. (1), (2) plus investment loans

Source: Kuvalin and Moiseyev 2011: 144.

as the most powerful obstacle to external borrowing. The unacceptable level of responsibility for borrowers, and the lenders' demand to have the right to control over the lenders' property and interference in their management are the other obstacles. These responses are consistent with the hypothesis about the high-risk premiums and other guarantees demanded by Russian banks for loans.

The acute shortage of high-quality workers is another problem for Russian enterprises. In 2011, the share of respondents referring to this issue amounted to 87.2 per cent (Kuvalin and Moiseyev 2011: 155). The shortage of high-quality workers was a salient feature of the 2000s. The share of enterprises citing this problem fluctuated during 1999–2011, between 81 and 95 per cent (ibid.: 154–5). Hence, there is a steady trend of high-quality workers being in short supply in Russia: 'Undoubtedly, this tendency is a significant threat to economic growth and the competitiveness of Russian production especially in the medium and long-term perspectives' (Kuvalin and Moiseyev 2007: 163). This is consistent with the idea that weaknesses in human capital investments by firms are an additional constraint reinforcing the limitations in their fixed capital stock (see Section 4.3.3).

Referring now back to the seventh hypothesis (see Section 6.1), one may see that the results of the surveys discussed above, provide evidence on the low quantity and poor quality of investment undertaken by Russian corporations, although these results do not provide direct evidence of the reasons for this outcome. The data presented in Figures 6.3 and 6.4 suggest that the majority of Russian enterprises consider their investment as insufficient to sustain their effective long-term growth, and even their current production. The perception of the high interest rates charged by Russian financial institutions is consistent with hypothesis 7(a), that is, 'The greater the potential for rent extraction at a borrowing firm estimated by the lender, the higher will be the risk premium charged by the former, and consequently the interest rate will be higher.'

There is no conclusive evidence on hypothesis 7(b), that is, 'Russian large insiders prefer shorter-term pay-back periods.' However, the data presented in Figures 6.5 and 6.6 and Table 6.2 showing the reliance of Russian firms on second-hand equipment confirms hypothesis 7(c) and indirectly supports hypotheses 7(b) and 7(d), which states that 'Large insiders generally undertake small investment projects in terms of the present values of their costs.' The conclusion drawn from the Rosstat survey about physical wear and tear rather than inefficiency being the prime cause of scrapping equipment, and from Figure 6.8 suggesting the low level of Russian businesses' innovative activities, is consistent with hypothesis 7, concerning the overall short-term time horizon of Russian corporations.

6.4   Case Study 1: Short-Sighted Big Insiders[7]

This case study of JSC Volgakabel, which provides an example of short-sighted big insiders, will show the links between informal control and inseparability of ownership and management (hypothesis 1 *a*); how the instability of control, stemming from an uneasy alliance between two groups of big insiders, leads to a short-term time horizon of the dominant groups (hypothesis 2); how development of the infrastructure of control stopped previous widespread theft at the enterprise (hypothesis 5); and how the short time horizon of big insiders led to investment strategies deficient in both size and quality (hypothesis 7).

6.4.1   Informal Control and the Inseparability of Ownership and Management

JSC Volgakabel is situated in Samara and produces different types of cable products. As of 1 January 2005, the company had 635 employees (Baker Tilly Rusaudit 2005a: 8). In the case of Volgakabel, there were two main 'insider' groups involved in a struggle for ownership and control: on the one hand, the pre-existing management, and on the other, the group of companies known as Samarskaya Obyedinennaya Kompaniya (SOK).[8] SOK is one of Russia's largest holding companies, its turnover amounting in 2003 to $1.7 billion, and in 2004, $2 billion. In the mid-2000s, SOK was associated with AvtoVaz which accounts for about 12 per cent of Russian automobile production and is the biggest producer of auto components in the Russian Federation (RF) (Gorelik 2005; Minin 2005). The principal owner of SOK is an entrepreneur from Samara, Yury Kachmazov (Finmarket 2005) who in 2005 belonged to *Forbes*'s list of the hundred richest people in Russia, with a personal fortune estimated to be $ 0.41 billion (*Forbes* 2005).

Ownership and control of the group of companies is totally integrated and concentrated, because Kachmazov owns 70 per cent of the group's assets and has been chairman of its Board of Directors for more than ten years (Gorelik 2005).

From the very beginning of its appearance on the market, SOK operated an aggressive policy of hostile takeovers: 'Its representatives have the habit of dropping in at the company suggesting that they organise the distribution of its output, then they *have been taking control over the financial flows* and later – the equity shares' (Gorelik 2005, emphasis added). The aggressive methods by which this control was exercised are elucidated by public scandals publicised in the mass media (*Samarskoye Obozrenyer* 2004a, 2005; Trifonov 2004). Apparently SOK is also actively involved in the 'privatisation of the state' (Kosolapov 2005; Kaschinsky 2005; *Novaya Gazeta v Ryazany* 2005), a process previously discussed in Section 3.2.4.

In 2000–04, SOK had consolidated 47.74 per cent of the shares in Volgakabel (*Samarskoye Obozrenyer* 2004b); this was the result of a long and persistent struggle with the previously dominant ownership/management group. SOK's takeover is not complete, the former owners still retain an exactly equal shareholding. More importantly, the latter retain the important top management positions: the chairman of the board of directors, the CEO and the commercial director all belong to the old dominant group. Both parties have agreed to preserve the balance of power by not attempting to purchase additional shares at the expense of the workforce (ibid.). Thus, ostensibly there exists an alliance between the two groups of large insiders.

Despite being in possession of exactly the same shareholding as the old owners, SOK's representatives are not on the Board of Directors, but they do occupy two very important management positions which enables them to control the size of the insider rent and the methods of its withdrawal. A consultant's report on the company indicated that the 'heads of the main functional areas are individuals loyal to the two major groups of owners' (Baker Tilly Rusaudit 2005a: 17–18, author's translation[9]). For example, the areas of sales and purchasing are supervised by the commercial director Akhmerov, who is a member of the previous management group, while his deputy Pakhomov represents SOK's interests. A similar structure holds for finance where the financial director Dolgusheva represents SOK, while the head of the planning department, Nefedova, is a protégé of the group of previous owners (ibid.).

The big insiders' power at Volgakabel became entrenched in a number of ways. In the 1990s, it was commonplace for managers to steal raw materials and products. Volgakabel's chief electrical engineer removed copper from the plant at the rate of a few tons per month, with the help of a sanitary engineering team hired specially for this purpose. At the beginning of the 2000s, a system of internal control was created at the enterprise with the purpose of establishing control over financial flows and controls to prevent theft as well. The plant is now surrounded by a barbed-wire fence, topped with surveillance cameras, and two checkpoints have been established to deter theft by employees, while another checkpoint controls vehicles leaving the site. In addition, an inventory control system has been established. These controls were followed up by prosecution of those caught stealing from the company. By 2005, one in ten of Volgakabel's jobs was in security. Of course, such a situation greatly increases overheads, but in general secures for the dominant group a strong control over the small insiders (ibid.: 37–40).

Control is maintained over selling prices and purchases through an informal distribution of decision making between the commercial director and his deputy head, again representing the two major groups of large insiders (ibid.: 18). Thus the management system created at JSC Volgakabel is characterised by a high level of centralisation. In the quality management system, a rigorous regulation of all business processes is imposed; all purchases must be authorised centrally by the purchasing department in Moscow, while the organisation of sales is similarly centralised (ibid.: 30).

Although the withdrawal of insiders' rent from the enterprise is disguised, some of its particular features are observable. Analysis reveals that there have been a number of contracts 'which could be considered as deals for the benefit of specific vested interests' (ibid.: 68). These include paying for the allegedly provided services to organisations controlled by Volgakabel's big insiders. Another possible channel of rent withdrawal is the peculiar way that Volgakabel's assets are managed. Consultants revealed that Volgakabel lent equipment to allegedly independent companies established by owners of Volgakabel. In these cases, Volgakabel itself operated just as an intermediary (ibid.: 85). Such types of relationship allow large insiders to avoid material responsibility in the event of failure to meet contractual commitments even when faced with legal action, and, at many enterprises, are used for rent withdrawal through manipulations of rental payments. Indirect evidence of rent extraction can be inferred from the words of SOK's vice-president Ofitserov, who notes that Volgakabel is 'self-sufficient and *if its means are not depleted by dividend payments* it is able to perform steadily and profitably' (*Samarskoye Obozrenyer* 2004b, author's translation). Such an apparently strange approach is more understandable if one takes into account that the dominant groupings realise their interests not through appropriation of dividend payments,[10] but through rent extraction. Share ownership serves the large insiders only to legitimatise control over the enterprise's financial flows. Although the exact size of insider rent withdrawn from Volgakabel is not known, one can get an impression of the size of financial flows, created by the company, from Table 6.3.

Table 6.3   Sales and profit of Volgakabel (in 1,000s of roubles)

	2003	2004	First quarter 2005
Revenue	14,485	17,360	4,260
Marginal profit*	2,737	2,822	412

* Marginal profit was obtained as a difference between sales and direct costs of production. For 2003–04, converted from roubles at the exchange rates for the last quarter of the years, for the first quarter of 2005 – at exchange rate for the same period.

Source: Baker Tilly Rusaudit 2005a: 106, 118.

In these conditions, where real control over the assets is informal, the two groups can only conclude an occasional truce, but they are unable to develop any consistent long-term strategy. First, their ends radically differ, because they all pursue their own rewards at the expense of their rivals. Secondly, neither group can be sure that the outcome of a long-term strategy will accrue to it and not to its rival. Thus, analysis of the ownership relations peculiar to Volgakabel leads to the conclusion that there is an unstable alliance of the two big insider groups dominating the firm. The existence of this unstable alliance is the major internal factor responsible for the company adopting a very short-term-oriented approach to its business strategy.

The time horizon adopted by Volgakabel's management is to an extent influenced by the position of the cable-producing industry in the national economy. More than 80 per cent of JSC Volgakabel's production costs comprise raw materials and semi-finished products (Baker Tilly Rusaudit 2005a: 110). The prime raw material used in this production process is refined copper, the price of which is tied to the indices of the London Metals Exchange through coefficients which the suppliers have determined. Because of this, cable production costs fluctuate with price changes on the world market. These are characterised by considerable volatility with a tendency to increase over time. This means that growth in costs is unpredictable and in this competitive market this leads to periodic decline of the marginal[11] profit on all of the main company's products. The consultants observe 'that raw materials prices grow faster than prices of the company's finished products. Besides, the elasticity of demand is such that the market will not allow for a price increase with every change in production costs' (ibid.: 118–19).

The cable industry's structure and the current condition of this market are additional important determinants of the company's short-term orientation: 'The cable industry of Russia is still fragmented without any dominant players and with a large number of medium sized companies' (ibid.: 58). In recent years, a significant horizontal and vertical integration has taken place in the industry, mostly through mergers and acquisitions. A few big holdings have already appeared. In total, by mid-2005, there were 36 big companies and a number of small ones, operating only about 60 plants, which means that holdings are still small in size (ibid.: 62). There is no significant presence of foreign investors in the market. On the whole, it can be noted that there is no company or group large enough to determine prices. Because of this, the market is still competitive and is unable to oppose or offset raw material price increases imposed by the big metallurgy companies, which means that the industry in question is another 'victim' of the former maintenance sector of the Russian economy.

Thus, the competitive character of the industrial market and its unfavourable position in the price structure are the major external factors, while the unstable equilibrium of the two principal insider groups is the major internal factor determining Volgakabel's development strategy.

6.4.2   The Company's Time Horizon

These internal and external conditions predetermine the strategic time horizons of Volgakabel. The Volgakabel management's time horizon is characterised by a distinct short-term orientation. Long-term planning is not practised at all, while in the medium term, 'the procedures of the company's planning for longer than a year horizon are partial and incomplete and predominantly do not operate in a coherent framework' (ibid.: 21). There are big gaps in Volgakabel's system of planning. The company, whilst emphasising the cost of current production, does not plan its longer-term investment, financial and production strategy. The month-by-month planning, that is, the short-term time horizon, is very different.

As the data (ibid.: 25) demonstrates, the planning procedures for the very short term are consistent with good business practice. The reliance on monthly rather than longer-term planning suggests that it is this time horizon that is prioritised by the dominant group. In this connection, the consultants have observed that 'The enterprise's leadership is primarily interested in the *operational horizon*' (ibid.: 28, emphasis added).

There is some further evidence of the short-term orientation of the two large insider groups controlling Volgakabel. The scheme of securing the business's assets with the help of 'dummy' firms, referred to above, makes business relations with this company highly risky. It does not enhance business reputation and respectability and prevents the establishment of mutually beneficial long-term relations with other businesses. These consequences would be unlikely to be neglected if the intention is to create viable and profitable long-term business relations. Despite the apparent rigorous adherence to business processes regulations and that 'at the enterprise all the procedures are fulfilled that are necessary to meet [Volgakabel's] operational targets, procedures designed for the long-term targets are not established' (ibid.: 16).

This short-term time horizon of JSC Volgakabel's management does not allow the company to make the most of the opportunities that are opening up in their industry. After the deep slump in demand for cable production in Russia, brought about by the economic crisis of the 1990s, the industry experienced a boom in the 2000s (ibid.: 61–2). This was connected with the Russian economy's revival, which had resulted in significant increase in orders for the industry during 2002–04. At a time when any significant competition from imports was virtually absent, the industrial outlook was fairly optimistic. Many companies sought to make use of these new opportunities by actively expanding in the internal market (for example, the JSC 'Chuvashkabel').

JSC Volgakabel set prices for its products at a level lower than their competitors. Analysts believe that it allowed the company to strengthen its positions in Povoljyer (the River Volga region), and in future – all over the country (ibid.). Meanwhile, 'Volgakabel for the present works only to preserve its current quality level ... of production reached in the last five to seven years' (ibid.: 61). This was a purely defensive strategy which did not permit the company to take advantage of new opportunities and in future it would likely lead to the loss of its market position.

The short-term orientation of Volgakabel had an explanation. The market's competitive character and the industry's position with respect to the specific problem of price structure made the expected profit very unstable, as referred to above. The company's managers explained to the consultants that it was the volatility of prices that made it difficult to plan in the medium term (that is, one year) and impossible in the long term (ibid.: 24). But these external factors – despite their very serious character – do not fully explain the company's short-termism.

Thus, where there is an unfavourable price structure and instability in the relationship between the large insiders, the uncertainty and risk of any long-term strategy increases and hampered the company's long-term development.

6.4.3 Volgakabel's Fixed Assets

Let us now turn to the question of the investment demand of the enterprise in question.

Consultants singled out two groups of assets: (*a*) the main buildings (29 units), (*b*) equipment used in the main production processes (219 units). The research revealed that 'the passive and active part of

Volgakabel's fixed assets [that is, buildings and equipment] (including rented units) was predominantly formed in the Soviet period' (ibid.: 41). The data suggest that the majority of the main buildings were constructed before 1965. In the 1980s and 1990s, only relatively small structures were built. The main part of the productive equipment was also installed before the mid-1980s, which meant that by the early 2000s the lifespan of the majority of Volgakabel's fixed assets exceeded 20 years, and for the buildings and structures, more than 40 years. Naturally, these assets had experienced a great deal of wear and tear: in advanced countries, as a rule, cable industry equipment is renewed every 5–7 years (ibid.: 42). In this industry in Russia, equipment retains efficiency for 10–20 years. Companies using older equipment than this experience a gradual decline in profitability and hence shrinkage of their potential internal investment funds (ibid.). Clearly, long-term competitiveness depends upon the renewal of these assets, and it may be implied that this was not one of Volgakabel's immediate objectives. It should also be noted that, in order to be successful, Volgakabel not only needed to move to new technologies but also, to radically expand productive capacity in order to meet the growing market demand. In the early 2000s, the capacity utilisation rate in Volgakabel's main production lines, apart from the cables with plastic insulation, fluctuated between 80 per cent and sometimes more than 100 per cent of engineer-rated capacity. This is explained by the growing demand for the enterprise's output. From the above and given the nature of these expanding markets, discussed above, it would appear that this company should have been expanding its capacity: 'In general, analysis of the productive capacity of JSC Volgakabel demonstrates that this enterprise can maintain its current capacity for a limited amount of time, but it is in urgent need of investment now' (ibid.: 46).

No significant investments were made by the company in recent years. As the consultants indicated, 'No active investment policy aimed at the creation of new productive capacity has been pursued, and no effort has been made to replace old equipment or install modern equipment. Indeed, from 2003 to the first quarter of 2005 *not a single large new investment project was realised*' (ibid.: 15, emphasis added). Investments that were undertaken were mainly directed at prolonging the life of ageing equipment. As a result, the overall level of assets and capacity was diminished and this capacity depreciation led to the permanent decrease in its residual value.[12] From a qualitative point of view, equipment was simply maintained at the technological level reached in Soviet times.

The short-term orientation of the enterprise's management undermined the organisation's investment process. Formally, Volgakabel had a 'Plan for Technical Development' (or investment plan) which contained a list of proposed investment projects (ibid.: 12–15), however the means of funding these projects were not clear. The plan only included the cost of the necessary equipment and not the expenses involved in their design, construction, installation and adjustment. More than this, the plan did not provide estimates of the future profitability of investments. As a result, it appeared to be impossible to prioritise the projects in terms of their profitability. The list of the largest investments included only seven pieces of equipment, either Russian or imported second-hand, all of which could be accomplished on the existing site. The scale of investments in question, that is, the purchase or modernisation of only seven units, can be seen to be small if compared to the 219 units revealed by the consultants' research. This plan was even more representative of the qualitative content of the projects in question. Virtually all of them were designed to eliminate bottlenecks at the most crucial points in the production lines. The payback period criteria for these projects were not established in the plan at all, indicating that extended payback periods were not considered. In addition, arbitrary and strict constraints were applied to investment costs,[13] even where these costs were sustainable and justified (ibid.). It may be concluded from this, that more expensive projects which were seen as necessary for production and potential profits, were rejected.

Apparently, the demand for investment funds by Volgakabel was negligible in comparison to the urgent need of the enterprise for radical expansion and the modernisation of the company's productive capacity.

In addition, it may be argued that the unfavourable position in the price structure, referred to above, and insider control nearly completely undermined Volgakabel's supply of investment funds. This can be derived from the evidence that, without exception, there was no source of financing indicated to achieve the company's investment plan. The resources which insiders left for enterprise development were sufficient only to accomplish the current maintenance of equipment and urgent repair work. Of course, price structure, which was beyond the power of the dominant owners, impedes accumulation of the necessary funds, but if insider rent had not been extracted, then some investment would still have been possible.

6.4.4 Some Conclusions

The case study of JSC Volgakabel shows that in order to uphold their balance of power the two groups of big insiders shared informal control over the major managerial positions, which corresponds to Hypothesis 1 of this chapter. In conditions of such equilibrium, neither party can be sure of its future position. This unsurety has been associated with the adoption of a short-term time horizon, which is reflected in the emphasis upon short-term production planning, short payback periods on investments undertaken, and neglect of the importance of the company's reputation by the dominant owners (Hypothesis 2). The theft of valuable materials was a chronic problem prior to the development of internal infrastructures of control. This past level of opportunism gives us a hint at the potential activities of small insiders which are currently suppressed by the system of control (Hypothesis 5). As a result of their short-termism, the big insiders in this enterprise adopted a short-sighted investment strategy, limited to maintaining equipment inherited from Soviet times and eliminating production bottlenecks by introducing second-hand equipment (Hypothesis 7, especially 7c).

6.5 Case Study 2: Medium-Term Big Insiders

This case study focuses on an oil-extracting enterprise which is controlled by a dominant group. Nevertheless, its time horizon is longer than that for a typical Russian company. We will look at the company's ownership structure, which is based on disguised informal mechanisms (Hypothesis 1) and a sophisticated scheme of insider rent extraction through a chain of offshore companies. Then the study will discuss the company's decision-making process as a part of the internal infrastructure of control imposed on the enterprise (Hypothesis 5).

This case study is especially interesting for the insights it provides on the conditions imposed on loans to the Russian corporate sector (Hypothesis 7a). Finally, the time horizon of the big insiders controlling this company will be discussed (Hypothesis 2).

The oil-extracting company JSC Petchoraneft produces crude oil extracted from a few sites in the Archangelskaya *oblast* (district) in the north of Russia. In March 2005, the company had twelve operating oil wells at its main site, which produced 312,000 tons of crude oil annually (Petchoraneft 2005a). At the time of study, Petchoraneft was an expanding company; its major infrastructure had been developed between 2000 and 2004, though more recent developments at this site involved less expensive investments than were previously undertaken. By 2005, Petchoraneft had extracted only 10 per cent of the site's oil reserves (Petchoraneft 2005b).

6.5.1 Disguised Control

The mechanism by which control over the company was exercised is reflected in Figure 6.10. As can be seen, the company's ownership structure was very complicated. Petchoraneft belonged to Nikol Ltd, but 100 per cent of the latter's shares were owned by Petchora Oil Holding Ltd, registered in Cyprus. This company in turn belonged to two organisations established in the British Virgin Islands. It should be noted that with the exception of Petchoraneft, not a single one of the mentioned companies possessed any production capacity. These 'empty' firms only redistributed Petchoraneft's financial flows. In addition, the offshore companies do not reveal their shareholders. Thus, it is impossible to identify the final owners of Petchoraneft, who have effectively disguised themselves behind this 'offshore cloud'.

Decision making on investments was completely centralised in the company's Moscow office (Baker Tilly Rusaudit 2005b: 16): 'Such distribution of responsibilities … assures reliable control over the financial flows and Petchoraneft is a highly centralised organisation with a concentration of the major managerial functions, and particularly of purchases and sales in its head office in Moscow' (ibid.: 12). The regional level of the management was responsible only for current production, or, as the analysts put it, 'material values without overstraining the Moscow office with managing production and construction' (ibid.).

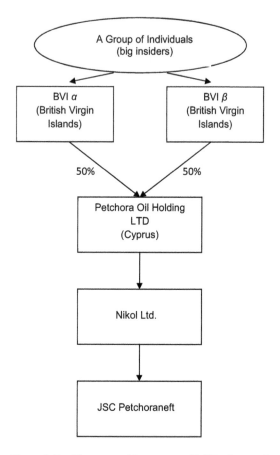

Figure 6.10   The ownership system at JSC Petchoraneft

The names of the companies *BVI* α and *BVI* β are pseudonyms.
Source: private correspondence.

Thus Petchoraneft was characterised by a sophisticated management system and a legal means of securing control by the dominant group over potentially highly profitable assets. From the perspective of the large insiders, these features become desirable as a means of securing regular rent extraction.

6.5.2   Rent Extraction

Of the major ways of withdrawing funds from Petchoraneft, the first is through oil sales (Petchoraneft 2005a). According to analysts, '*JSC*

Petchoraneft transferred ownership of part of its financial flows while selling oil Nearly all its deliveries were conducted through intermediaries including those of its offshore owners' (Baker Tilly Rusaudit 2005b: 54, originial emphasis). This is demonstrated in Table 6.4.

Table 6.4   Major buyers of Petchoraneft on the world market

Company	Essence of contracts	Differential ($ for a barrel)	Country of registration	Return from 2003 to the first quarter 2005 before VAT and export duties ($ mil.)
1. Merk Company Ltd	Provided intermediary services in selling oil	2.5–6.45	Russia	32.8
2. Eastern Oil Trade Ltd	Sold oil in 2004–05	7.4–10.95	British Virgin Islands	9.1
3. Europetroleum Energy SA	Sold oil in 2004–05	3.59–8.85	British Virgin Islands	7.8
4. Sibneft Oil Trade Company Ltd	Sold oil in 2004	5.2	British Virgin Islands	1.2

Rouble sums are converted to US$ using the average exchange rate for the entire period in question.

Source: Baker Tilly Rusaudit 2005b: 49–53.

The price of oil was determined at the level set by the London Commodity Exchange minus a discount. If Russian tax agencies asked why the oil was sold cheaper than the market price, Petchoraneft would reply that the foreign buyer would pay for transportation and hence obtain his profit. Although this sounds reasonable, the trick is that the first buyer did not transport anything, but resold the oil to a real buyer at market prices. The discount was used to accumulate funds in offshore companies (ibid.). A similar scheme was used for deliveries inside Russia. Oil was delivered to the oil-processing enterprises. Not a single delivery was made directly; everything went through the intermediary firms (ibid.: 51–3). For example, the latter sold crude oil to the JSC Moscow Oil-Processing Plant in exchange for petrol, which was later resold. In reality, Petchoraneft was selling oil to intermediaries for prices about 15 per cent lower than the market level, and the difference was accumulated by offshore companies (ibid.).

The second way of extracting funds was connected to the purchase of expensive goods and services. In 2000–04, the offshore company Casita Enterprises Ltd, registered in Cyprus, was paid $6,337,350 for allegedly providing geological services (ibid.: 213). According to the analysts, services of the same quality could be provided by Russian firms at a much cheaper rate. Even worse, there is evidence that these services were fictitious and were used only for conducting financial transactions (ibid.). Another unusual partner for Petchoraneft was a firm hired to estimate the market value of the company's property; the charges for this valuing were much higher than the current market level (ibid.: 217). Thus, Petchoraneft's big insiders created a coherent mechanism for withdrawing funds from the company. The first method permits extraction of funds on a regular basis, whilst the second enables the periodic withdrawal of larger sums of money.

6.5.3   Generation of Investment Funds

According to the consultants, Petchoraneft implements a coherent strategy of modernisation and expansion of its productive capacities in order to secure all the necessary conditions for increasing its rate of crude oil extraction (ibid.: 69). As a result, not only are additional oil wells drilled, but the entire necessary infrastructure is constructed as well. This is the reason why the company has modern fixed capital. The wear and tear of fixed capital belonging to Petchoraneft as a whole amounts to less than 16 per cent of the company's balance sheet value (ibid.), which, as one could have seen earlier, is very low by Russian standards. The created productive capacities permitted increasing oil extraction until 2010, when a gradual decline of production was projected to begin (Petchoraneft 2003: 1). This meant that the major investments at this site had already been undertaken and further large-scale investment would not be necessary. This is an example of large insiders who have a longer-term strategy, whose behaviour reflects this perspective. Nevertheless, their strategy exhibited some features which are not consistent with a long-term maximising organisation.

Analysis of the financial sources for investment in Petchoraneft reveals an unexpected situation. Taking into account that this company belonged to the privileged sector of the Russian economy, one could expect that it relied primarily on internally generated funds for financing its investment. In reality, the company financed its large-scale investment programme through external borrowing. The company's debts grew by nearly 10 per cent on average every quarter from January 2003 to April 2005 (Baker Tilly Rusaudit 2005b: 141). External borrowing had amounted to approximately $58.3 million at the end of this period. At the same time, the residual value of the company's real assets was only $31.8 million as of April 2005 (ibid.: 70). It appears that Petchoraneft's debts were nearly twice the size of its assets. About 83 per cent of the borrowed funds were in long-term foreign currency commitments and about 15 per cent in short-term rouble loans (ibid.). Table 6.5 presents the details of the large credit agreements signed by the company in question as of April 2005.

According to the data in Table 6.5, external borrowing was provided at a very high interest rate, about 10 per cent annually, which was much more expensive than available abroad. Particularly representative is the LIBOR interest rate plus 4.4 per cent. (LIBOR stands for London Interbank Offered Rate and is the benchmark for the short-term interest rates of the world financial markets.) This permits us to single out the volatile component (LIBOR) separating the world market rate from the premium. The latter is nothing less than the risk premium and the provision of loans is accompanied by a complex scheme of guarantees. This includes guarantees agreements and use of securities such as a company's equities, assets, stocks of crude oil and so on. Conditions for providing loans include strict control on the part of banks over the borrower's financial activities. The latter is required to provide, on a regular basis, accounting reports prepared for the taxation bodies; information about the other company's securities and debts and so on. In essence, it is a monitoring of the borrower by the lender.

These strict conditions reflect the specific risks which banks encounter when providing loans to Russian companies. These risks do not include any political risks. Over the time horizon within which these agreements operated – until 2006–07 – no elections or other incidences of social turmoil were envisaged. The high interest rates and the complicated system of securities can be explained by the specific risks incurred with insider control. This was a result of the fundamental instability of this type of corporate governance. Thus Petchoraneft's large insiders could withdraw all the profits, financing their investments with externally borrowed funds. Since the company

Table 6.5 Some of Petchoraneft's debt commitments

Bank lender	Type of commitment	Amount of funds (thousands of US$)	Annual interest rate %	Comments
1. Vnesheconombank	Long-term loan in foreign currency	17,000	Before paying the first instalment 9.5	Loan agreement from 26 April 2004
			And after – 9.0	Date of payment: 27 August 2007
				Security:
				1. Guarantee agreement with JSC Y
				2. Guarantee agreement with JSC Z Holding Co. Ltd (Cyprus)
				Security agreement between the bank and JSC Z Holding Co. Ltd (Cyprus), amounts to $33.9m – 26% ordinary registered shares (51,239 units)
2. Vnesheconombank	Long-term loan in foreign currency	23,000	Before paying the first instalment 9.5	Loan agreement from 27 October 2004
			And after – 9.0	Date of payment: 9 February 2008
				Security:
				1. Guarantee agreement with JSC Z Holding Co. Ltd (Cyprus)
				2. Guarantee agreement with JSC 'A kompaniya'
				3. Agreement between the bank and JSC Z Holding Co. Ltd (Cyprus), ordinary registered shares of the JSC 'X' on the sum of $26.1m – 20% ordinary registered shares (39,415 units)
				4. Agreement on using real estate property (mortgage) as security on the sum of $9.0m.

3. International Moscow Bank Ltd	Long-term loan in foreign currency	10,000	LIBOR rate plus 4.4%	Not later than in 30 calendar days from the signing of the agreement the borrower should insure real estate against all risks of losing and damaging it in favour of the security holder on the sum not less than $8.9m and convey to the security holder the original insurance papers and proofs of insurance payments. Loan agreement from 25 February 2005 for the targeted financing of the current investment projects. Date of payment: 31 December 2006. Security: 1. Agreement on provision of shares as securities between the JSC 'W' and the bank at a sum of $4.5m – 7.73% of ordinary registered shares (16,135 units). 2. Agreement on provision of shares as securities between the R Company Ltd and the bank at sum of $5.5m – 9.45% of ordinary registered shares (19,706 units). 3. Agreement on security at the sum of $1.3m, including equipment on $0.2m, real estate on $1.3m. 4. Agreement on security at the sum of $0.75m – oil goods on the sum of $0.8m
4. Petro-Russo Co. Ltd	Interest rates on debts in foreign currency	10,000	-	Borrowing agreement from 3 August 2003. Date of returning: 3 August 2005. Conditions: 15% annually on the main sum and 5% annually on the sum of problem loans.

Names of some companies have been changed.

Source: Baker Tilly Rusaudit 2005b: 141–8.

in question belonged to the privileged sector of the Russian economy, the external capital market was available to it.

6.5.4   Some Conclusions

From the case study above, one can draw the following conclusions. Petchoraneft's ownership structure showed how the 'offshore cloud' helps to disguise the company's real owners. This means that large insiders, although disguised, could exercise informal control over the enterprise, thus ensuring that the owners maintained a degree of management control (Hypothesis 1). The dominant owners developed a sophisticated scheme of insider rent extraction through a chain of offshore companies. They preferred to extract internally generated funds rather than invest them, which is in itself evidence of their short-term time horizon. Although the company belonged to the privileged sector of the Russian economy, and hence enjoyed higher than average profits, its dominant group rejected long-term growth maximisation in favour of the medium-term period. This is consistent with Hypothesis 2. Rent extraction by Petchoraneft's large insiders created the potential for intensive intra-firm conflicts at this company, which is why decision making was rigorously centralised as a part of the internal infrastructure of control imposed on the enterprise (Hypotheses 4 and 5). Belonging to the privileged sector of the Russian economy, Petchoraneft had access to the external capital market, although high risks associated with insider control led to additional risk premiums charged by lenders (Hypothesis 7).

6.6   Case Study 3: an Acute Struggle Between Big Insiders and Short Termism

This case study analyses the position of the Volgograd JSC Chimprom. The company became the object of a fierce struggle between a few groups of particularly strong big insiders, which is why this case exhibits the nature of informal control (Hypothesis 1) and particularly highlights the role of external infrastructure of control with particular vividness. This example of the instability of control, peculiar to the uncertain domination over this enterprise (Hypothesis 2), enables us to explore how this led to big insiders' withdrawal of particularly large amounts of rent (Hypothesis 3). Against this backdrop, the relatively weak development of the internal infrastructure of control enables us to explore the sophisticated, multi-level system of appropriation of rent by small insiders (Hypotheses 4 and 5). The devastating results which this type of insider control has for investment strategy (Hypothesis 7) is also examined.

6.6.1   The Struggle of Big Insiders for Control Over Chimprom

Only in recent years has the chemical industry become the subject of conflict between Russian big insiders. According to Lemeshko (2006), this was due to the previously low profitability in this sector. Indeed, on average, fixed capital stock has depreciated by 58.8 per cent and more than 60 per cent of its output is uncompetitive in the world market (ibid.). Between 2002 and 2006, events in the world market became favourable for Russian chemical enterprises due to higher energy prices in comparison with Russia's, and the price increase on some chemical materials produced by Russian firms as a result of demand shifting from western European producers (Krjuchkova 2005). A major consequence of this new situation facing the industry was an intensification of the struggle for control over the enterprises by competing groups of big insiders (Seregin 2005). The struggle for control over Chimprom is summarised in Figure 6.11.

The major peculiarity of the Chimprom ownership structure was that 51 per cent of the company's shares were in state ownership (represented by Mingosymuschestvo[14]), while the remainder were traded on the open market (Andronova 2005; Anisimov 2006; Bitsev 2004). As illustrated below, rival groups of big insiders struggled to obtain a blocking holding and control over the top managerial positions. Functionaries from Mingosymuschestvo successfully played on the conflicts between the big insiders. From Soviet times until April 2003, Leonid Kutyanin was VJSC Chimprom's general executive. According to Snigirev (2004), the functionaries from Mingosymushestvo were eager to get rid of him, but this was difficult because Kutyanin was backed by the influential Moscow businessman Valery Khaykin. The latter was the president of the GIVA insurance company and a counsellor to the Ministry of Industry and Science (Minpromnauka), where he had widespread connections with important functionaries. His business methods were based on hostile takeovers of enterprises

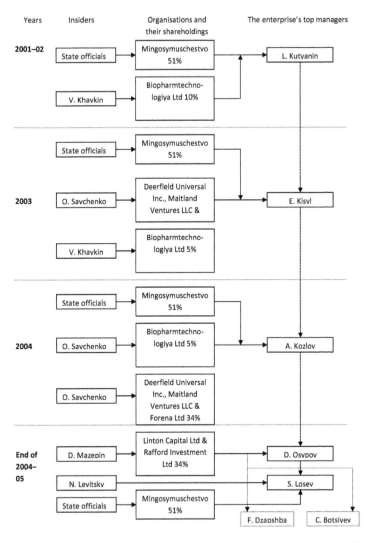

Figure 6.11 Struggle of big insiders for control of Volgograd JSC Chimprom

Source: Drawn from the publications referred to in this section.

followed by asset stripping (ibid.). The cases described by Snigirev are typical examples of rent extraction by very short-term-oriented dominant groups.

The same functionaries from Minpromnauka who helped Khaykin in his takeovers, were the state representatives on Chimprom's Board of

Directors. Every time the issue of Kutyanin's dismissal was raised, these state representatives blocked his removal (ibid.). In the early 2000s, Khaykin declared his aim to create a state pharmaceutical holding under the aegis of Minpromnauka (Lemeshko 2003). The holding was to include Chimprom, as well as other large chemical enterprises. In 2002, Khaykin managed to buy 5.09 per cent of the total amount of shares belonging to the company's trade union (Snigirev 2004), paying only 25 roubles per share (less than US$1 at the time), while a share's market value was 800 roubles (nearly $30) (ibid.). The new owner of the shareholding was Biopharmtechnologia Ltd, which was controlled by Khaykin (Svyatoslavskaya 2004). The Khaykin-Kutyanin group tried not to lose their chances to enrich themselves, as the later prosecution of Kutyanin indicated (Vershinina and Samoilenko 2004). Abuses of power were revealed in various forms, including the theft of finances provided from the federal budget for conversion from military to civilian production at Chimprom (ibid.). In the course of the interregnum following the removal of Kutyanin, a rival group of big insiders joined the struggle.

In 2001, a new group of companies started buying Chimprom's shares. The group was under the control of Oleg Savchenko, owner of the JSC Evropeyskaya Podshipnikovaya Corporatsiya (the European Ball-Bearing Corporation) and a member of the Russian Federation's State Duma (Bitsev 2004). It was reported in the mass media that Savchenko became a big businessman after heading the Chukotka Economy Foundation in the 1990s, from which he had withdrawn $35 million (ibid.). The structures controlled by Savchenko then took over a few ball-bearing companies, whose fixed assets were immediately stripped and parts of their land holdings sold (ibid.). In 2003, Savchenko declared that he intended to create a chemical holding (Kolesnikov 2003), and in that year, he became an owner of 30 per cent of Chimprom's shares (Svyatoslavskaya 2004). In the spring of 2003, as a result of court action, the sale of the trade union's shares to Khaykin was abrogated, and businesses controlled by Savchenko obtained this holding for 10 million roubles (about $342,000 at the time) (ibid.). The new big insider appointed to the position of the Chimprom commercial director was Alexander Mitrofanov, who represented Savchenko's interests (Bitsev 2004). The latter was under legal prosecution for illegally bankrupting another chemical enterprise, where he had previously been a financial director (ibid.). One can infer from this information that Savchenko and Mitrofanov are experienced big insiders, who specialised in hostile takeovers, with a tendency to asset strip their controlled enterprises. Their activities at Chimprom support this conclusion.

As was mentioned in the press, 'As a first step the new shareholders established their control over the current management of the enterprise' (ibid.). Kutyanin was temporarily left in his position of general executive, but the real control shifted to the commercial director Mitrofanov (ibid.). Also in 2003, after entrenching his position in the company, Savchenko initiated his struggle against Kutyanin (Lemeshko 2003). Auditing revealed significant abuses of power by the executives (see below) and Kutyanin was displaced, with his functions transferred to Evgeny Kysil who was associated with Savchenko (Kolesnikov 2003).

Meanwhile, Khaykin was backed in his struggle against Savchenko's grouping by external powerful forces, namely all those whose incomes were jeopardised by the impending change in ownership: functionaries, who had previously benefited from bribes, bankers involved in investing 'conversion' money, intermediaries helping to transfer finances, 'roofs' covering the participants, and even the governor of Volgogradskaya *oblast* (Volgograd) Maksyuta (Vershinia and Samoylenko 2004). The most important support was provided by governmental functionaries at the highest level. Under Mikhail Kasyanov (Russian Prime Minister, May 2000–February 2004), this role was played by Kopeykin, deputy head of the federal government machinery (apparatus); Svinarenko, former first deputy of Minpromnauka; Milovidov, the financial markets' department head, and director of property relations of the federal government machinery (ibid.), and Ivanov, department head of the chemical industry's industrial and innovation policy in Minpromnauka (Snigirev 2004). These powerful functionaries recommended that Prime Minister Kasyanov replace Chimprom's general director (Vershinia and Samoylenko 2004). Their candidate was Aleksey Kozlov, who had never worked in the industry and had no production management experience at all, but did represent the interests of Khaykin's group (ibid.). To weaken their rivals, Khaykin's group initiated a criminal prosecution of the former executives and Kysil was sued for inflicting damage on Chimprom amounting to

600 million roubles (about $20.1 million at the end of 2003); Kysil was eventually sentenced to three years' imprisonment suspended (Osyka 2005).

This was a serious blow for Savchenko, but further events have shown that he also had powerful allies in state structures (Bitsev 2004). Kozlov's appointment was opposed by Guslev, the deputy minister of property relations; Borodin, adviser to the same minister and the chair of Chimprom's board of directors, and Medvedev, the former first deputy of the same minister (ibid.). However, despite their high positions in the governmental hierarchy, they failed to protect Savchenko, and in March 2004, Kozlov became Chimprom's general executive (Snigirev 2004). The company's new head immediately instigated court actions against the offshore companies, representing Savchenko among the shareholders (Savyatoslavskaya 2004), and their shares were suspended (Lemeshko 2003). The struggle of the Khaykin and Savchenko groups for control over Chimprom demonstrates the importance of an external infrastructure of control which plays a crucial role in securing control over enterprises in Russia. The nature of these institutions reflects their informal character.

Meanwhile, the Khaykin group's triumph was only short-lived. In November 2004, Savchenko's disputed shares were bought by another pair of offshore companies: Linton Capital Ltd and Rafford Investment Ltd, which were controlled by a famous businessman and former state functionary, Dmytri Mazepin (Kommersant 2005). In the 1990s, Mazepin occupied a number of top managerial positions in big companies and successively was: an adviser, a deputy, and the first deputy chairman of the Russian Federal Property Fund (Andronova 2005). In 2004, in his role as a director of Construction Bureau Ltd, he announced his plan to create a holding in the chemical industry and started buying large shareholdings in this sector's companies (Gileva 2005). Chimprom was of interest to Mazepin because it was a supplier to enterprises he had already purchased (Seregin 2005). Kozlov, in November 2004, retired from his position as Chimprom's general executive and became a member of the board of directors in one of Mazepin's other companies (Regnum 2005), which meant that he left Khaykin for a more promising employer. In any case, Khaykin was crowded out of Chimprom. Despite this achievement, imposing his own control over the enterprise proved to be a much more difficult task for Mazepin. He was promoting both candidates suggested for the general executive position – Osipov and Dzapshba – and the first was appointed only temporarily (*Kommertcheskaya Nedvijimost* 2006). The reason for this was that Mazepin's control over Chimprom was being challenged by new, strong rivals.

These rivals were led by a young, ambitious businessman, Nikolay Levitsky. His rapid rise in Russian big business was connected to classic hostile takeovers in the 1990s with the widespread usage of law-enforcing agencies in pressuring shareholders reluctant to give up their property rights (Komrakov and Stolyarov 2005; Efimova 2005). In 2004, Levitsky, together with a famous Russian oligarch Victor Vekselberg, established a chemical company Synntech Group. Vekselberg was listed as one of the ten wealthiest people in Russia, with business interests in oil, non-ferrous metallurgy, banking and other industries (NEWSru.com 2004). The two partners started creating their own group of chemical companies using the same methods to pressurise shareholders and managers (Efimova 2005). The interests of Mazepin and the Levitsky-Vekselberg groups clashed in a number of chemical companies (Malkova 2005; Anisimov 2006; Komrakov and Stolyarov 2005; Efimova 2005), as illllustrated in Figure 6.12. This struggle with powerful rivals complicated Mazepin's obtaining control over Chimprom. In June 2005, his protégé Osipov was forced to retire and a new figure was appointed as a temporary general executive – Losev (Vestnik Chimproma 2005), who was regarded as representing the Levitsky-Vekselberg group's interests (Osyka 2005).

The complicated situation at Chimprom exemplifies modern Russian business practices. The Mazepin group possesses a blocking shareholding, while Letitsky-Vekselberg has seized control over the management. This means that neither of the two groups is entrenched at the enterprise. All these rival groups of big insiders managed to establish control over Chimprom for only a brief time period, which inevitably led to a short-term orientation and induced them to withdraw as much finance as they could.

6.6.2 Rent Extraction by Big Insiders

Although the methods and size of rent withdrawals are disguised by big insiders, some information came into the public domain

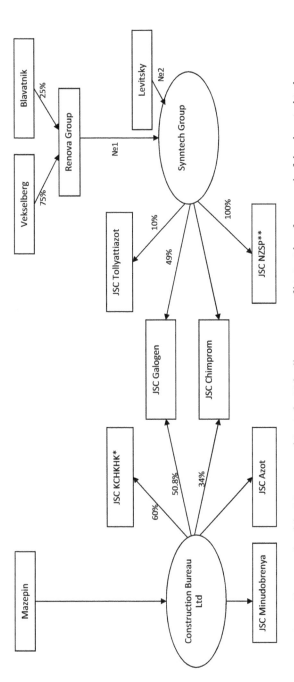

Figure 6.12 The struggle of the Mazepin and Levitsky-Vekselberg groups of big insiders for control of the chemical industry

JSC KCHKHK – JSC Kirovo-Chepetsky Chimitchesky Combinat after B. Konstantinov
JSC NZSP – JSC Novocherkassky Zavod Syntetitcheskykh Productov

Percents above the arrows show the share holdings of the two rival groups in the corresponding companies.

Based on the following sources: Malkova 2005, Anisimov 2006, Komrakov and Stolyarov 2005, Efimova 2005.

due to revelations instigated by rivals. It appears that the Khaykin-Kutyanin group specialised in the theft of state finances which had been provided for conversion from military to civilian production (Vershinia and Samoylenko 2004). Of the $2–5 million provided annually for conversion in the period 1999–2002, not more than 50 per cent was actually spent for this purpose. The claimed expenditure on conversion was four times greater than the actual cost and theft amounted to millions of dollars (ibid.). In 2002, auditors found that obviously ruinous bond schemes were financed, prices manipulated and the profitability of the enterprise that year dropped from 16.48 to 0.52 per cent (Kolesnikov 2003).

The Savchenko-Kisyl group was no better. It appropriated part of the finances provided for some target programmes, for instance, a part of $63 million issued by the US government for eliminating the chemical weapons stored at Chimprom (Bitsev 2004). In 2003, a strategic stock of coke disappeared (about $369,000); 30 million roubles (about $1 million) from the Russian government, also provided for eliminating chemical weapons, were withdrawn; the building of the enterprise's central office building was sold for 6 million roubles (about $201,00) without authorisation, and so on (Trofimov 2004). According to the new general executive Kozlov (2004), the enterprise was preparing for a feigned bankruptcy, which would mean no taxes or wages would be paid. The Savchenko-Kisyl group's major channel for extracting rent from Chimprom was 'Chimpromtrading' Ltd (ibid.). Ostensibly, this trading company was established to sell Chimprom products for a very modest remuneration (ibid.). However the real role of this firm was very different (Trofimov 2004). The functions of both purchases and sales were passed to Chimpromtrading. It has been previously explained that these are two classical methods for extracting rent by big insiders. Price manipulation ensued. According to the new general executive, 'Prices were significantly either overvalued or undervalued in favour of the trading house' (Kozlov 2004). For instance, technical soda was sold to Chimpromtrading at a price 60 per cent less than the market level (ibid.). In total, from April 2003 to March 2004, Chim-promtrading obtained 600 million roubles profit (about $21.1 million in 2003), while Chimprom losses amounted in 2004 to 155 million roubles (about $5.2 million) (Bitsev 2004). As a result, by March 2004, the recurring finances of the enterprise were reduced to 20 per cent of their norm. This means that the Savchenko group was preparing Chimprom for bankruptcy, in order to later purchase it at a negligible price (Kozlov 2004).

Under general executive Losev, the situation did not change radically. The enterprise's products were still sold to intermediaries at undervalued prices (Osyka 2005). As a result of six months of his tenure, Losev reduced Chimprom to a nearly bankrupt state. According to Gubkin, a member of the State Duma, this was a 'premeditated decrease of the assets value prior to privatisation [of the state shareholding] in the interests of the particular individuals desiring to obtain Chimprom at a cheap price'. By 'particular individuals', Gubkin meant the Levitsky-Vekselberg group (ibid.). How rent extraction by big insiders affected Chimprom's financial flows can be seen from Table 6.6.

Table 6.6   Profits and losses of Chimprom

Variable	2000	2001	2002	2003	2004	First quarter 2005
Gross revenue, thousands of roubles	2,302,776	2,760,515	2,781,522	2,636,495	3,158,967	859,173
Gross profit, thousands of roubles	555,421	721,840	416,637	342,010	516,885	82,652
Net profit after taxes	74,057	153,990	4,554	178,107	115,662	−25,352

(residual profit, loss), thousands of roubles

Source: Chimprom 2005: 22–3.

The data show the company's persistent decline of return and profit in the last five years. In this period, as has been shown above, the industry had experienced recovery along with the economy as a whole. Meanwhile, net profit turned into losses at Chimprom over this period. Due to this, profitability of the firm's own capital declined from 12.9 in 2001 to −8.2 per cent in 2004, and profitability of both fixed assets and sales became negative; in 2003, Chimprom's losses per share amounted to $8.70, and in 2004, $6.00 (Chimprom 2005: 22–3). At the same time, it should be noted that in 2004, the return on sales had grown by 19.8 per cent compared with the previous year, and production price at the same period increased by 18.3 per cent (ibid.). Hence, even the increase in the company's income was more than offset by rent extraction and tax payments.

6.6.3   Rent Extraction by Small Insiders

The large amounts of rent extracted by big insiders from Chimprom were accompanied by opportunistic behaviour among its employees and managers. Weaknesses in Chimprom's management contributed to this. The accounting information from the production departments is largely false. There are a number of reasons for this. In 2004, more than 80 per cent of control equipment at the enterprise had exceeded its designed product lifespan and was obsolete (Baker Tilly Rusaudit 2004: 8). This led to inaccurate measurement of raw materials stocks, and accounting for internal flows of materials was much worse than accounting for external deliveries (ibid.: 15–16). The internal accounting system did not allow for control of production inputs and created ample opportunities for falsifying accounting (ibid.: 19). One glaring flaw in the managerial system was that individuals who potentially had the opportunity for theft, oversaw the people tasked with accounting (ibid.: 16). Accounting procedures were of low quality and were open to abuse (ibid.: 15). Comparing this deeply flawed management system with Volgakabel and Petchoraneft's highly efficient centralised systems, one can infer that the acute struggle of big insiders may have been a factor that prevented them from establishing a reliable internal infrastructure of control. Chimprom's small insiders tried to retain their chances for financial gain.

In 2003–04, a whole hierarchy of theft by small and medium-sized insiders was established at Chimprom (Makeyev 2005). At the lowest level, theft was organised by rank-and-file workers trying to supplement their low wages by spiriting away the company's tools, construction materials and any products which had market value. At the second level were foremen and the shop-floor heads. Using the gaps in the accounting system, discussed above, they overvalued expenditure on materials in the production process, appropriating the excessive materials. Later, using the company's workforce, they produced additional products from the appropriated materials and equipment, and sold them on. The next level of theft emerged when opportunists from the production departments established connections with their colleagues in the central office, especially the purchasing department. The production departments ordered raw materials which were allegedly used in production in their partners' shops. In reality, no materials were bought, the money was shared among the group of small insiders, and fictitiously included in production costs. The next level consisted of medium insiders from the company's central office, who established their own firms, providing raw materials to, and/or purchasing products of, Chimprom. Their method of rent extraction, through price manipulation, was essentially the same as that used by big insiders, the difference only being the scale of these activities (ibid.).

As can be seen from this example, small and medium-sized insiders extract their portion of rent due to their control over various components of the company's financial flows, just as their big insider colleagues do. For this purpose, they have even established partnerships and firms that can be treated as the elements of their own infrastructure of control and rent extraction.

6.6.4   Fixed Assets and the Character of Chimprom's Investments

The main indicator of the time horizon and investment strategy of the big insiders, who have dominated Chimprom, is the condition of the company's productive capacity, which is illustrated in Table 6.7. Chimprom's accounts show the high level of wear-and-tear of the company's fixed assets, which lost more than 60 per cent of their original value. Note that machinery, tools and equipment are very heavily degraded, by more than 70 per cent of their original value. However, these figures do not reveal the full picture; as was explained in Section 1.2, old fixed assets are generally undervalued in Russia, while new assets are valued at current prices. As a result, the value of fixed assets is artificially lowered, which helps to reduce property taxes. This undervaluation of assets is probably the reason why it was announced at Chimprom's Board of Directors' meeting that the wear-and-tear of its fixed assets as a whole in 2005 amounted to 80 per cent (Sokolova 2005). This figure itself is an indicator of short-termism and a deeply flawed investment strategy.

For example, the water supply and circulation system, vital for chemical production, was constructed as early as the 1950–60s, and

Table 6.7 Value, structure, and wear and tear of Chimprom's fixed assets*

Type of fixed assets	Replacement value** (US$ millions)***	Percentage share of the whole stock	Size of depreciation*** (US$ millions)	Percentage share of the whole stock	Wear and tear in %
1. Buildings	68.5	57.75	37.9	51.55	55.29
2. Machinery, tools and equipment	44.8	37.72	32.4	44.04	72.32
3. Transport	5.4	4.53	3.2	4.41	60.41
4. Other fixed assets	0.9	0.75	0.2	0.27	2.23
Replacement value in whole, and depreciation in total	118.7		73.5		
Wear-and-tear in total					61.94

*   As of 1 April 2005.

**   Replacement value is measured in mixed prices: old equipment in prices at the last re-evaluation of fixed assets and new equipment in current prices.

***   The corresponding sums in roubles were converted to US$ at the exchange rate of 28.5 to 1, which was the going rate in the middle of 2005.

Source: Chimprom 2005, p. 21.

has since then only been maintained, not replaced (Roptanova 2004a). In 2005, carbide production at Chimprom was the biggest in Europe, and yielded net profits which off-set losses of a number of other production lines (Roptanova 2004b). Despite the vital importance of this particular production line, it also dates back to the 1950–60s and was continually under repair (ibid.). Investments were only undertaken in cases when equipment, which was yielding significant profits, was at the edge of breaking down completely (see, for example, Maximova 2004; Roptanova 2005). One of Chimprom's shop-floor heads, Knyazev, commented:

> At our enterprise the major productive equipment is overwhelmingly obsolete. Due to various reasons it often breaks down. Meanwhile almost no funds were provided in recent years to purchase any new equipment. The approach to the provision of raw materials was similar – they were purchasing what was cheapest. (Maximova 2004)

6.6.5 Some Conclusions

The struggle for informal control over Chimprom was focused on its top management positions, which suggests that it precluded the separation of ownership and control (Hypothesis 1). In this case, the informal control of big insiders was particularly unstable (Hypothesis 2). This led to a short-term time horizon and intensive rent extraction from the company's financial flows (Hypothesis 3). Withdrawal of funds by big insiders, under relatively weak internal infrastructure of control, induced a four-tier system of rent extraction by small and medium-sized insiders, thus demonstrating an increase in intra-firm conflicts (Hypotheses 4 and 5). This short-term time orientation and a large-scale rent extraction caused a deficient investment strategy. Chimprom's big insiders elected to favour cheap investment projects of inferior quality with relatively short pay-back periods (Hypothesis 7).

6.7 Conclusion

In this chapter, some empirical evidence has been provided to substantiate the hypotheses based on the main propositions of the Russian model of corporate governance suggested in this book. The lack of direct data on the informal relationships peculiar to Russian enterprises, and unreliability of the official data on accumulation of capital in Russia (see Section 6.2) compelled us to rely on surveys of Russian companies and a number of case studies. These provided insights into the intrinsic mechanisms of Russian enterprises from different perspectives.

Hypothesis 1 was that informal control was associated with the inseparability of ownership and management. All three case studies have provided evidence on this connection. However, whether the causal link is that (a) the former causes the latter, or (b) the reverse, cannot be conclusively deduced from this study. As has already been mentioned above (Section 6.2), these two hypotheses are observationally equivalent. Nevertheless, the Chimprom case suggests that the inseparability of ownership and management in this company was not an aim in itself for the rival groups of big insiders, but was a by-product of their efforts to impose their domination over the company.

Hypothesis 2, stating that the fundamental instability of insider control leads to a short-term time horizon of large insiders, was supported by all three case studies. The case of Chimprom demonstrates that in the course of a severe struggle for control, the rival groups of dominant owners did not concern themselves with long-term investment strategies. The case of Volgakabel suggests that even if the rival groups reach a temporary alliance, they are too suspicious about their rival's potential opportunistic behaviour to develop any sound long-term investment policy. However, the case of a relatively prosperous company, namely Petchoraneft, indicated that with stable insider control, large insiders can adopt a longer-term time horizon.

Hypothesis 3 maintained that the shorter the time horizon of big insiders, the greater the share of the firm's funds extracted as rent. This could not be demonstrated conclusively, because large insiders of all three companies maximised the present value of present and future rent extraction. Even Petchoraneft, belonging to the privileged sector of the Russian economy, financed its investment through borrowed money, which suggests that all the profit was withdrawn from the company. Thus, the proposition that longer-term-oriented large insiders extract less rent in the short run is based only on logical considerations. The author hopes to investigate this problem more rigorously in future.

Hypothesis 4 expressed the idea that the greater the portion of a firm's financial flows appropriated by large insiders, the more intensive are the intra-firm conflicts. In the case of Chimprom, where short-term rent extraction was particularly high, evidence was found of highly developed opportunistic practices, leading even to small and medium-sized insiders creating elements of their own infrastructure of control. In the case of Volgakabel, it has been shown that prior to establishing a highly developed internal infrastructure of control, this enterprise suffered from widespread theft. Petchoraneft has a highly centralised decision-making management, capable of preventing any abuses on the part of small insiders. Nothing is known about whether this company experienced a period of significant opportunism from its employees in the past, but it is surmised that the privileged-sector companies, with greater financial flows at their disposal, can pay higher wages and thus decrease the potential for intra-firm conflicts.

Hypothesis 5 argued that the greater the potential for intra-firm conflicts, the greater is the infrastructure of control developed. The Volgakabel case study demonstrated how the development of the infrastructure of control reduced small insiders' previous disruptive and criminal activities. This suggests that the current internal infrastructure of control corresponds to the potential threat of opportunism, the size of which can be estimated from the previous experience. Lack of a reliable internal infrastructure at Chimprom left the activities of small and medium insiders unchecked.

Hypothesis 6 asserted that increased intra-firm conflicts increase the probability of a hostile takeover. None of the three case studies provide significant evidence to support this proposition. However, when the large insiders' conflicts with workers were discussed in Chapter 4, it was demonstrated how a rival group of large insiders tried to take over VCBK, exploiting worker unrest. In addition, the four levels of opportunistic behaviour found at Chimprom suggest that small insiders are able to accumulate capital, just like their big-insider colleagues, and even eventually become medium-size insiders. Theoretically, this can lead to challenging the entrenched group's dominant position on the part of medium insiders.

Hypothesis 7 maintained that the shorter the time horizon of big insiders and the greater the portion of funds attributable to rent extraction, the lower will be the size and the quality of the firm's investment. The surveys (see Section 6.3) provided evidence of the deficiency in Russian corporations' investment strategies. They suggest that the majority of Russian enterprises consider their investment insufficient to sustain their effective long-term growth. The other survey reveals that Russian enterprises do not consider a shortage of effective productive capacity to be a significant limitation to their increase in production, even in conditions of the national economy's recovery. This apparent contradiction is resolved by data demonstrating that Russian companies find cheap ways to expand their fixed assets, for example, investing in low-quality equipment. This suggests that inferior investment strategies are predominant in the Russian economy's corporate sector. Though the general evidence from the surveys implies short-termism, it does not establish a direct link to flawed investment strategies. Such direct links are provided by case studies. Volgakabel and Chimprom demonstrate classical examples of short-termism, while Petchoraneft's narrative illustrates that even big insiders of the privileged sector are limited to a medium-term time horizon.

In conclusion, the particular type of corporate governance peculiar to modern Russian corporations has become a major institutional obstacle to the investment required for the national economy's effective economic growth.

Conclusion

The conundrum of Russian capitalism was formulated in the current work as follows: why are Russian owners not interested in long-term investments and make their choice in favour of inferior investments? As I attempted to show in this book, the answer can be found only in the nature of the new social system which emerged in post-Soviet Russia. On the one hand, the nascent Russian capitalism is rooted in the degeneration of Stalinist bureaucracy which increasingly obtained informal control over economic resources under central planning. On the other hand, it is rooted in the influence of financialised western capitalism, in which corporations seek to maximise short-term shareholder value rather than long-term growth. These double origins of Russian capitalism are captured by the notion of insider rent, being a type of short-term income appropriated by the dominant groups due to their control over the firms' financial flows.

Being a concrete form of surplus value, insider rent reflects the essence, the most characteristic features, of modern Russian society. This type of income is a sort of 'genetic code' of Russian capitalism, embodied in all its major organs. It was demonstrated that insider rent withdrawal determines the firms' objectives, the system of inter- and intra-firm conflicts, the time horizon of management, the investment strategies of companies, the price structure in the economy and, eventually, the mechanism of economic growth. As a consequence of the 'ascent from abstract to concrete', Russian capitalism is understood not as a chaotic heap of particular phenomena and processes, but as an ordered social system, demonstrating organic unity and inner logic of composition. Last, but not least, the insider rent model illustrates the limitations of capitalism as a social system, and serves as a proof of the historical necessity to seek an alternative development path.

Indeed, from the perspective of Russian capitalism provided in the present work, one may conclude that the radical market reforms failed, if one assumes that their aim was to establish a more efficient economic system than the Soviet one. Indeed, if the insider model suggested in the current book is correct, than the tendency to technological stagnation and worker impoverishment is imprinted in Russian big business's very foundations. This means that the Russian people's bitter experience of the last two decades rehabilitates the *relative* value of national planning.

The same lesson can be drawn from international experience. The core western countries managed to overcome the 'Great Depression' of the 1930s through adopting Keynesian-style state regulation of the national economy, without doubt prompted greatly by the Soviet experience. In contrast, 'deregulation', beginning in the 1980s, led to the current world economic crisis. Although there were growing indications of the coming financial meltdown, neoclassical mainstream economists failed to discern them and to realise their importance. This testifies that *economic thinking that considers markets as self-sufficient and rejects planning offhand does not fit modern society's needs*. From this arises the issue of developing an alternative model of a planned-market economy, in which social control over big business is established, while regulation of prices, profits and wages secures the conditions of long-term growth.

The above does not mean that the author suggests a simple return to Soviet-pattern planning. As was demonstrated above (see ch. 2), Soviet planning was characterised by overcentralisation, limiting the economic activities of the masses, and by the arbitrary power of the state bureaucracy. This led to the USSR's failure in its economic competition with the West and facilitated the onset of the big insiders. Instead, I suggest seeking an optimal combination of planning and the market. This combination's particular arrangements can be discovered only through learning-by-doing. However, some major features of the new system can be anticipated by theoretical analysis.

Planomernost as an economic notion means the deliberately maintained proportionality of the national economy.[1] Planomernost stems from Marxian reproduction schemes, in which economic growth was treated as a result of the interplay of the different departments (sectors, industries) of the national economy. Proportionality means the state of balance, of the harmonised structure of different spheres of the economy. The most important external indication of proportionality is full employment of labour and technical resources. The value and technological conditions of growth (see ch. 5) reflect proportionality from the perspectives of the price structure and technologies. I believe that this can be achieved in the framework of some sort of 'plan-market' economic model.

Such a model possesses a number of particular features. *The social essence* of the plan-market economy is determined by *domination of labour*, which loses its nature as hired labour and becomes something which can be called 'possessive labour'.[2] *The main objective* of the model in question is maximisation of labour welfare through the increase of both real wages and public goods (medicine, education, defence, law enforcement, sustainable environment and the like). The major condition of this is public control over the simultaneous determination of prices, investments and wages in the corporate sector. In consequence, the value and technological conditions of growth will be met. Such a system has some important institutional preconditions.

One possible approach to reforming corporate governance in order to address the problem of insider control and intra-firm conflict in Russian corporations would be to implement the continental model as opposed to the American model. The essence of a new system of corporate governance is to search for a compromise between the interests of the different stakeholders while recognising their legal rights. The first precondition for this is judicial reform, making law enforcement effective, including the enforcement of contractual commitments through the courts. Apart from that, this new system of law enforcement should fight corruption, and thus destroy the external infrastructure of control of big insiders. This new Russian system of corporate governance could take into account the advantages of the continental model. The German system can provide an important clue as to how to move the controlling power over management from big insiders to other stakeholders.

In Germany, there is typically a two-tier Board of Directors model made up of 'supervisory' and 'managerial' bodies (Henderson 1993: 280–82). This so-called 'co-determination' means that if a company has more than 2,000 employees, its supervisory board is formed by representatives of shareholders and workers on equal terms (ibid.). The supervisory board elects and controls the Board of Directors. With such a system, the power exercised by Russian big insiders over their enterprises would be undermined if supervisory boards were introduced which represented employees, minority shareholders, banks, consumers and the state. These measures can help destroy the internal infrastructure of control on the part of big insiders. Here one can draw some lessons from the recent reforms of corporate governance in Europe and the US.

The major perceived problem with corporate governance in Europe is connected to the existence of a dominant shareholder who controls the majority of votes (Morck et al. 2005). On the one hand, a dominant owner has power to control managers; on the other, he or she can abuse this power, using corporate resources for their own advantage and damaging the minority shareholders' interests (ibid.). This moves the continental system closer to the Russian situation. One of the major abuses of power by a dominant shareholder is 'self-dealing' or 'tunnelling' (Johnson et al., 2000). This refers to the transfer of value from the companies, even where the owner possesses only a small portion of the cash-flow rights, to a company where he possesses a large portion of such rights (ibid.). This is very similar to one rent extraction method practiced by Russian big insiders. A notorious example of expropriation of a company's resources by the dominant shareholder using self-dealing is the Parmalat case of 2003 (Enriques and Volpin 2007: 123–5).

In the wake of such conflicts, a number of corporate law reforms were enacted in France, Germany and Italy. Strengthening internal governance mechanisms through increasing the Board of Directors' power in organising auditing, disclosure of information and the like, seeks to give directors more ability to challenge dominant shareholders (Denis and McConnell 2003). Recent developments in US law increase the minority shareholders' role in corporate governance (Bebchuk 2005), while other revisions to corporate law in both Europe and the US have imposed on companies additional obligations to disclose information in four key areas: a) corporate governance; b) self-dealing and insider trading; c) executives' compensation; d) financial reporting (Enriques and Volpin 2007: 134–6). Another area of reform is the strengthening of public enforcement structures, including the supervisory authority's powers, sanctions in cases of market abuse, enforcement of financial reporting and auditing, and imposing on corporations a code of conduct guiding their behaviour (Paine et al. 2005). The Sarbanes-Oxley Act adopted by the US Congress in 2002 revises regulations covering the auditing of US public companies. According to this act, the Public Company Accounting Oversight

Board (PCAOB), which oversees and regulates auditing, must enlist auditors 'to enforce existing laws against theft and fraud by corporate officers' (Coates 2007: 91). In addition, this law 'required CEOs to sign off on their companies' financial statements, strengthened the role of the Board of Directors, forbade cosy relationships between accountants and executives, and mandated that companies and their auditors assess the effectiveness of internal control' (Feldman 2005: 134).

These developments in western corporate law give a clue to the major reforms needed in Russia. The introduction of a 'co-determination' system of the German type would enable a supervisory board to represent presently disenfranchised groups: employees, minority shareholders, consumers, suppliers, lenders and state officials at municipal and/or federal levels. Being empowered to elect and monitor the activities of the company's Board of Directors and top-tier managers, the supervisory board would be a representative body for seeking a compromise of interests of the different stakeholders. Public disclosure of information is another important aspect of western experience which is relevant here. In Russia, this should be aimed at information which is crucial to reveal big insiders' hidden activities. This should include the obligatory disclosure of shareholders' interests in offshore companies as a necessary precondition to eliminate the 'offshore clouds' which disguise the ultimate owners of Russian businesses. Information about firms' financial flows should be susceptible to rigorous scrutiny by members of supervisory boards. The latter should be empowered to control companies' major dealings with intermediary firms, monitoring their prices and other conditions of these deals. To counter these auditing companies being dominated by big insiders, the Russian Federation's Accounting Chamber should be given the same powers as the American PCAOB in overseeing activities of the companies providing these services. Such measures can change the dominant pattern of corporate governance in Russia, making key decision making, including decisions on investment, more open and less susceptible to informal control. As a result, the current inseparability of ownership and control would be weakened, and the combined power of stakeholders' interest will gradually replace big insiders' domination over enterprises. In that case, the instability of insider control will be removed and the institutional preconditions for a longer-term time horizon of management may emerge.

These measures can potentially provide the institutional foundations for a new system of indicative planning as indeed formulated in Eichner's approach (1976: 278–88). The latter is based on his megacorp model, assuming that decisions on the distribution of a firm's income, investment and pricing are made simultaneously (see Ch. 1). The key to this system is an industrial committee, where representatives of the state, managers, shareholders and trade unions seek compromise on the level of wages, investments and prices in the planning period. This gives a clue to the creation of conditions which prevent the appropriation of rent by any dominant group, while securing a balance of the long-term interests of stakeholders. Such a system should eliminate the privileged sector's favourable price structure.

The main aim of the suggested public policy measures taken as a whole is to create the institutional and external preconditions for the Russian economy's long-term growth, increasing the welfare of the Russian population, not the corrupted elite.

Notes

Introduction

1. This is how the official version of Marxism-Leninism was referred to in the Soviet Union.
2. *Zeitschrift für Weltgeschichte*, 2009, Vol. 10, No. 2.
3. I prefer to label the social system which actually existed in the USSR 'the Soviet system' rather than 'Communism', 'Socialism', or 'State socialism', since the degree to which it was socialist is debatable.

1 Global Accumulation and the Capitalist World-system

1. This is an exemplary exercise in the Hegelian dialectics of quality and quantity (see his *Science of Logic*). Taken from the standpoint of its quality, or of its useful application in a particular branch of the economy, labour manifests itself in a concrete form. In this sense, it is heterogeneous. But taken from the standpoint of its quantity, or of the expenditure of a worker's muscular and nervous energy, labour manifests itself in a purely abstract form. In this sense, it is absolutely homogeneous across different industries.
2. This is simply another manifestation of the duality of labour, from which the double nature of capital originates at the new stage of ascent from the abstract to the concrete. Neoclassical theoreticians grope their way toward this idea when they strive to reconcile the obvious heterogeneity of capital in its physical form with the necessity to treat it as an absolutely homogeneous, malleable good: every second new drops of water tumble down, but Niagara remains the same. It is not that these theoreticians engage in a vague, unintentional search for an understanding of the dialectical nature of capital, but that they fail to distinguish between the two aspects of labour, making the neoclassical metaphor meaningless. From this standpoint, Joan Robinson's critique of the homogeneity assumption of the neoclassical theory of capital is relevant, but should be seen as transitional to a Marxian approach that embraces both aspects of reality.
3. The fact that FDI skyrocketed after the collapse of the Soviet system says a lot about the nature of the Cold War. It is commonly maintained in the West that the capitalist world confronted the 'moral evil' of communism. There is no need to deny that Soviet society suppressed human rights. This was morally unacceptable not only from a liberal, but still more so from a Marxian perspective. But as the above citations and data on FDI testify, the USSR restricted the ability of the global capitalist system to exploit vast populations in whole regions of the world. With the demise of the Soviet

Union, the forces of capital were released unfettered and on a global scale, increasing human suffering across the world and bringing about the quick degeneration of world capitalism into a largely unproductive, parasitic system. Though by no means a perfect society, the USSR nevertheless represented an obstacle to the 'moral evil' of capitalism.

4. Readers might be puzzled by the notion of negative net dividends, which in the crisis years of 2008 and 2009 years exceeded −300 per cent. Net dividends mean gross dividends minus taxes, and refer to the sum of money actually obtained by a shareholder. The practice is now widespread of paying dividends partly in cash and partly in shares. This remarkable fact reflects the situation in which a bullish stock market means shareholders are interested less in dividends per se than in growing share prices. While obtaining only part of their dividends in cash, shareholders must pay taxes on the whole sum of their income. If, for instance, only 10 per cent of dividends are paid in cash and the tax rate is 30 per cent, the net dividend will be negative in the sum of −20 per cent of gross income (see more in Cassidy 2009).

5. The term 'moral hazard' refers to a propensity for offsetting risk using other people's money, if the possible adverse consequences can be shifted to a third party. For instance, if an investment fund manager happens to be a relative of a finance minister or some other influential state functionary, then the fund may be in a position to undertake highly risky speculative operations. In the best case scenario, the fund is profitable, while in a bad case, it can count on government help. The classical case of moral hazard is the massive bailout, after the onset of the 2008–09 crisis, of US banks that were considered 'too big to fail'.

6. The neoclassical 'marginal productivity' theory of distribution maintains that in a market economy both capital and labour are remunerated strictly according to their contribution to production (by their corresponding marginal products, in neoclassical parlance). Hence, no one can be exploited under capitalism.

7. This was expressed brilliantly by the unorthodox Bolshevik Victor Serge: 'The enemies of the working class have adopted Marx's contribution very widely. Rulers, industrial and financial potentates, and mob leaders at times urge the burning of Marx's works and throw Marxists in jail, but they understand social realities no less well than Marxist economists and politicians. While their hired professorate refutes the theory of surplus value, they defend the share withdrawn by the privileged classes from society's income with no less energy and determination' (Serge 2001: 129–30).

8. Here the reference is to the workforce producing goods for export.

9. 'The world may be moving inexorably toward one of those tragic moments that will lead future historians to ask, why was nothing done in time? Were the economic and policy elites unaware of the profound disruption that economic and technological change were causing working men and women? What prevented them from taking the steps necessary to prevent a global social crisis?' (Kapstein 1996: 18).

2 From Central Planning to Capitalism

1. The social system which resulted from the Russian revolution of 1917 is often referred to as: 'Communism', 'Socialism', or 'State socialism'. These terms are obscure due to the difference attributed to them in different schools of thought. Also, to what extent the USSR was socialist is a highly controversial issue. (See opinion of the present author below.) That is why in this book the term 'The Soviet social system' or 'The Soviet system' will be used to designate the actual society which existed in the USSR.

2. Sergey Vitte (1849–1915) was the Russian finance minister (1892–1903) and later the Chair of the Committee of Ministers (1903–06) and the Chair of the Council of Ministers (1905–06). He introduced the 'gold standard' to Russia in 1897, to attract foreign capital in nascent Russian industry. Due to this arrangement, foreign capital was able to obtain profits investments in Russia in gold.

3. In 1861, the per capita national income in constant prices was in Britain 4.5 times, in the US 6.3 times, in Germany 2.5 times, and in France 2.1 times higher, than in Russia. In 1913, this lag reached 4.9, 8.7, 3.1 and 2.5 times correspondingly (Gregory 1982: 155–7). Notwithstanding that Russia possessed the largest population, territory and mineral resources in the aforementioned group of countries, its share in their aggregate industrial production amounted to only 4.2 per cent at the beginning of the twentieth century (Boffa 1994: 17).

4. 'Under pressure from richer Europe, the Russian state swallowed up a far greater relative part of the people's wealth than in the West, and thereby not only condemned the people to a twofold poverty, but also weakened the foundations of the possessing classes. Being at the same time in need of support from the latter, it forced and regimented their growth. As a result, the bureaucratized privileged classes never rose to their full height, and the Russian state thus still more approached an Asiatic despotism' (Trotsky 2008: 5).

5. 'The 20th century experienced the first wave of the great revolutions conducted in the name of socialism (Russia, China, Vietnam, Cuba) and the radicalization of the liberation struggles of Asia, Africa and Latin America (the peripheries of the imperialist/capitalist system) whose ambitions were expressed in the Bandung project (1955–80)' (Amin 2011: 59).

6. We may arrive at such a conclusion after considering the differences between Lenin and Stalin on economic policy, relations between the workers and peasants, party regime, the place of Soviets in power system, issue of nationalities (Slavin 2010). The range of issues raised and the contrast between the two positions assume two opposing strategies of constructing socialism.

7. Trotsky emphasised the prime importance of a victorious world revolution as a condition of constructing socialism in Russia, while Bukharin underscored the necessity to increase peasants' welfare as the crucial precondition to successful modernisation. However important they were, we should not exaggerate these differences and treat them as completely opposite. Indeed, Trotsky largely considered Russia's

successful industrialisation to be crucial to the attainment of world revolution. For this purpose, he championed the increasing centralisation of resources by the state. On the other hand, Bukharin had fully realised that only world socialism could guarantee Soviet Russia's survival. He believed that the success of the 'world village' (colonial peoples) in its struggle with the 'world city' (central powers) would depend on whether the USSR demonstrated harmonious relations between the city and the village. With different emphases on the role of state and market in a mixed economy, both approaches recognised the need for industrialisation and were fully aware of the capitalist world-system context.

8. This does not mean that I blame only Russian peasantry in that revolution went astray. The Bolsheviks' political culture had a strong authoritarian ingredient. In and of itself, it was a product of a clandestine struggle which this party waged against the tsarist repressive, and in many ways, medieval state. This was acknowledged by one of the brightest maverick Bolsheviks – Martem 'yan Ryutin – the leader of an anti-Stalinist opposition group. He observed that the Bolsheviks had had a strong immunity against 'right-wing opportunism', but they had displayed a weak immunity against 'left-wing opportunism', under which term he understood betrayal of workers' interests to the 'dictatorship of a leader' (Ryutin 1992).

9. See an excellent account of the problem in Carabelli (1988). The author examines the philosophical foundations of 'fundamental uncertainty' and then demonstrates that the whole body of Keynesian economic thought is derived from this idea.

10. It was named after its founder – professor and chair of political economy in MSU Nicolas Tsagolov (1904–85). For an evaluation of this school's legacy from the standpoint of the methodology of 'critical realism', see in S. Dzarasov (2010).

11. In 1960, Pakistani President Bhutto visited the Soviet republic of Uzbekistan to take part in a summit with Indian politicians mediated by the USSR. Bhutto's biographer wrote, 'The next day they motored to the historic city of Tashkent. The vast Soviet countryside, with its massive multi-storeyed apartment blocks and agricultural development, made a deep impression. In Tashkent they found time to pray at the famous Jamia Masjid [mosque]' (Taseer 1979: 42).

12. The later history of the KPRF (the Communist Party of the Russian Federation), completely integrating into the new social system as an alleged opposition, shows this threat was enormously exaggerated. At no point in Russian post-Communist history did Communists dare to challenge the capitalist system, always coming to terms with the existing power.

3 Russian Big Business: Corporate Governance and the Time Horizon

1. INTOSAI is the International Organisation of Supreme Audit Institutions. Its main aim is to provide a forum for sharing experiences and improving the quality of state audits around the world. These Guidelines are suggested by the INTOSAI Working Group on the Audit of Privatisation,

which is chaired by Sir John Bourn, head of the United Kingdom National Audit Office.

2. The Accounting Chamber, established in 1995, is a ministry of the Russian Federation and the highest organ of financial control in the country. It is in charge of monitoring the propriety of usage of the state budget finances. Control over the efficiency of state property management is also among the prime tasks of this government body. The Accounting Chamber is not entitled to undertake any practical measures following its investigations, but only to provide the revealed evidence to the law enforcement agencies. Reports of the Accounting Chamber's auditors and experts, regularly published in its Bulletin, are generally regarded by independent specialists as a highly reliable source of information reflecting the current state of the Russian economy.

3. Imperial, Inkombank, Oneximbank, Capital Saving Bank, Menatep and AKB International Financial Corporation: virtually none of these organisations still exist, although many of their former owners still belong to the Russian business elite.

4. At this time, Boris Yeltsin was the Russian Federation's president.

5. A 'pyramid scheme' is a kind of investment fund (and scam) advertising enormous returns on vouchers deposited in it, which was in widespread use in Russia in the 1990s. Initially founders of such funds would pay high interests, but only to attract new clients. They used vouchers to obtain profitable assets, but not to enrich their investors. Such structures are called 'pyramids' because they pay interest to older investors at newcomers' expense, growing disproportionately, but only until a certain moment when they declare bankruptcy and disappear. After appropriating the securities and money of hundreds of thousands of people, the majority of pyramid schemes foundered, but their protagonists avoided any criminal prosecution and enjoyed their accumulated wealth. Some were arrested, but no one returned the money taken from the investors. A pyramid scheme corresponds to the western 'Ponzi scheme'.

6. This association includes analysts from the leading Russian and foreign economic institutions, providing consulting services to the state agencies such as the Academy of the National Economy Attached to the Russian Federation Government, the Institute for the Economy in Transition, the Canadian International Development Agency and others. (The names of organisations are given as they were at the moment of the corresponding publication referred to above in 2001.)

7. 'Ownership and Control Over the Enterprises (2004) World Bank', *Voprosy Economiky*, No. 4. Some specialists think that World Bank experts underestimated the sale volumes of Russian enterprises controlled by large oligarchic groups because the latter apply schemes enabling them to hide some returns in the course of tax evasion (Klepach and Yakovlev 2004: 37–8).

8. The question of the 'excess' subsidiaries needs further comment. In the Soviet period, enterprises had numerous auxiliary low or no-profile subdivisions. which helped to compensate for shortages of many important resources. The prime function of these structures was the provision of resources which were difficult to obtain from the state.

Under current conditions, these segments became inefficient because of low-capacity utilisation rates. As a result, companies started eliminating them, but these subsidiaries also embraced R&D departments, high-tech areas of production and the social services, which were on the accounting balance of many Soviet enterprises. Frequently, this process inflicted damage both upon the companies and the population as a whole.

9. The somewhat ambiguous term 'administrative resource' means support of the state bureaucracy – federal, regional, or local – usually obtained through bribery.

4 Rent Withdrawal, Social Conflict and Accumulation

1. The exact form of such income appropriation will be discussed subsequently.
2. It was one of the biggest banks in Russia at that time.
3. Research was undertaken in 1995–2001 by one of the leading institutions in this field in Russia 'State University – High School of Economics'. Research was supported by the Russian Federation's Ministry of Economy, the Russian programme of economic research (EERC), the Institute of the Transition Economies of the Bank of Finland (BOFIT) and the Institute of Strategic Analysis and Entrepreneurial Development with financial assistance of the World Bank.
4. Note that 987,000 roubles were paid to a bank; 313,000 roubles were accrued to a financial company, and 20,000 roubles paid for bonds in the amount of 150,000 roubles, which is exactly 1.5 per cent of the initial 10 million roubles.
5. 'Kickback' is an illegal reverse payment (bribe) to the gas suppliers for deliveries exceeding contractual commitments.
6. I am indebted to the professor of the Moscow State University Victor Cherkovets for posing this question and suggesting a solution to it.
7. In the Marxian theory of commodity value c denominates the constant costs or the part of fixed capital assets consumed in course of production (depreciation), v – variable costs or wage share, and s – surplus value, accruing to capitalists.
8. This is a figure for the 'white' or officially documented wage payments. In Russia, there was the widespread practice of 'black' or undocumented wage payments, especially in the 1990s. According to official estimates, the total share of wages reached in 2010 an impressive 50.6 per cent (Rosstat 2011: 402). However, this figure includes so-called 'concealed workers' compensation' and 'concealed, mixed incomes'. Under the latter term, the difference is meant between the total expenditures on all household needs, including their financial assets, and formally registered incomes (ibid.: 391). Including 'hired labour' in the wider category of 'households' and including financial assets in wages, Russian statistics 'improve' the image of the national capitalism, but mislead the analysts who artificially appreciate workers' incomes.
9. See discussion of this in more details in: Dzarasov and Novojenov, 2005: 348–67.

5 Insider Rent and Conditions of Growth in the Russian Economy

1. 'Proportional' here has a meaning close to the concept of equilibrium, connoting the state of the national economy when the output of any sector exactly equals the demand for its product.

2. Yaremenko 1997, 1998, 2001. See analysis of this theory in the context of alternative economics framework in Dzarasov 2002.
3. The first edition of this book appeared as early as 1981.
4. One may object to the above on the grounds that insider rent is treated as a semi-feudal phenomenon assuming extra-economic coercion, which contradicts the Marxian assumption of the personal judicial freedom of the workforce under capitalism. However, here the methodology of ascent from the abstract to the concrete comes into play. In *Das Kapital*, Marx analyses capitalism in its abstract form, while nowhere in the real world does such pure capitalism exist. Any empirically given form of capitalism contains some non-capitalist elements, predetermined by its individual history, culture and geography. This fact gives rise to varieties of capitalism. Since insider rent is a concrete form of income, it not only can, but it should diverge in some respects from its abstract essence. Insider rent and surplus value are related as the form and the essence. (For more, see Dzarasov 2012.)

6   The Accumulation of Capital by Russian Corporations: Some Empirical Evidence

1. The value of fixed capital installed in each year divided by the value of total capital stock at the end of that year. Both terms are measured in full book values, without taking into account the loss of value due to wear and tear.
2. The value of fixed capital scrapped during a year divided by the value of total capital stock at the beginning of that year. Both terms are measured in full book values, without taking into account the loss of value due to wear and tear.
3. Private communication.
4. This period reflects the average condition for the whole sector of the economy, and it is quite reasonable for a rational, long-term oriented capitalist firm, especially if one takes into account the possibility of gaining a share of industrial market through only partial modernisation (about one-fifth, on average) of existing capacities.
5. Replacement value is measured in mixed prices: old equipment in prices at the last re-evaluation of fixed assets and new equipment in current prices.
6. This information is from Kuvalin in private correspondence.
7. The following three case studies are based on an unpublished manuscript: Dzarasov R. and D. Novojenov, 'An Empirical Study of Investment strategies of Russian Corporations'. In order to preserve commercial confidentiality, some companies' titles and individuals' names were changed.
8. Samara United Company: its abbreviation 'SOK' means 'Juice' in Russian.
9. In 2005, the auditor-consulting firm Baker Tilly Rusaudit conducted an analysis of the condition of the company in question according to the due diligence procedure. All citations of this source are the author's translation.

10. Since they own jointly 95 per cent of this company's total shares, it might be thought that they would use dividends as a way of extracting their insider rent. This practice can be found in some other companies where large insiders dominate the share capital, however it does expose their rents to taxation.
11. That is, the price of a product minus direct unit costs. It characterises contribution of production of every kind in covering of the fixed costs and formation of the net profit.
12. Original value of equipment minus wear-and-tear.
13. They are unjustified, of course, only from the standpoint of the company's long-term perspectives, but they are perfectly justified from the standpoint of the big insiders' demand for the current rent withdrawal.
14. Ministry of State Property.

Conclusion

1. In Soviet economic theory, planomernost was strictly distinguished from the process of planning. The latter is nothing but a number of steps carried out by the state bodies, while the former is a feature of economic development in which the economy avoids slumps due to permanently maintained proportions (equilibrium) of the national economy.
2. Under the category of 'labour', I mean not only manual labour, but all social groups whose incomes are based on wages: engineers, rank-and-file managers, teachers, doctors, researchers, and so on. These groups create real economic values, as opposed to those parasitic social classes who only redistribute in their own favour the products of alienated labour in the form of insider rent.

Bibliography

Abe N. and Iwasaki I., 2010, 'Organisational culture and corporate governance in Russia: a study of managerial turnover', *Post-Communist Economies*, Vol. 22, No. 4, December, pp. 449–70.

——, Dolgopyatova T. and Iwasaki I., 2007, 'Internal Control Systems of Russian Corporations', *IERHU Discussion Paper Series B No. 36*, Tokyo: The Institute of Economic Research Hitotsubashi University.

Aerni V., de Juniac Ch., Holley B., and Nang T., 2007, *Tapping Human Assets to Sustain Growth. Global Wealth 2007*, Boston, MA: Boston Consulting Group.

Afanas'ev Vl., A. Hal'chinskyi and V. Lant's'ov, 1986, *Karl Marx's Great Discovery: the Dual-Nature-of-Labour Doctrine: its Methodological Role*, Moscow: Progress Publishers.

Aganbegyan A., 1988, *Sovietskaya ekonomika – vzglyad v budischeye (The Soviet economy – a glimpse of the future)*, Moscow: Ekonomika.

Alekseyev, 2001, 'Prozrachnost' (Transparency), *Kommersant*, 1 October.

Alexandrovich S. (ed.) (2001) *Privatizatsiya, konkurentnaya Sreda I Effektivnost Managmenta (Na Primerer TEK) Privatization, Competitive Environment and Management Efficiency (At the Example of the Fuel-Energy Complex)*, Report of the Expert Journal, May (Moscow: Expert).

Amin S., 2011, *Ending the Crisis of Capitalism or Ending Capitalism?* Cape Town etc.: Pambazuka Press.

——, 2010, *The Law of Worldwide Value*, New York: Monthly Review Press.

Andrianov V., 1999, *Rossia: Economichesky I investitsionny potentsial (Russia: Economic and Investment Potential)*, Moscow: Economika.

Andronova A., 2005, *Volgogradsky Chimprom, Obzor Kompanii (Volgograd Chimprom, Study of a Company)*, Moscow: CenterInvestGroup, 12 January.

Anisimov S., 2006, 'Torg Zdes Ne Umesten' (Bargaining Is Irrelevant), *Noviyer Izvestia*, 3 February.

Argumenty I Facty (Sanct Peterburg), 2000, 'Krisha' (The Roof), 20 September.

Arrighi G., 2010, *The Long Twentieth Century. Money, Power and the Origins of our Times*, London and New York: Verso.

Aslund A., 2007, *Russia's Capitalist Revolution. Why market reform succeeded and democracy failed*, (Washington, DC: Peterson Institute for International Economics).

——, 1999, 'Why Has Russia's Economic Transformation Been So Arduous?', Paper delivered to the World Bank Annual Conference on Development Economics, (Washington, DC: World Bank).

Aukutsionek S., 2003, 'Proizvodstnenniyer Moshnosti Rossiyskikh Predpriyatyi' (Productive Capacities of Russian Enterprises), *Voprosy Ekonomiky*, No. 5, pp. 122–36.

Avdasheva S. and Dolgopyatova T., 2010, 'Evolutsia Rossiyskoi Firmy i Korporativnogo Upravleniya: v Poiskakh Effektivnogo Sobstvennika' (Evolution of a Russian Firm and Corporate Governance: Seeking an Efficient Owner), in Nureyev R. (ed.) *Ekonomitcheskiyer Sub'yekti Post-Sovetskoi Rossii (Institutsionalnyi Analyz): Desat' Let Spustya*, Moscow: Moskovsli Obschestvenniy Nautchnyi Fond, pp. 10–43.

——, Golikova V., Sugiura F. and Yakovlev A., 2007, 'External Relationship of Russian Corporations', *IERHU Discussion Paper Series B*, Tokyo: The Institute of Economic Research, Hitotsubashi University.

Auty R., 2001, 'Transition Reform in the Mineral-Rich Caspian Region Countries', *Resources Policy*, No. 27, pp. 25–32.

Bair J. (ed.), 2009, *Frontiers of Commodity Chain Research*, Stanford, CA: Stanford University Press.

Baker Tilly Rusaudit, 2004, *Printsipy Proizvodstvennogo Utcheta Na Volgogradskom OAO Chimprom (The Principles of Production Accounting at Volgograd JSC Chimprom)*, (Volgograd-Moscow).

——, 2005a, *Otchet po Resultatam Provedeniya Protsedury Due Diligence OAO Volgakabel(Report on the Results of Implementation of the Due Diligence Procedure to the JSC Volgakabel)*, Moscow.

——, 2005b, *Otchet po Resultatam Provedeniya Protsedury Due Diligence OAO Petchoraneft(Report on the Results of Implementation of the Due Diligence Procedure to the JSC Petchoraneft)*, Moscow.

Barnes A., 2006, *Owning Russia. The struggle over factories, farms, and power*, (Ithaca, NY and London: Cornell University Press).

Bazarov V., 1989, 'Printsipy postroyenniya perspectivnogo plana' (Principles of the perspective planning), in Koritski E. (ed.), *Kakim byt' planu: discussii 20-kh godov: stat'I I sovremennyi kommentariy (What should a plan be like: the 1920s debates: papers and comments)*, Leningrad: Lenizdat.

Bebchuk L., 2005, 'The Case for Increasing Shareholder Power', *Harvard Law Review*, Vol. 118, No. 3, pp. 833–917.

Belikov I., 2004, *Corporate Governance in Russia: Who Will Pay for it and How Much?*, (Moscow: Russian Institute of Directors).

Berglof E. and von Thadden E.-L., 1999, 'The Changing Corporate Governance Paradigm: Implications for Transition and Developing Countries', CERP Working Paper No. 263.

Berle A. and Means G., 1968 [1932], *The Modern Corporation and Private Property*, New York: Harcourt, Brace & World, Inc.

Bessonov V., 1999, 'Ob Evolutsii Tsenovikh Proportsiy v Protsesser Rossiyskikh Ekonomitcheskikh Reform' (On the Evolution of the Price Proportions in the Course of Russian Economic Reforms), *Ekonomitcheskiy Zhurnal HSE*, Vol. 3, No. 1, pp. 42–81.

BFM.ru, 2010, 'SKP Otsenil Uscherb ot Raiderstva' (The General Attorney Office's Investigations Committee Estimated the Damage of Raiding), *BFM.ru*, 11 February, <http://bfm.ru/news/2010/02/11/skp-ocenilo-ushherb-ot-rejderstva-za-2-5-goda-v-4-mlrd-rublej.html>, accessed 7 February 2012.

Bitsev O., 2004, 'Khimitcheskaya Ataka. Chinovniki Vsemy Putyami Derjat Gosudarstvo na Rasstoyanii ot Yego Je Sobstvennosti' (A Chemical Attack. Functionaries Use All Means to Keep the State Off Its Own Property, *Novaya Gazeta*, No. 18, 18 March.

Black B., 2001, 'The Corporate Governance Behaviour and Market Value of Russian Firms', *Emerging Markets Review*, Vol. 2, pp. 89–108.

——, Love I. and Rachinsky A., 2006, 'Corporate Governance Indices and Firms' Market Values: Time Series Evidence from Russia', *Emerging Markets Review*, Vol. 7, pp. 361–79.

Blair M., 1993, 'Financial Restructuring and the Debate about Corporate Governance', in Blair M. (ed.), *The Deal Decade. What Takeovers and Leveraged Buyouts Mean for the Corporate Governance*, Washington, DC: The Brookings Institution, pp. 1–18.

——, 1995, *Ownership and Control: Rethinking Corporate Governance for the Twenty-First Century*, Washington, DC: The Brookings Institution.

Blanchard O., 1998, *The Economics of Post-Communist Transition*, Oxford: Clarendon Press.

Blinder A., 2007, 'Free Trade's Great, but Offshoring Rattles Me', *Washington Post*, 6 May, <http://www.washingtonpost.com/wp-dyn/content/article/2007/05/04/AR2007050402555.html?nav=rss_print/outlook>, last accessed 20 May 2012.

Blokhin A., 2002, *Institutsionalniye Usloviya I Factory Modernizatsii Rossyiskoi Economiky (Institutional Conditions and Factors of Modernisation of Russian Economy)*, Moscow: MAX-Press.

Bochkarev A., Kondratyev V. and Krasnova V., 1998, *Sem Not Managementa (The Seven Management Notes)*, Moscow: Journal Expert Ltd.

Boffa J., 1994, *Istoriya Sovetskogo Soyuza*, Vol. 1 of 'The History of the Soviet Union'. Moscow: Mezhdunarodniyer Otnosheniya.

Borisov V., 1999, 'Mashinostroyenie: Modernizatsiya I Konkurentosposobnost' (Engineering: Restructuring and Competitiveness), *Economist*, No. 7, pp. 65–74.

——, 2000, Mashinostroyenie V Vosproizvodstvennom Protsesse (Engineering in Reproduction Process), (Moscow: MAKS-Press).

—— and Pochukayeva O., 2011, 'Modernizatsiya Obrabatyvayuschey Promyshlennosty RF na Osnover Ustiychivogo Razvitiya Itechestvennogo Mashinostroyeniya' (Modernization of RF Manufacturing on the Bases of Sustainable Development of Russian Engineering), *Problems of Forecasting*, No. 2, pp. 55–63.

Brenner R., 2009, *What is Good for Goldman Sachs is Good for America. The Origins of the Present Crisis*, Los Angeles, CA: Center for Social Theory and Comparative History, UCLA.

——, 2003, *The Boom and the Bubble. The US in the World Economy*, London and New York: Verso.

Broadman H., 1999, 'Comments on Ownership and Control in Russian Industry', Report given at the Conference on Corporate Governance in Russia, (Moscow: OECD and World Bank), <http://www.oecd.org/dataoecd/55/46/1921794.pdf>, last accessed 5 December 2007.

Carabelli A., 1988, *On Keynes's Method*, London: The Macmillan Press Ltd.

Cassidy D., 2009, 'Declaring Negative Dividends', *Forbes.com*, 3 November, <http://www.forbes.com/2009/03/11/reit-dividend-payout-personal-finance-investing-ideas-irs-ruling.html>, last accessed 23 May 2012.

Chernigovski M., 2005, 'S Kratkim Vrajeskim Visitom' (With a Brief Inimical Visit), *Kommersant-Dengy*, 23 March.

Chimprom, 2005, *Kvartalny Otchet Volgogradskogo Otkrytogo Aktsionernogo Obchestva Chimprom za: 1 Kvartal 2005 Goda (Quarterly Report of the Volgograd Joint Stock Company Chimprom for First Quarter 2005)*.

Coates J., 2007, 'The Goals of the Sarbanes-Oxley Act', *Journal of Economic Perspectives*, Vol. 21, No. 1, Winter, pp. 91–116.

Consortium on the Questions of Applied Economic Researches, 2001, *Transformation of the Property Rights and Comparative Analysis of the Russian Regions*, Moscow: Consortium on the Questions of Applied Economic Researches.

Davydova M. and Romanova L., 2003, 'Chistka Gasproma' (Gasprom Purges), *Gazeta*, 19 February.

Deitch M., 2006, 'Tyatr Absurda' (Theatre of Absurdity), *Moskovski Komsomolets*, 24 April.

Denis D. and McConnell J., 2003, 'International Corporate Governance', *Journal of Financial and Quantitative Analysis*, Vol. 38, No. 1, pp. 1–36.

Deryabina M., 2001, 'Restrukturizatstiya Rossyiskoi Ekonomoky Cherez Pereraspredeleniye Sobstvennosty I Kontrolya' (Restructuring the Russian Economy through the Redistribution of Property and Control), *Voprosy Economiky*, No. 10. pp. 2–9.

Desai P., 2006, *Conversations on Russia. Reform from Yeltsin to Putin*, Oxford: Oxford University Press.

—— and Goldberg I., 2000, 'The Vicious Circles of Control: Regional Governments in Privatised Russian Enterprises', World Bank Working Paper No. 2287, February, Washington, DC: World Bank.

Deutscher I., 1963, *The Prophet Outcast. Trotsky: 1929–1940*, London, NY and Toronto: Oxford University Press.

Dolgopyatova T., 2001, 'Modely I mechanizmy Korporativnogo Kontrolya V Rossyiskoi Promyshlennosty. Resultaty Empiritcheskogo Issledovaniya' (Models and Mechanisms of Corporate Control in Russian Industry. Results of Empirical Research), *Voprosy Economiky*, No. 5, pp. 46–60.

——, 2002, 'Modely I Mechanizmy Korporativnogo Kontrolya Na Rossiyskikh Predpriyatiyakh' (Models and Mechanisms of Corporate Control at Russian Enterprises), Mimeo, SUHSE Working Paper 1/2002/05, Moscow: State University Higher School of Economics.

——, 2003b, 'Ownership and Control Structures As Viewed By Statistics and Surveys', *The Russian Economic Barometer*, Vol. XII, No. 3, pp. 12–20.

——, 2005, 'Evolution of the Corporate Control Models in the Russian Companies: New Trends and Factors', SUHSE Working Paper WP1/2005/04, (Moscow: State University Higher School of Economics).

Dorofeyev E., 2001, *Modely Tsenoobrazovaniya Na Rossyiskom Fondovom Rynker (Models of Pricing at the Russian Securities Market)*, Candidate Degree in Economics Thesis, (Moscow: Central Institute of Economics and Mathematics of Russian Academy of Sciences).

Dyck A., 2002, *The Hermitage Fund: Media and Corporate Governance in Russia*, Harvard Business School, 17 October, N2-703-010.

Dzarasov R., 2012, 'Insider Rent Makes Russian Capitalism: a Rejoinder to Simon Pirani', *Debatte: Journal of Contemporary Central and Eastern Europe*, Vol. 19, No. 3 (December), pp. 585–97.

——, 2011a, 'Eichnerian Megacorp and Investment Behaviour of Russian Corporations', *Cambridge Journal of Economics*, Vol. 35, No. 1, pp. 199–217.

——, 2011b, 'Werewolves of Stalinism: Russia's Capitalists and their System', *Debate: Journal of Contemporary Central and Eastern Europe*, Vol. 19, Nos 1–2, pp. 471–9.

——, 2010, *Mekhanism Nakopleniyar Kapitala I Investitsionniyer Strategyi Rossiyskikh Korporatsiy (The Mechanism of Accumulation of Capital and Investment Strategies of Russian Corporations)*, Doctoral Thesis, Moscow: Moscow State University.

——, 2002, 'The Theory of Qualitative Heterogeneity of Resources and Alternative Economics', *Studies on Russian Economic Development*, Vol. 13, No. 5, pp. 462–72.

—— and Novojenov D., 2003, 'Investitsionnoyer Povedeniyer Rossyiskikh Korporatsyi V Usloviyakh Insaiderskogo Kontrola' (Investment behaviour of Russian Corporations in Conditions of Insider Control), *Management in Russia and Abroad*, No. 5.

——, 2005, *Krupnyi Bizness I Nakopleniyer Kapitala V Sovremennoi Rossii (Big Business and the Accumulation of Capital in Modern Russia)*, Moscow: Editorial URSS.

Dzarasov S., 2010a, 'Critical Realism and Russian Economics', *Cambridge Journal of Economics*, Vol. 34, Issue 6, pp. 1041–56.

——, 2010b, 'The Post-Keynesian alternative for the Russian economy', *Journal of Post-Keynesian Economics*, Vol. 33, No. 1, pp. 17–40.

Efimova E., 2005, 'Tolliyattiazot Pereshel V Kontrnastupleniyer' (Tolliyattiazot's Wages Counteroffensive), *RBC Daily* (internet edition), 17 November, <http://www.rbcdaily.ru/2005/11/17/industry/211675>, last accessed 30 April 12.

Eichner A., 1991, *The Macrodynamics of Advanced Market Economies* (Armonk, NY: M.E. Sharpe).

——, 1976, *The Megacorp and Oligopoly: Micro Foundations of Macro Dynamics* (Cambridge: Cambridge University Press).

——, 1973, 'A Theory of the Determination of the Mark-up Under Oligopoly', *Economic Journal*, Vol. 83, December, pp. 1185–244.

Ellis L. and Smith K., 2007, 'The Global Upward Trend in the Profit Share', Basel, Switzerland: Bank for International Settlements, Working Paper 231.

Enriques L. and Volpin P., 2007, 'Corporate Governance Reforms in Continental Europe', *Journal of Economic Perspectives*, Vol. 21, No. 1, Winter, pp. 117–40.

Erl D. and Sabyrianova K., 2001, 'Equilibrium Delays of Wages: Theoretical and Empirical Analysis of the Institutional Trap', in Maleva T. (ed.), *Wages and Forfeit: the Problem of Delays of Labour Remuneration*, Moscow: Moscow Carnegie Center.

Expert, 2002, 'Joint Project. Rating of the Biggest Companies According to their Sales Volume', No. 37.

Fadeyev V., 2002, 'Kapital I Bogatstvo' (Capital and Wealth), *Expert*, No. 47.

Fedorinova Y., 2004, 'Bogaty Traider Evrazholding' (A Wealthy Evrazholding Trader), *Vedomosty*, 20 July.

——, 2006, 'Auditiry Ne Poverily Evrazu' (Auditors have not trusted Evraz), *Vedomosty*, 3 February.

Fedorov E., 2011, '95% Rossyiskoi Promyshlennosty Prinadlezhit Inostrannym Offshoram' (95% of Russian Industry Belongs to Foreign Offshore Sites), <http://www.efedorov.ru/node/904>, accessed 6 February 2012.

Feldman A., 2005, Surviving Sarbanes-Oxley *Inc.Magazine*, September, Vol. 27, Issue 9, pp. 132–8.

Fey C., Adaeva M. and Vitkovskaia A., 2001, Developing a Model of Leadership Styles: What Works Best in Russia?, *International Business Review*, Vol. 10, pp. 615–43.

Finmarket, 2005, *Krupneishim Aktsionerom Gruoppy SOK Yvlyaetsya Yury Kachmazov (The Biggest Shareholder of the SOK Group is Yury Kachmazov)* <http://www.finmarket.ru/z/nws/news.asp?rid=1&fid=87664&l=43&id=366147&ref=AnketaOrg>, last accessed 28 April 2012.

Forbes (Russia), 2005, *Rating Sotny Bogateishih Ludey Rossii (Rating of One Hundred of the Richest People in Russia)*, May, No. 14.

Frank A.G., 1972, *Lumpen-Bourgeoisie: Lumpen-development. Dependence, Class, and Politics in Latin America*. New York and London: Monthly Review Press.

Freeland C., 2011, *Sale of the century. The inside story of the second Russian revolution*, (London: Abacus).

Freeman R., 2010, What really ails Europe (and America): the doubling of the global workforce', *The Globalist*, 5 March <http://www.theglobalist.com/storyid.aspx?StoryId=4542>, last accessed 20 May 2012.

Frydman R., Gray C. and Rapaczynski A. (eds), 1996, *Corporate Governance in Central Europe and Russia. Volume 1. Banks, Funds, and Foreign Investors*, (Budapest: Central European University Press).

Gaidar Y., 1995, Rossiya na Pereputyer. Vostochnaya Despotiya Ily Burjuaznaya Demokratiya? (Russia at the Crossroads. Oriental Tyranny or Bourgeois Democracy?), *Izvestia*, January 10.

Gel'man V. and I. Tarusina, 2003, 'Studies of political elites in Russia: an overview' in: Gel'man V. and A. Steen (eds), *Elites and democratic development in Russia*, London: Routledge, pp. 187–205.

Gileva L., 2005, Schastye Ot Mazepina (Happiness from Mazepin), *Kapital Weekly. Ekonomitchesky Ejenedelnik*, No. 10 (509), 30.03.

Gimpelson V., 2004, Defitsit Kvalifikatsii I Navykov Na Rynker Truda (Nedostatok Predlojeniya, Ogranicheniya Sprosa Ili Lojniyer Signaly Rabotodatelei?) (Deficit of Skills and Qualification at the Labour Market (Insufficient Supply, Demand Limitations or False Employers' Message?)), *Voprosy Economiky*, No. 3, pp. 76–91.

Gladyshevsky A., Maksimtsova S. and Rutkovskaya E., 2002, 'Investitsionniyer Reservy Ekonomicheskogo Rosta' (Investment Reserves of Economic Growth), *Problems of Forecasting*, No. 5, pp. 14–28.

Golikova V., Dolgopyatova T., Kuznetsov B., and Simachev Y., 2003, 'Spros na Pravo v Oblasty Korporativnogo Upravleniya: Empiricheskiyer Svidetelstva' (Demand for Rights on the Corporate Governance: Empirical Evidence), in: *Razvitiyer Sprosa na Pravovoyer Regulirovaniyer Korporativnogo Upravleniya v Chastnom Sektorer (Development of Demand for Legal Regulation of the Corporate Government in the Private Sector)*, Series 'Scientific Reports: Independent Economic Analysis', No. 148, Moscow: 'Projects for the Future' Fund.

Gorbunov A. (ed.), 1997, *Ofshorniyer Firmy V Mejdunarodnom Bizneser: Printsipy, Shemy, Metody (Offshore Firms in International Business: Principles, Schemes, Methods)*, (Moscow: DS EXPRESS Inc.; Company 'Eurasian region').

Gordon L., 1995, *Nadejda Ily Ugroza?: Rabocheyer Dvijeniyer Y Profsoyuzy V Perekhodnoi Rossii (Hope or Threat?: Worker Movement and Trade Unions in Transition Russia)*, (Moscow: Russian-American Foundation of Trade Union Research and Training).

Gorelik S., 2005, Eprty Nashly SOKinogo Otsa (Experts Have Found SOK's Father), Utro.ru, Internet edition, 05.04, No. 95 (1859) <http://www.utro.ru/articles/2005/04/05/424960.shtml>, last accessed 28 April 2012.

Goriaev A. and Zabotkin A., 2006, Risks of Investing in the Russian Stock Market: Lessons of the First Decade, *Emerging Markets Review*, Vol. 7, pp. 380–97.

Goskomstat, 2001, *Rossiyski Statistitcheski Ezhegodnik, 2001. Statistitcheskiy Sbornik* (Russian Statistical Yearbook, 2001), Moscow: Gosudarstvenniy Komitet po Statisiker.

Gregory P., 1982, *Russian National Income, 1885–1913*, Cambridge: Cambridge University Press.

Grinberg R., 2007, *Rynochniyer Reformy v Rossii: Ojidaniya, Rezultaty, Perspectivy (Market Reforms in Russia: Expectations, Results, Perspectives)*, Moscow: Institute of Economics of the Russian Academy of Sciences.

Grishankov D., 2004, 'Shest Protsentov Novboi Ekonomiky' (Six Per Cent of the New Economy), *Expert-Online*, No. 37 (437) (October), pp. 1–4 <http://expert.ru/expert/2004/37/37ex-osntex4_28537/>, last accessed 5 October 2013.

Grosfeld I. and Hashi I., 2004, *The Emergence of Large Shareholders in Mass Privatised Firms: Evidence from Poland and the Czech Republic*, (Milano: Nota Di Lavoro).

Guriev S., Lazareva O., Rachinsky A. and Tsukhlo S., 2003, *Corporate Governance in Russian Industry*, (Moscow: New Economic School).

Harvey D., 2006, *Limits to Capital*, London: Verso.

——, 2003, *The New Imperialism*, Oxford, New York: Oxford University Press.

Hashi I., 2004, Pravovaya Osnova Korporativnogo Upravleniya v Postsotsialisticheskikh Stranakh (The Legal Base of Corporate Governance (A Comparative Analysis of Post-Socialist Countries' Experience)), *Problemy Teorii I Practici Upravleniya* (Theoretical and Practical Aspects of Management), No. 3, pp. 48–56.

——, Kozarzewski P., Radygin A., 2004, *The Legal Framework for Effective Corporate Governance and Evolving Ownership Structure in Privatised Companies in Poland and Russia: A Comparison with other Transition Economies*, Staffordshire University, mimeo.

Heinrich A., Lis A. and Pleines H., 2005, Corporate Governance in the Oil and Gas Industry. Cases from Poland, Hungary, Russia and Ukraine in a Comparative Perspective, *KICES Working Papers No. 3*, December, (Koszalin: Koszalin Institute of Comparative European Studies).

Hellman J., Jones G. and Kaufmann D., 2000, 'Seize the State, Seize the Day'. State Capture, Corruption, and Influence in Transition, *World Bank Policy Research Working Paper* No. 2444, September.

Henderson R., 1993, *European Finance*, London: McGraw-Hill.

Henry J., 2012, *The Veblenian Predator and Financial Crises: Money, Fraud, and a World of Illusion*, AFEE Conference WP, 5 January, Chicago.

Ho K., 2009, *Liquidated. An Ethnography of Wall Street*, Durham and London: Duke University Press.

Hopkirk P., 1990, *The Great Game. On secret service in High Asia*, London: John Murray (Publishers) Ltd.

Ilyin, V., 1998, *Vlast i Ugol: Shakhterskoyer Dvijeniyer Vorkuty (1989–1998) (Power and Coal: Miners' Movement in Vorkuta (1989–1998))*, Syktyvkar: Syktyvkar University Press.

IMF, *World Economic Outlook April 2005*, Washington: International Monetary Fund.

INTOSAI, 1998, Guidelines on the Best Practice for the Audit of Privatisation, WGAP <http://www.nao.gov.uk/intosai/wgap/home.htm>, last accessed 4 April 2007.

Iskyan K., 2002, 'Russian Thaw', *Global Finance*, February, Vol. 16, Issue 2, pp. 32–5.

Ivanova M., 2011a, *Marx, Minsky and the Great Recession*, Istanbul University: Second International Conference in Political Economy, WP.

——, 2011b, Money, Housing and World Market: the Dialectic of Globalised Production, *Cambridge Journal of Economics*, Vol. 35, No. 5, pp. 853–71.

Izyumov A. and Vahaly J., 2008, 'Old Capital vs. New Investment in Post-Soviet Economies: Conceptual Issues and Estimates', *Comparative Economic Studies*, No. 50, pp. 79–110.

Jagannathan R., Kapoor M., and E. Schaumburg, 2009, *Why are We in a Recession? The Financial Crisis is a Symptom, not the Disease!*, NBER WP 15404, Cambridge, MA.

Johnson S., La Porta R., Lopez-de-Silanes F., and Shleifer A, 2000, Tunneling, *American Economic Review*, Vol. 90, No. 2, pp. 22–7.

Juravskaya E, and Sonin K., 2004, Ekonomika i Politika Rossyiskikh Bankrotstv (Economy and Policy of the Russian Bankruptcies), *Voprosy Economiky*, No. 4, pp. 25–37.

Kabanov K. (ed.), 2012, *Dominirovaniyer Bankovskogo Raiderstva ede Tendentsiya v Zakhvater i Peredeler Sobstvennosty v Rossii v Period 2009-2011 gg.* (Domination of Bank Raiding as a Tendency in Acquisition and Redistribution of Property in Russia in the Period of 2009–11), Moscow: The National Anticorruption Committee.

Kagarlitsky B., 2007, *Empire of the Periphery: Russia and the World-System* London: Pluto Press, 2007.

Kalecki M., 1971, *Selected Essays on the Dynamics of the Capitalist Economy*, Cambridge: Cambridge University Press.

Kapelushnikov R., 2001, Sobstvennost i control v Rossyiskoi Promyshlennosty (Ownership and Control in the Russian Industry), *Voprosy Economiky*, No. 12, pp. 109–26.

——, 1999, Krupneishiyer i Dominiruyuschiyer Sobstvenniky v Rossyiskoi Promyshlennosty: Svidetelstva Monitoringa REB (The Biggest and Dominant Owners in the Russian Industry: Testimony of the REB [Russian Economic Barometer] Monitoring), *Voprosy Economiky*, No. 10, pp. 54–67.

——, 1998, *Rossyisky Rynok Truda: Adaptatsiya Bez Stabilizatsii (Russian Labour Market: Adaptation without Stabilisation)* <http://www.libertarium.ru/libertarium/10779>, last accessed 17 June 2005.

—— and Demina N., 2005, Vliyaniyer Kharakteristik Sobstvennosty na Resultaty Ekonomicheskoi Deyatelnosty Rossyiskikh Promyshlennykh Predpriyatyi (Effect of the Property Ownership on the Performance of the Russian Industrial Enterprises), *Voprosy Ekonomiky*, No. 2, pp. 53–68.

Kapstein E., 1996, Workers and the World Economy: Breaking the Postwar Bargain, *Foreign Affairs*, Vol. 75, No. 3, pp. 16–37.

Karyagina T., 1990, Tenevaya Ekonomika v SSSR (Shadow Economy in the USSR), *Voprosy Ekonomiky*, No. 3, pp. 112–23.

Kaschinsky Y., 2005, Polurassekretilsya (Semi-Unveiled Himself), *Kuryer*, (Ulyanovsk newspaper), 04.26.

Katasonov V., 2002, *Begstvo Kapitala iz Rossii (Capital Flight from Russia)*, (Moscow: Ankil).

Kay J., 1993, *Foundations of Corporate Success*, (Oxford: Oxford University Press).

Keasey K. and Wright M., 1993, Issues in Corporate Accountability and Governance, *Accounting and Business Research*, 91a: 291–303.

——, Thompson S. and Wright M., 2005, *Corporate Governance: Accountability, Enterprise and International Comparisons*, (Chichester: John Wiley & Sons).

——, Thompson S. and Wright M., 1997, *Corporate Governance: Economic, Management and Financial Issues*, (Oxford: Oxford University Press).

Khanin G. and Fomin D., 2007, 'Potrebleniyer i Nakopleniyer Osnovnogo Kapitala v Rossii: Alternativnaya Otsenka' (Consumption and Accumulation of Fixed Capital in Russia: An Alternative Appraisal), *Problems of Forecasting*, No. 1, pp. 26–51.

Khrennikov I., 2003, '"Evrazholding" Navel Poryadok' ('"Evrazholding" Have Put Things in Order'), *Vedomosty*, 16.09.

Klebnikov P., 2000, *Godfather of the Kremlin*, Orlando et al.: Harcourt, Inc.

Kleman C., 2003, 'Neformalniyer Praktiky Rossyiskikh Rabotchikh' (Informal Practices of Russian Workers), *Sociologicheskiyer Issledovaniya*, No. 5, pp. 62–71.

Klepach A. and Yakovlev A., 2004, 'O Roly Krupnogo Biznesa v Sovremennoi Rossyiskoi Ekonomiker (Kommentaryi k Dokladu Vsemyrnogo Banka)' (On the Role of the Big Business in the Modern Russian Economy (commentary to the World Bank Report)), *Voprosy Ekonomiky*, No. 8, pp. 36–43.

Klimantova G. and Mukhetdinova N., 2001, 'Politika Dokhodov I Jiznennyi Uroven Rossyiskogo Naseleniya v 1990-ye Gody' (Income Policy and Living Standards of the Russian Population in the 1990s) <http://www.budgetrf.ru/Publications/Magazines/VestnikSF/2001/vestniksf139-08/vestniksf139-08030.htm>, last accessed 21 May 2006.

Kokoritch V., 2004, 'Rossyisky Rynok Truda: Kak Eto Slutchilos?' (Russian Labour Market: How Did It Happen?), *Epigraph* (Economic Weekly), No. 27 (477), 16 July, <http://www.epigraph.info/articles/19821/>, last accessed 24 September 2007.

Kolennykova O., Cosalse L. and Ryvkina R., 2004, 'Kommertsializatsiya Slujebnoi Deyatelnosty Rabotnikov Militsii' (Commercialization of the

Official Activities of the Militiamen), *Sociologycheskya Issledovanya*, No. 3, pp. 23–35.

Kolesnikov A., 2003, 'Chimprom Na Vydanyer' (Chimprom for A Wedding), *Expert*, 14.07.

Kommersant, 2005, *Vchera na Vneocherednom Sobranii Aktsionery Volgogradskogo OAO "Chimprom" Izbraly Stanislava Loseva Generalnym Directorom (Yesterday at Their Extraordinary Meeting Volgograd Chimprom Shareholders Voted for Stanislav Losev As Their General Director)*, 20 July.

Kommertcheskaya Nedvijimost 2006, *Chimprom Gotovitsya k Prodaje (Chimprom Is Preparing for Sale)* <www.knm.ru/index.php?a=news&b=11598>, last accessed 30 April 12.

Komrakov and Stolyarov, 2005, 'Dva Pretendenta na "Tolliyattiazot"' (Two Claimants on "Tolliyattiazot"), *Vedomosty*, No. 320 (1511), 7 December.

Kondratyeva M., 2006, 'Raidery: Kak Syest Chujoi Biznes?' (Raiders: How to Consume Someone's Business), *Russki Newsweek*, 12 June.

Kornev A., 2005, 'Potentsial Rosta Promyshlennosi: Formyrovaniyer Stoimosty Mashin I Oborudovaniya' (Potential of Industrial Growth: Formation of the Value of Machinery and Equipment), *Problems of Forecasting*, No. 1, pp. 62–71.

—— and Lavrenev N., 2011, 'Formirovaniyer Investitsiy Razvitiya v postkrizisniy Period' (Investments Formation in Post-crises Period), *Problems of Forecasting*, No. 1, pp. 63–78.

Kosolapov A., 2005, '"Yesli Drug Okazalsya Vdrug …" Informatsionniyer Voiny v Samarer Burlyat Kak Mutniyer Veshniyer Vody …' ("If a Friend Suddenly Proved to Be …" Information Wars in Samara Are Seething, As the Troubled Spring Waters …), IT Periodical Samara Segodnya, 19 April <http://news.samaratoday.ru/showNews.php?id=55829>, last accessed 28 April 12.

Kostin V., 2005, 'Opyt Ispolzovaniya Macrostrukturnykh Modelei v Analyzer Ekonomiky Rossii' (Application of the Macro-structural Models to Analysis of Russian Economy), in: Korovkin A. (Editor), *Trudy INP RAN (Works of the INP RAN)* (Institute of Forecasting of the Russian Academy of Sciences), Moscow: MAX-PRESS, pp. 221–32.

Kotz D., 2001, 'Is Russia Becoming Capitalist?', *Science and Society*, Vol. 65, No. 2, Summer, pp. 157–81.

—— and Weir F., 2007, *Russia's Path from Gorbachev to Putin. The Demise of the Soviet System and the New Russia*, New York: Routledge.

——, McDonough T. and M. Reich (eds), 1994, *Social Structures of Accumulation. The Political Economy of Growth and Crisis*, Cambridge: Cambridge University Press.

Kozina I., 2001, 'Profsouzy v Kollektivnykh Trudovukh Konfliktakh' (Trade Unions in Collective Labour Conflicts), *Sociologicheskiyer Issledovaniya*, No. 5, pp. 46–59.

Kozlov, 2004, 'Na Zavoder Zakonchilos Vremya Bezvlastiya' (The Time of Anarchy Is Over at the Enterprise), *Kommersant-Nijneyer Povoljyer*, No. 103, 12 April.

Krasavin A. and Makeev N., 2006, 'Dochky-Matery: Zachem Gazpromy Nyjen "Mejregiongas"' (Daughters of the Mother. What for "Gasprom" Needs "Mejregiongas"), *Kompaniya*, 25.08.

Krjuchkova, 2005, Slivaysa Kto Mojet (Let Merge All who Can), *Expert-Ural*, No. 20 (192), 30 April.

Krugman. P., 2009, *The Return of Depression Economics and the Crisis of 2008*, New York, London: W.W. Norton & Company.

Kurz H. and Neri S., 2001, 'Sraffa and von Neumann', *Review of Political Economy*, Vol. 13. No. 2, pp. 161–80.

Kuvalin D. and Moiseyev A., 2006, 'Rossiiskiyer Predpriyatiya v Nachaler 2006 Goda: Investitsionnaya Situatsiya' (Russian Enterprises in the Beginning of 2006: Situation with Investment), *Problemy Prognozirovaniya*, No. 5, pp. 111–24.

——, 2007, 'Rossiiskiyer Predpriyatiya v Serediner 2006 Goda' (Russian Enterprises in the mid-2006), *Problemy Prognozirovaniya*, No. 2, pp. 156–75.

——, 2010, 'Rossiiskiyer Predpriyatiya v Nachaler 2010 Goda: Vzglyady na Problemy Postkrizisnogo Razvitiya' (Russian Enterprises in the Beginning of 2010 Year: Views at the Problems of Post-crisis Development), *Problemy Prognozirovaniya*, No. 5, pp. 124–41.

——, 2011a, 'Rossiiskiyer Predpriyatiya v Serediner 2010 Goda: Medlenniyer Uluchsheniya Na Phoner Vysoloy Ekonomicheskoy Neopredelennosty' (Russian Enterprises in the Middle of 2010: Slow Improvement at the Backdrop of Economic Uncertainty), *Problemy Prognozirovaniya*, No. 2, pp. 140–57.

——, 2011b, 'Rossiiskiyer Predpriyatiya v Nachaler 2011 Goda: Tekuschiyer Problemy I Investitsionnayar Siyuatsiya' (Russian Enterprises in the Beginning of 2011: Current Problems and Investments), *Problemy Prognozirovaniya*, No. 5, pp. 139–57.

——, 2012, 'Rossiiskiyer Predpriyatiya v Serediner 2011 Goda: Adaptatsiya k Postkrizisnym Usloviyam' (Russian Enterprises in the Middle of 2011: Adaptation to Post-srises Conditions), *Problemy Prognozirovaniya*, No. 3, pp. 132–52.

——, Kuznetsova O. and Kuznetsov A., 2001, 'The Virtues and Weaknesses of Insider Shareholding', in: A. Kuznetsov (ed.), *Russian Corporations: The Strategies of Survival and Development*, (New York: Haworth Press).

Lane D., 2011, *Elites and Classes in the Transformation of State Socialism*, New Brunswick (USA), London: Transaction Publishers.

Lapavistas C. and I. Levina, 2011, *Financial Profit: Profit from Production and Profit upon Alienation*, Research on Money and Finance, Discussion Paper No. 24.

La Porta R., Lopez-De-Silanes F. and Schleifer A., 1999, 'Corporate Ownership Around the World', *The Journal of Finance*, Vol. LIV, No. 2, April, 471–517.

Latynyna Y., 2002, 'Skhema Prachechnoi Mejprombanka. Pugacheva Ulichily v Moshennichestver' (Mejprombank 'Laundering' Scheme. Pugachev's Fraud Is Revealed), *Novaya Gazeta*, 27 May.

——, 2003, 'Vnutrividovaya Borba Gosudarevykh Ludei' (Intra-Species Struggle of the State Officials), *Novaya Gazeta*, 10 February.

Lavigne M., 1999, *The Economics of Transition. From Socialist Economy to Market Economy*, Basingstoke and New York: Paulgrave.

Lazareva O., Rachinsky A. and Stepanov S., 2007, 'A Survey of Corporate Governance in Russia', *CEFIR/NES Working Paper No. 103*, Moscow: Centre for Economic and Financial Research at New Economic School.

Lazonick W., 2011a, *Reforming the Financialized Business Corporation*, University of Massachusetts Working Paper, January.

——, 2011b, 'How GE and Jeff Immelt are Failing to Reinvigorate the U.S. Economy', *The Globalist*, 3 May <http://www.theglobalist.com/StoryId. aspx?StoryId=9113>, last accessed 5 October 2012.

—— and O'Sullivan, M., 2000, 'Maximizing Shareholder Value: a New Ideology for Corporate Governance', *Economy and Society*, Vol. 29, No. 1, pp. 13–35.

Lee F., 1998, *Post Keynesian Price Theory*, Cambridge: Cambridge University Press.

Lemeshko A., 2003, Shareholders Share Volgograd Chimprom, *Vedomosty*, 23 July.

——, 2006, 'Rossiyu Jdet Vtoroi Chimicheski Peredel' (The Second Redistribution of Property in Chemistry Is Impending for Russia), *RBC Daily* (Internet Edition), 12 January <http://www.rbcdaily.ru/2006/01/12/ industry/213451>, last accessed 30 April 12.

Levina E., 2006, *Lobbyrovaniyer Interesov Integrirovannykh Struktur v Sovremennoi Rossii (Lobbyism of Interests of Integrated Groups in Modern Russia)*, Moscow: INDEM Foundation.

Lustgarten A., 2012a, 'A Stain that Won't Wash Away', *The New York Times*, 20 April, p. 12.

——, 2012b, *Run to Failure: BP and the Making of the Deepwater Horizon Disaster*, New York and London: W.W. Norton & Company Inc.

Mair D. and Laramie A., 2002, 'Full Employment: Gift Horse or Trojan Horse?', *Review of Social Economy*, Vol. LX, No. 4, pp. 567–93.

Makeyev R., 2005, 'Vorovstvo Melkikh Insaiderov Na Volgogradskom OAO "Chimprom"' (Small Insiders' Theft at Volgograd JSC 'Chimprom'), An Interview, 16 September, author's archive.

Malkova I., 2005, 'Mazepin I Renova ne Podelyli Chimiyu' (Mazepin and 'Renova' Failed to Share Chemistry), *Vedomosty*, No. 228 (1509), 5 December.

Mallin C., 2004, *Corporate Governance*, Oxford: Oxford University Press.

Mandel J. and Nougayrede D., 2004, 'The IFLR Guide to Mergers & Acquisitions. Russia: General Overview', *International Financial Law Review. A Supplement*.

Marx K., 1959 [1894], *Capital*, Vol. III, New York: International Publishers.

Maximov B., 2002, 'Polojeniyer Rabochikh i Rabocheyer dvijeniyer v Rossii 1990-kh Godov' (Conditions of Workers and Worker Movement in Russia of 1990s), in Buzgalin A., Churakov D., Shultser P. (eds), *Rabochyi Klass i Rabocheye Dvijeniyer Rossii: Istoriya i Sovremennost (The Working Class and the Worker Movement in Russia: History and Modernity)*, Moscow: Slovo.

Maximova Z., 2004, 'Bolshaya Otdacha Nachinaetsya s Malykh Vlojenyi' (Large Returns Start From Small Investments), *Vestnik Chimproma*, 1 October.

Mayetnaya E. and Shipitsina N., 2004, '"Sashky" na Tsarctver. Noviyer Rossyiskiyer Millionery' ("Sashkies" ruling. New Russian millionaires), *Moskovski Komsomolets*, 17 December.

McCarthy D. and Puffer S., 2002, 'Corporate Governance in Russia: Towards a European, US, or Russian Model?', *European Management Journal*, Vol. 20, No. 6, December, pp. 630–40.

——, 2003, 'Corporate Governance in Russia: a Framework for Analysis', *Journal of World Business*, Vol. 38, pp. 397–415.

McDonough T., Reich M. and D. Kotz (eds), 2010, *Contemporary Capitalism and its Crisis. Social Structure of Accumulation Theory for the 21st Century*, Cambridge: Cambridge University Press.

Menshikov S., 2007, *The Anatomy of Russian Capitalism*, Washington, DC: Executive Intelligence Review News Service.

——, 2006, *Koreyskaya Model' Dlya Kremlevskoy Gruppy*, (The Korean Model for the Kremlin Group) <http://rusref.nm.ru/Korean.htm>, accessed 21 April 2011.

——, 2004, *Anatomiya Rossyiskogo Kapitalizma (Anatomy of the Russian Capitalism)*, Moscow: Mezjdunarodnya Otnoshenya.

Michie J., 1995, Introduction, in: J. Michie and J.G. Smith (eds), *Managing the Global Economy*, Oxford: Oxford University Press.

Mickiewicz T., 2006, 'Corporate Governance in Russia and Poland in Comparative Perspective: An Introduction', in Mickiewicz T. (ed.), *Corporate Governance and Finance in Poland and Russia*, Basingstoke: Macmillan Publishers Limited, pp. 3–22.

Milberg W., 2008, *Shifting Sources and Uses of Profits: Sustaining U.S. Financialization with Global Value Chains*, CEPN/SCEPA Conference, University of Paris – 13, 17–18 January.

—— and D. Winkler, 2010, 'Financialisation and the Dynamics of Offshoring in the USA', *Cambridge Journal of Economics*, Vol. 34, Issue 2, pp. 275–93.

Miles D., 1995, 'Testing for Short Termism in the UK Stock Market: A Reply', *Economic Journal*, Vol. 105, No. 432, September.

Minin A., 2005, 'Odnym Milliarderom Bolsher' (One Billionaire More), *Expert On-line*, 11 April, No. 14 (461) <http://www.expert.ru/printissues/expert/2005/14/14ex-news343/>, last accessed 28 April 12.

Mogil'nitskyi B., 2009, 'Russlaya revolutsiya v perspective dolgogo vremeny: noviyer podkhody k yeye osmysleniyu' (The Russian revolution in the long-term perspective: new approaches to reconsidering), in Sorokin A. (ed.) *Okt'abr' 1917. Vyzovy dlya XXI veka* (October 1917. Challenges for the 21st century), Moscow: LENAND.

Mohun S., 2009, 'Aggregate Capital Productivity in the US Economy, 1964–2001', *Cambridge Journal of Economics*, Vol. 33, No. 5, pp. 1023–46.

Morck R., Wolfenson D. and Yeung B., 2005, 'Corporate Governance, Economic Entrenchment and Growth', *Journal of Economic Literature*, Vol. 43, No. 3, pp. 655–720.

Morozov A. and M. Sundberg, 2000, *Russia: issues in public expenditure policy*, Conference on post-election strategy, Moscow: The World Bank, 5–7 April.

Mysharin A., Sharonov A., Lapidus B., Chichagov P., Burnusov N. and Macheret D., 2001, *Programma Strukturnykh Reform na Jeleznodorojnom Transporter (s kommentariyamy) Programme of the Structural Reform at the Railways (With commentaries)*, Moscow: MTSFER.

Nell G., 2011, 'Rent-Seeking, Hierarchy and Centralisation: Why the Soviet Union Collapsed So Fast and What it Means for Market Economies', *Comparative Economic Studies*, Vol. 53, pp. 597–620.

NES, PwC in Russia and CTI PwC, 2010, *Innovatsionnaya Aktivnost' Krupnogo Biznesa v Rossii (Innovative Activities of Big Business in Russia)*, Moscow: New Economic School, PricewaterhouseCoopers in Russia and Centre for Technologies and Innovations PwC.

NEWSru.com, 2004, *Biographiya Viktora Vekselberga: Shirokyi Krug Interesov (Biography of Viktor Vekselberg: Wide Range of Interests)*, 26 April.

Nikolski A., 2006, Raiderstvo na Grany Myateja (Raiding at the Edge of Riots), *Vedomosty*, No. 30(1557), 21 February.

Nornikel, 2003, 'Godovoi Otchet OAO "Norilskyi Nikel" za 2003 God' (Annual Report of the JSC Gorno-Metallurgitcheskaya Companya 'Norilski Nickel' for 2003) <www.nornik.ru>, last accessed 5 April 2005.

Novaya Gazeta v Ryazany 2005, 'Gruppu SOK Obvinyaut v Prichastnosty k Korruptsionnomu Skandalu v Ryazanskoi Oblasty' (The Group SOK is Implicated in the Corruption Scandal in Ryazan District), 22 February <http://www.newspaper.ryazan.ru/zag07.html>, last accessed 14 April 2006.

Novikova L., 2006, 'MERT Ostanovit Korporativniyer Voiny' (MEDT Will Stop the Corporate Wars), *Gazeta*, No. 13, 13 January.

Noviye Izvestiya 2000, 27 'Tysyach Stolichnikh fyrm I Predpriyatyi Zaregistrirovano po utrachennym Documentam' (27 Thousand Firm in Capital Are Registered With the Lost Identity Documents), 8 September.

Novojenov D., 2003a, *Upravlenier Investitsiyamy v Rossyiskikh Korporatsiyakh v Usloviyakh Dominirovaniya Insaiderov (Managing Investments in Russian Corporations under Domination of Insiders)*, Candidate Degree in Economics Thesis, Moscow: Institute of Economics of Russian Academy of Sciences.

——, 2003b, 'Organizatsionniyer structury v Rossyiskoi Ekonomiker' (Organizational Structures in Russian Economy), *Ekonomist*, No. 12, pp. 45–57.

Ofer G., 1987, 'Soviet economic growth: 1928–1985', *Journal of Economic Literature*, December 1987, Vol. 25, Issue 4, pp. 1767–883.

Oman C., 2001, 'Corporate Governance and National Development', OECD Development Centre. Technical Paper, No. 180, September.

Orhangazi O., 2008, 'Financialisation and Capital Accumulation in the Non-Financial Corporate Sector: A Theoretical and Empirical Investigation on the US Economy: 1973–2003', *Cambridge Journal of Economics*, No. 32, pp. 863–86.

Osyka, 2005, 'Formular Khimicheskogo Bunkrotstva' (A Chemical Bankruptcy Formula), *Trud*, No. 236, 16 December.

Paine L., Deshpandé R., Margolis J. and Bettcher K., 2005, 'Up to Code: Does Your Company's Conduct Meet World-Class Standards?', *Harvard Business Review*, December, Vol. 83 Issue 12, pp. 122–33.

Pajuste A., 2007, 'Do Good Governance Provisions Shelter Investors from Contagion? Evidence from the Russian Crisis', *Economics of Transition*, Vol. 15, No. 4, pp. 807–24.

Papper J., 2000, *'Oligarkhy': Ekonomicheskaya Khronika, 1999–2000 ('Oligarchs': Economic Chronicles, 1999–2000)*, Moscow: State University: High School of Economics.

——, 2002a, 'Rossyisky Krupnyi Bizness Kak Ekonomicheskyi Phenomen: Osobennosty Stanovleniya I Sovremennogo Razvitiya' (Russian Big Business as an Economic Phenomenon: Peculiarities of Its Emergence and Modern Development), *Problems of Forecasting*, No. 1, pp. 29–46.

——, 2002b, 'Rossyisky Krupnyi Bizness Kak Ekonomicheskyi Phenomen: Spetsifitcheskiyer Cherty, Modely Ego Organizatsii' (Russian Big Business as an Economic Phenomenon: Specific Features, Models of Its Organization), *Problems of Forecasting*, No. 2, pp. 83–97.

Petchoraneft, 2003, *Profil Dobichy Srednekharyaginskogo Mestorojdeniya (Extraction Profile of Srednekharyaginsky Site)*, Moscow: The Central Office of Petchoraneft.

——, 2005a, 'Informatsiya ob OAO Petchoraneft' (Information on JSC Petchoraneft), (Moscow: The Central Office of Petchoraneft).

——, 2005b, 'Otsenka Dokhodnosty OAO Petchoraneft and NBNK' (Appraisal of Profitability of JSC Petchoraneft and of NBNK), Moscow: The Central Office of Petchoraneft.

Pirani S., 2008, *The Russian Revolution in Retreat, 1920–24. Soviet workers and the new communist elite*, Abingdon and NY: Routledge.

——, 2010, *Change in Putin's Russia. Power, money and people* (London: Pluto Press).

Ponomarev D., 2003, 'Evrazholding Uyekhal na Kypr' (Evrazholding Left for Cyprus), *Kommersant*, Vol. 166, No. 2769, 15 September.

Pollin R., 2007, 'Global Outsourcing and the US Working Class', *New Labor Forum*, Vol. 16, No. 1, pp. 122–5.

Popov V., 2004, 'Sobstvennost I Upravleniyer v Rossyiskom Krupnom Biznese' (Ownership and Management in the Russian Big Business), Interview, 6 July, author's archive.

Prokhorova N., 2005, 'Rossyiskyi Bizness Napolovinu Kriminalnyi' (Russian Business Is Half Criminal*)*, *Ytro. Ru, 2005*, 5 October <http://www.utro.ru/articles/2005/10/05/483090.shtml>, last accessed 23 March 2007.

Pugh G., 1998, 'Financial Systems and Industrial Performance', in Shackleton L. and Lange T. (eds), *Germany: An Economy in Transition*, Oxford: Berg.

Radygin A., 1992, 'Spontaneous Privatisation: Motivations, Forms and Stages', *Studies on Soviet Economic Development*, Vol. 3, No. 5, pp. 341-7.

——, 1998, 'Rossyiskaya Privatizatsiya: Natsionalnaya tragediya yli Institutsionalnaya Baza Postsovetskikh reform?' (Russian Privatization: National Tragedy or the Institutional Base of the post-Soviet Reforms?), *The Russian World*, No. 3, Vol. VII.

——, 1999, 'Pereraspredeleniyer Prav Sobstvennosty v Postprivatizatsionnoi Rossii' (Redistribution of the Property Rights in the Post Privatized Russia), *Voprosy Economiky*, No. 6, pp. 57–73.

——, 2001, 'Sobstvennost I Integratsionniyer Pritsessy v Korporativnom Sectorer' (Nekotoriyer Noviyer Tendentsii) (Property and Integration Process in the Corporate Sector (Some New Tendencies)), *Voprosy Economiky*, No. 5, pp. 26–45.

—— and Entov R., 1999, *Institutsionalniyer Problemy Razvitiya Korporativnogo Sektora: Sobstvennost, Kontrol, Rynok Tsennykh Bumag (Institutional Problems of the Corporate Sector Development: Property, Control, Securities Market)*, WP No. 12 P, Moscow: Institute of Economics of the Transition Period.

—— and Sydorov I., 2000, 'Rossyiskaya Korporativnaya Ekonomika: Sto Let Odinochestva?' (Russian Corporate Economy: One Hundred Years of Solitude?), *Voprosy Ekonomiky*, No. 5, pp. 45–61.

——, Entov R. and Shmeleva N., 2002, *Problemy Sliyanyi i Poglocshenyi v Korporativnom Sektorer (The Problems of Mergers and Takeovers in the Corporate Sector)*, WP No. 36 P, Moscow: Institute of Economics of the Transition Period.

Rawlinson P., 2010, *From Fear to Fraternity. A Russian Tale of Crime, Economy and Modernity*, London: Pluto Press.

Razmi A. and Blecker R., 2008, 'Developing Country Exports of Manufactures: Moving Up the Ladder to Escape the Fallacy of Composition?', *Journal of Development Studies*, Vol. 44, No. 1, pp. 21–48.

Regnum, 2005, 'Prejneyer Rukovodstvo Volgogradskogo "Chimproma" Ostavilo Zavod bez Strategii Razvitiya, Schitayet Glava Predpriyatiya' (The Head of the Enterprise Believes That the Former Top-managers Have Left the Company Without Development Strategy), 27 July <http://www.regnum.ru/news/489723.html>, last accessed 30 April 2012.

Reznik I., 2002, 'V Mejregiongaz Nagryanuly Revizory' (Inspectors Arrived in Mejregiongaz Unexpectedly), *Vedomosty*, 17 October.

RIA-Analitika, 2011, 'Altayskie sem'i zhivut bednee vsekh'. Moscow, RIA Novosti, 13 April <http://www.rian.ru/markets/20110413/364047513.html>, accessed 18 April 2011.

Rimashevskaya N., 2006, 'Nekotoriyer Problemy Sotsialnogo Reformirovaniya v Rossii' (Some Problems of the Social Reforms in Russia), *Problems of Forecasting*, No. 2, pp. 3–18.

Rizzi, B., *The Bureaucratisation of the World* (London: Tavistock, 1985 [1939]).

Rodrick D., 2011, 'Labour markets: the unexpected frontier of globalization', *The Globalist*, 31 May <http://www.theglobalist.com/printStoryId.aspx?StoryId=9156>.

Roptanova E., 2004a, 'Ony Soshlys: Voda I Kholod. Realizuetsya Energosberegayuschaya Programma Chimproma' (They met together: Water and Cold. Energy Saving Programme Is Exercised at Chimprom), *Vestnik Chimproma*, 1 October.

——, 2004b, 'Skovanniyer Odnoi Tsepyu' (Fixed by the Same Chain), *Vestnik Chimproma*, 15 October.

——, 2005, 'Voda Stanet Yescher Chischer. Chimprom Vosstanovil Postavky Jidkogo Chlora na Rossyiskiyer Vodokanaly' (Water Will Become Even More Pure. Chimprom Resumed Deliveries of the Liquid Chloral to Russian Water Supply Systems), *Vestnik Chimproma*, 24 June.

Rosstat, 2004a, *Natsionalniyer Scheta Rossii v 1996–2003 Godakh (National Accounts of Russia in 1996-2003 years)*, Moscow: The Federal State Statistics Service.

——, 2004b, *Russia in Figures, 2004. Concise Statistical Handbook*, Moscow: Federal State Statistics Service.

——, 2005a, *Investitsii v Rossii, 2005, Ctatistitcheskyi Sbornik (Investments in Russia, 2005, Statistical Yearbook)*, (Moscow: Federal State Statistics Service).

——, 2005b, *Mejdunarodniyer Sopostavleniya Valovogo Vnutrennego Produkta za 1999–2000 i 2002 Gody, Statisticheskyi Sbornik (International Comparisons of the Gross Domestic Product for 1999-2000 and 2002 Years, Statistical Yearbook)*, Moscow: Federal State Statistics Service.

——, 2005c, *Promyshlennost Rossii, 2005, Statisticheskyi Sbornik (Industry of Russia, 2005, Statistical Yearbook)*, Moscow: Federal State Statistics Service.

——, 2008a, *Promyshlennost' Rossii, 2008. Statistitcheskiy Sbornik* (Industry of Russia, 2008. Statistical Handbook), Moscow: Federal State Statistics Service.

——, 2008b, *Sotsial'noe Polozhenie i Uroven' Zhizni Naseleniya Rossii, 2008. Statisticheskiy Sbornik* (Social State and Living Standards of the Russian Population, 2008. Statistical Yearbook), Moscow: Federal'naya Sluzhba Gosudarstvennoy Statistiki.

——, 2010a, *Promyshlennost Rossii, 2010, Statisticheskyi Sbornik (Industry of Russia, 2010, Statistical Yearbook)*, Moscow: Federal State Statistics Service.

——, 2010b, *Russia in Figures, 2010. Statistical Handbook*, Moscow: Federal State Statistics Service.

——, 2010c, *Sotsial'noe Polozhenie i Uroven' Zhizni Naseleniya Rossii, 2010. Statisticheskiy Sbornik* (Social State and Living Standards of the Russian Population, 2010. Statistical Yearbook), Moscow: Federal'naya Sluzhba Gosudarstvennoy Statistiki.

——, 2011a, *Investitsii v Rossii, 2011. Statistitcheskiy Sbornik* (Investments in Russia, 2011. Statistical Handbook), Moscow: Federal State Statistics Service.

——, 2011b, *Natsionalniyer Scheta Rossii v 2003–2010 Godakh. Statistitcheski Sbornik* (National Accounts of Russia in 2003–2010. Statistical Handbook), Moscow: The Federal State Statistics Service.

——, 2011c, *Russia in Figures, 2011. Statistical Handbook*, Moscow: Federal State Statistics Service.

——, 2011d, *Trud I Zanyatost' v Rossii, 2011* (Labour and Employment in Russia, 2011. Statistical Yearbook), Moscow: Federal'naya Sluzhba Gosudarstvennoy Statistiki.

——, 2012a, *Promyshlennost Rossii, 2010, Statisticheskyi Sbornik (Industry of Russia, 2010, Statistical Yearbook)*, Moscow: Federal State Statistics Service.

——, 2012b, 'Investitsionnaya Aktivnost' Organizatsiy' (Investment Activity of Organisations), *Statistitcheskiy Bulluten*, No. 1 (182), pp. 20–28.

—— RF, Minobrnauky RF and SU-HSE, 2009, *Indikatory Innovatsionnoi Deyatel'nosty: 2009. Statistitchesky Sbornik* (Indicators of Innovative Activity: 2009. Statistical Handbook), Moscow: The Federal State Statistics Service, Minobrnauky RF and SU-HSE.

Rozmainsky I., 2002, *Osnovniyer Kharakteristiky Semeyno-Klanovogo Kapitalisma v Rossii na Rubejer tysyacheletyi: Institutsionalno-postkeynesianskyi Podkhod (The Major Characteristics of the Family-Clan Capitalism in Russia at the Edge of Millennium: Institutional-Postkeynesian Approach)* <http:// ie.boom.ru/Rozmainsky/family.htm>, last accessed 5 June 2006.

——, 1999, *Ogranichennost Metodologicheskogo Individualisma, Obscestvennaya Ideologiya I Kollaps Investitsyi v Rossii (Limitations of the Methodological*

Individualism, Social Ideology and Investment Collapse in Russia) < http:// ie.boom.ru/Rozmainsky/irozmain.htm>, last accessed 13 August 2006.

Rudyk E., Kremenetski J. and Bulavka L., 2000, 'Rabochyi Protest v Rossii: Opyt I Problemy' (Worker Protest in Russia: Experience and Problems), Moscow: Economic Democracy.

Rutkevitch M., 2004, 'Vozrastaniye sotsial'noi napryazhennosty k kontsu sovetskogo perioda' (Growth of the social tensions to the end of the Soviet period), *Sotsiologotcheskiye issledovaniya*, No. 7, pp. 62–70.

——, 1999, 'O sotsial'noi structure sovetskogo obchestva' (On social structure of the Soviet society), *Sotsiologotcheskiye issledovaniya*, No. 4, pp. 19–28.

Ryutin M., 1992, *Na koleny ner vstanu (I will not stand on my knees)*, Vilnyus: Gosizdat politicheskoi literatury Litovskoi SSR.

Samarskoye Obozrenyer 2004a, *Istochnyk Bedstvyi SOKa Propal (The Source of SOK Misfortunes Disappeared)*, 26 July < http://news.samaratoday.ru/ showNews.php?id=27798>, last accessed 28 April 2012.

——, 2005, *Igorya Ejova Osvobodily ot Obvinenyi (Igor Ejov Was Cleared of Accusations)*, 16 August < http://www.samarskoeobozrenie.ru/ document/1540>, last accessed 15 April 2006.

Satarov G. (ed.), 2004, *Antikorruptsionnaya Politika: Uchebnik (Anticorruption Policy: a Textbook)*, Moscow: RA 'SPAS'.

—— and Parkhomenko S., 2001, *Raznoobraziyer Stran I Raznoobraziyer Korruptsii (Diversity of Countries and Diversity of Corruption)*, Moscow: INDEM Foundation.

Semenov V., 1960–70, 'Sotsial'naya stratificatsiya' (Social stratification), in Konstantinov F. (ed.), *Philisophskaya Entsiklopediya*, Vol. 4, Moscow: Sovetskaya entsiklopediya.

Seregin V., 2005, 'Mazepin Skupayet Phtoroplasty' (Mazepin buys phtoroplasts), *RBC Daily*, 28 February < http://www.rbcdaily. ru/2005/02/25/industry/38075>, last accessed 30 April 2012.

Serfati C., 2008, 'Financial Dimensions of Transnational Corporations, Global Value Chain and Technological Innovation', *Journal of Innovation Economics*, Vol. 2, No. 2, pp. 35–61.

Serge V., 2001, 'Syla I Predely Marxizma', in Serge V., *Sotsialistitchesky Gumanizm Protiv Totalitarizma*, Moscow: NPTS 'Praxis'.

Serra N., Spiegel S., and Stiglitz J., 2008, 'Introduction: from the Washington Consensus towards a new global governance', in Serra, N., and Stiglitz, J. (eds), *The Washington Consensus Reconsidered: Towards a Global Governance*, Oxford: Oxford University Press, pp. 3–13.

Shalayev S. (ed.), 2002, *Opyt I Praktika Raboty Profsouznykh Komitetov v Sovremennykh Usloviyakh (Experience and Practice of the Trade Union's Committees in Modern Conditions)*, Moscow: Research Trade Union Centre.

Shanin T., 1986, *Revolution as a Moment of Truth* (Vol. 2 of 'The Roots of Otherness: Russia's Turn of Century'), London: Macmillan.

Shastitko A. (ed.), 2008, *Natsional'ny Doklad po Korporativnomu Upravleniyu. Vypusk 1 (The National Report on Corporate Governance. Issue 1)*, Moscow: National Council on Corporate Governance.

—— (ed.), 2009, *Natsional'ny Doklad po Korporativnomu Upravleniyu. Vypusk 2 (The National Report on Corporate Governance. Issue 2)*, Moscow: National Council on Corporate Governance.

Shiller R., 2008, *The Subprime Solution. How Today's Global Financial Crisis Happened, and What to Do about It*, Princeton, NJ and Oxford: Princeton University Press.

Shleifer A. and Vasiliev D., 1996, 'Management Ownership and Russian Privatization', in Frydman R., Gray C., Rapaczynski A. (eds), *Insiders and the State*, Vol. 2 of 'Corporate Governance in Central Europe and Russia' (Budapest: Central European University Press), pp. 62-77.

Shokhina E., 2002, 'Neulovymyer' (The Elusive), *Expert*, No. 45, pp. 60–63.

Sixsmith M., 2010, *Putin's Oil. The Yukos affair and struggle for Russia*, New York: Continuum International Publishing Group Ltd.

Slavin B., 2010, *Lenin protiv Stalina. Posledniy boi revolutsionera (Lenin against Stalin. The last battle of a revolutionary)*, Moscow: Editorial URSS.

Skorobogatov A., 1998, *Ekstensivnyi Rost bankovskogo Sectora I Upadok Kreditnoi Efery v Sovremennoi Rossii (Extensive growth of the Banking Sector and decline of the Crediting Sphere in Modern Russia)*, February <http://ie.boom.ru/scorobogatov>, last accessed 13 August 2006.

Smirnova I., 2002, 'Otnosheniya Mejdu Sobstvennikamy i Upravlentsamy Torgovogo Predpriyatiya' (Relations between the Owners and Managers in Trading Enterprises), Interview, 13 August, author's archive.

Snigirev V., 2004, 'Na Chimprom Idet NaJIVA' (NaJIVA Comes to Chimprom), *Noviyer Izvestia*, 19 March.

Sokolova A., 2005, 'Aktsionery Chimproma Sverili Plany Kandidatov na Post Generalnogo Direktora' (Chimprom Shareholders Discussed the Plans of Competitors for the Position of the General Director), *Vestnik Chimproma*, 4 February.

Somov N., 2006, 'German Greff: Raiderstvo Raiderstvu Rozn' (German Greff: Raiding is Different from Raiding), *Noviyer Izvestiya*, 19 May.

Sprenger C., 2002, 'Ownership and Corporate Governance in Russian Industry: A Survey', *EBRD Working Paper No. 70*, January, London: European Bank for Reconstruction and Development.

Stepashin S. (ed.), 2004, *Analyz Protsessov Privatizatsii Gosudarstvennoi Sobstvennosty v Rossyiskoi Federatsii za Period 1993-2003 Gody (Ekspertno-Analyticheskoyer Meropriyatiyer) (Analysis of the Processes of Privatization of the State Property in Russian Federation During the Years 1993-2003 (Expert-Analytical Report))*, Moscow: Olyta Publishing House.

Stolyarov, B., 2002, 'Rynok Korruptsionnykh Uslug' (Market of the Corruption Services), *Vedomosty*, 22 May.

Svyatoslavskaya, N., 2004, 'Aktsii Chimproma Vzyali pod Arest' (Chimprom Equities Are Put Under Arrest), *Kommersant*, No. 137, 29 July.

Symatchev Y. and Drugov Y., 1999, *Pravovoyer Obespetcheniyer Ekonomicheskikh Reform, Predpriyatiya (Legislation Support for the Economic Reforms, Enterprises)*, Moscow: Institute of Economics of the Transition Period.

Tarler E., 1958, *Evropa v epokhu imperializma (Europe in the age of imperialism)* CW, Vol. V, Moscow: Izdatelstvo Akademii Nauk SSSR.

Taseer S., 1979, *Bhutto: a political biography*, London: Ithaca Press.

Timofeyev A., 2000, 'Osobennosty Strategicheskogo Managementa v Energo-Proizvodyashei Kompanii' (Specifics of Strategic Management of the Energy-Producing Company), *Energetic*, No. 6, pp. 6–7.

——, 2003, 'Problemy Upravleniya Personalom v Sovremennoi Rossii' (The Problems of Human Resource Management in Modern Russia), Interview, 26 February, author's archive.

Trifonov, V., 2004, 'SOK Zastrakhovalas ot Obvinenyi, Zabrav v Upravleniyer ZAO Investflot' (SOK Secured itself from Accusations of Taking 'Investflot' in Trusted Managing), *Kommersant*, 19 October.

Trofimov S., 2004,' Kuda Uplyly Milliony? V Kameru Vremennogo Izolyatora Preprovojden Byvshyi Generalnyi Director Proizvodstvennogo Obiyedineniya Chimprom Evgenyi Kysil' (Where Have the Millions Gone? The Former General Director of the Production Unit Chimprom Evgeny Kisyl Is Put Under Interrogation), *Volgograd Pravda*, 13 May.

Trotsky L., 2008, *The Overthrow of Tsarism*, Vol. 1 of 'The History of the Russian Revolution', Chicago, IL: Haymarket Books.

——, 2004, *The Revolution Betrayed*, New York: Dover Publications.

TsPT, 2008, *Reiderstvo kak Sotsial'no-Ekonomitcheski I Polititcheski Phenomen Sovremennoi Rossii (Raiding as a Social-Economic and Political Phenomenon of Modern Russia)*, Moscow: Tsentr Politicheskikh Tekhnologyi.

T'ut'ukin S., 2002, *Menshevizm: stranitsy istorii (Menshevizm: the pages of history)*, Moscow: ROSPEN.

Ukhov S., 2006, 'Yuri Borisov: Raiderstvo Eto Kupyt na Grosh Pyatakov' (Yuri Borisov: Raiding Buys Cheap and Sells Dear), *Izvestiya*, 20 July.

Ustyuzhanina E., Yevsyukov S., and Petrov A., 2010, *Sostoyaniyer i perspectivy razvitiya korporativnogo sectora v Rossii (The current state and perspectives of development of the corporate sector in Russia)*, Moscow: CEMI RAS.

Uzyakov M., 2000, *Transformatsiya Rossyiskoi Ekonomiky I Vozmojnosty Ekonomicheskogo Rosta (Transformation of the Russian Economy and Possibilities of Economic Growth)*, (Moscow: ISEPN Publishers).

Valtukh K., 2000, 'Neobkhodima Mobilizatsionnaya Ekonomicheskaya Strategiya' (Mobilizing Economic Strategy is Necessary), *ECO*, No. 11., pp. 3–15.

Varfolomeyev A., 2003, 'Nikelevaya Golodovka' (The Hunger for Nickel), *Institute of Globalization Issues*, 11 February.

Veblen T., 1936 (1904), *The Theory of Business Enterprise*, New York: Charles Scribner's Sons.

Vernengo M., 2001, 'Sraffa, Keynes and "The Years of High Theory"', *Review of Political Economy*, Vol. 13, No. 3, pp. 343–54.

Vernikov A., 2007, 'Corporate Governance and Control in Russian Banks', *UCL-SSEES Economics Working Paper No. 78*, July, London: University College London – School of Slavonic and East European Studies.

Vershinina O. and Samoilenko N., 2004, 'Ne Dlya Vas, Kozlov, Volgogradskyi Chimprom' (Volgograd Chimprom, Mr Kozlov, Is Not For You), *Tribuna*, 18 March, p. 5.

Vestnik Chimproma, 2005, 'Stanislav Losev: Vperedy Bolshaya Rabota' (Stanislav Losev: A Lot of Work Lies Ahead), 8 July.

Vinogradova H. and Kozina I., 2011, 'Otnosheniyar Sotrudnichestva I Konflikta v Predstavleniyakh Rossiyskikh Rabotnikov' (The Relations of Cooperation and Conflict in the Perception of Russian Workers), *Sotsiologicheskiyer Issledovaniya*, No. 9, pp. 30–40.

Vodyanov A., Kvolynskaya N., Gazeev M., Gujnovski L., Ejov C., Orlov R. and Chernyavski A., 2000, *Neftyannoi Komplex Rossii I Ego Rol v Vosproizvodstvennom Processer (Russian Oil Producing Complex and Its Place in Reproduction Process)*, Moscow: Expert.

Voitsekh, I., 2005, 'Korruptsia Syedaet Poloviny VVP' (Corruption Consumes Half of GDP), *Ytro. Ru*, 25 July <http://www.utro.ru/articles/2005/07/25/461430.shtml>, last accessed 5 April 2007.

Volkonsky V., 1998, *Institutsionalniyer Problemy Rossyiskikh Reform (Institutional Problems of the Russian Reforms)*, Moscow: Dialog-MSU.

—— and Kuzovkin, A., 2002, 'Disparitet Tsen v Rosii i v Nirer' (Price Disparity in Russia and in the World), *Problemy Prognozirovaniya*, No. 6, pp. 11–28.

Vorobyev, S., 2005, 'Metody Otyema Sobstvennosty: Uslugy i Tseny' (Methods of Takeover: Services and Prices), *Kompanya*, 24 October.

Voskoboynikov I., 2004, 'O Korrektirovker Dynamiki Osnovnykh Fondov v Rossyiskoi Ekonomiker' (About the Corrections of the Dynamics of Fixed Capital in Russian Economy), *Economic Journal of HSE*, No. 1, pp. 3–20.

Vuylsteke C., 1994, *Tekhnika Privatizatsii Gosudarstvennykh Predpriyatyi. Tom 1, Metody I Instrumenty (Techniques of Privatization of State-Owned Enterprises. Vol. 1, Methods and Implementations)*, Technical Paper No. 89, The World Bank, Moscow: Publishers Group 'Progress', 'Universe'.

Whitefield S., 1993, *Industrial Power and the Soviet state*, Oxford: Oxford University Press.

Woodruff D., 1999, *Money Unmade. Barter and the fate of Russian capitalism*, Ithaca, NY and London: Cornell University Press.

Xing Y. and N. Detert, 2010, 'How iPhone Widens the United States Trade Deficit with the People's Republic of China', Asian Development Bank Institute, Working Paper No. 257, December (Paper revised May 2011).

Yakovlev A., 2002, 'Ekonomika "Chernogo Nala" v Rossii: Spetsifika I Mashtaby Yavleniya, Otsenky Obshestvennykh Poter' (The 'Black Cash' Economy in Russia: Specifics and Phenomenon Scale, Estimation of the Social Losses), *Voprosy Statistiky*, No. 8, pp. 3–16.

——, 2004, 'Evolution of Corporate Governance in Russia: Government Policy Vs. Real Incentives of Economic Agents', *Post-Communist Economies*, Vol. 16, Issue 4, pp. 387–403.

Yaremenko G., 2005, 'Nekotoriyer Problemy Sovremennoi Politiky Dokhodov Naseleniya v Rossii' (Some Problems of the Modern Income Policy in Russia), *Problems of Forecasting*, No. 3, pp. 94–101.

Yaremenko Y., 1997, *Teoriya i metodologiya issledovaniya mnogourovnevoi ekonomiki (The theory and methodology of studying of the multilevel economy)*, Moscow: Nauka.

——, 1998, *Ekonomicheskiyer Besedy (Economic Discussions)*, Moscow: Centre for Research and Statistics of Science.

——, 2001, 'Ekonomicheskiy Rost. Strouktournaya Poliytika' (Economic Growth. Structural Policy), *Problems of Forecasting*, No. 1, pp. 6–14.

Zakharov N., 2004, 'Sotsio-Kulturniyer i Professionalniyer regulyatory Povedeniya Rossyiskogo Chinovnika' (Socio-Cultural and Professional Regulators of the Russian Civil Servants Behavior), *Sociologicheskya Issledovanya*, No. 4, pp. 34–52.

Index

'accumulation by dispossession',
18–19, 23, 40
and value chains, 26–30
and the global crisis, 34–9
Amin, Samir, 28, 45–6, 263, 269
Arrighi, Giovanni, 22, 269
Aslund, Andres, 54, 91, 154, 269
'ascent from the abstract to the
concrete', 16–17, 19, 40, 149, 261,
267
average longevity of equipment, 203–4

Barnes, Andrew, 61, 68, 84, 88, 270
Bazarov, Vladimir, 51, 270
Berezovsky, Boris, 2–5
Berle, Adolf, 20–1, 270
Bhutto, Zulfikar Ali, 264, 28
big (large) insiders
definition of, 10
brief exposition of the concept,
10–14
and a danger of hostile takeover, 12
and Russian model of corporate
governance, 97, 100, 104–5, 107,
110–11, 113–14, 116, 118–21
and instability of insider control,
123–5, 128–32
and insider rent extraction, 133–9,
141–52, 155–7, 268
and social conflicts, 157–9, 161–3,
165–7
and accumulation of capital,
167–70, 169, 207–8, 211, 216,
220–4, 227, 230–2, 234–5,
238–42, 244–9, 251–4, 256
time horizon of, 170–4, 197–8
and conditions of growth, 188–90,
192–3, 195
and the suggested reform of
corporate governance, 256–9
Brenner, Robert, 23, 37, 271
Brezhnev, Leonid, 56–7, 60, 62
British Petrolium (BP), 33, 280
Bukharin, Nicolas, 46, 263–4

bureaucracy, 2, 8–9, 42–3, 45, 47–50,
55–6, 58, 61, 62–3, 67–9, 72,
77–9, 89, 94, 151, 154, 256, 266
ministerial bureaucracy, 61
Stalinist bureaucracy, 117, 255
Bureacracy's power over society, 8
Bureaucratisation of the World, The, 49,
284
Burnham, James, 49–50

Capture economy, 114–16
central planning, 8–9, 42–3, 45–7, 49,
51, 53–5, 57–61, 63–7, 69, 71,
73, 75, 77–9, 117, 154, 255, 263
the crisis of, 58–60
Chains of firms, 107–12
see also 'offshore clouds'
Chubais, Anatoly, 71
'Commodity fetishism,' the Marxian
theory of, 51
compensation, effect of, 180, 192, 194
conditions of growth, 175–95, 256–7
Corporate governance
definition of, 81–2
American and Continental models
of, 24, 26, 33, 82–3, 92
reforms of, 258–9
Russian model of
brief exposition of, 10, 14
detailed exposition of, 92–4,
96–7, 99–107, 125, 130–1, 135,
148, 197, 235, 251, 254
suggested reforms of, 257–9
Crimean War, the, 44

de-industrialisation, 27, 35, 39
degree of monopoly theory, 151–2,
178, 181, 190–2, 195
see also mark-up
direct control over top-management,
112–14
dividends
of US corporations, 7, 15, 20, 40
net dividends (of US corporations),
24–5, 30–1, 262

of Russian corporations, 97, 136–8, 146, 149, 157, 168, 172, 268

Djilas, Milovan, 50

dominant groups, 11, 80, 106, 118, 122, 124, 133, 143, 154, 158, 165, 169, 173–5, 191–3, 221, 240, 255

see also big (large) insiders

duality of labour, 16, 18–19, 40, 261

Eichner, Alfred, 12, 20, 176, 194, 273

exploitation
    of labour, 6–7, 16–17, 26, 38, 39–42, 53, 153, 155–6, 163, 190
    of periphery, 16, 18, 37, 38, 148

fictitious capital, 22

financial markets, 7, 19, 21–2, 40, 102, 236, 242

financialisation, 6, 16, 22–3, 32, 39, 41, 197

fixed capital stock, 6, 51, 198, 201, 203–8, 214, 220, 239

foreign direct investment (FDI), 26–7, 261

Frank, Andre Gunder, 156, 274

Freeland, Chrystia, 10, 84, 90, 274

fundamental uncertainty, 50–1, 53, 264

Global Commodity Chain approach, 191–2

Global production networks, 16, 40

'Golden Age of Capitalism', 15, 20, 22–3

'golden rouble,' 44
    see also Golden standard

Golden standard, 263

goodwill, 21, 32, 190
    see also intangible assets

Gorbachev, Mikhail, 9, 42–3, 57, 62–9, 66–7, 75, 78, 137, 278

'Great Game', The, 44, 276

Great Recession, The, 31, 276

Harvey, David, 18–19, 22, 275

Hay, Jonathan, 71

Ho, Karen, 25

hostile takeover (s), 10, 12, 23, 114, 116, 122, 124–30, 132, 134, 171–2, 174, 197–8, 222, 239, 242, 244, 253

'imperialist rent', 28, 38

inceparabiliy of ownership and control (management), 10, 13, 112, 131, 135, 197, 221, 252, 259

indicative planning, 260

industrialisation
    of the periphery, 6, 38
    of the Tsarist Russia, 42, 44
    of the Soviet Union, 46, 48, 53, 264

informal control
    of bureaucracy over resources, 8, 42–3, 60, 64, 67, 69, 78–9
    over assets on the part of private owners, 9, 13, 78, 94, 97, 100, 113, 157, 161, 170–1, 190, 197, 207, 230, 238, 251–2, 255, 259
    evolution of, 60–3

infrastructure of control
    definition of, 10–11, 14
    and big insiders, 100, 105–6
    and Russian model of corporate governance, 107, 111, 117–18, 120–1, 124, 128, 130–2
    and insider rent extraction, 150–2
    and corporate conflicts, 160–1, 166–7
    and instability of insider control, 171, 174
    and price disparity and modification of insider rent notion, 185, 190–1
    and accumulation of capital (case-studies), 196, 198, 221, 230, 238–9, 243, 248–9, 251, 253, 257–8

insider rent
    brief exposition of the concept, 11, 13–14
    definition of, 133–4, 139
    methods of extraction, 144, 147
    the nature of, 149–51, 153–6, 255, 267–8
    and corporate conflicts, 158–9, 161, 163, 165
    effects of, 167–70, 174
    and conditions of growth, 175, 178, 189–90, 192–3
    and investment strategies, 196, 208, 211–12, 222, 224, 230, 238

insiders and outsiders, the general
    concept of, 82–3
instability of insider control, 13, 107,
    134, 197, 252, 259
intangible assets, 21–2, 32, 190, 192
    see also goodwill
internal funds, 7, 24–5, 31, 40, 106,
    136, 234, 238
investment funds
    of American corporations, 7–8, 24,
    40
    of Russian corporations, 134, 141,
    158, 167–8, 196, 211–12, 228–9
investment strategies, 13–14, 16, 26,
    30–1, 33, 162, 190, 198–9,
    207–8, 216, 218, 221, 252,
    254–5
Ivanova, Maria, 27, 276

Jennings, Steven, 71–2
Jordan, Boris, 70–2

Kagarlitsky, Boris, 44, 276
Kalecki, Mikhal, 151–2, 178, 191, 277
Karyagina, Tatyana, 62, 277
Keynes, John M., 50–1, 176, 289
Khodorkovsky, Mikhail, 68
Kotz, David, 9, 55, 60, 66, 75, 152–3,
    278, 281
Krugman, Paul, 34

Lane, David, 9, 56–7, 71, 279
Laramie, Anthony, 152, 179, 280
Lenin, Vladimir, 45–6, 48, 263, 287
Litvinenko, Alesander, 5
'loans-for-shares' auctions, 4, 91

Mair, Douglas, 152, 179, 280
'marginal productivity theory', 35, 37,
    262
mark-up, 12, 144, 147, 151, 169, 191–2
    see also degree of monopoly theory
Marshallian representative firm, 19–20
Marx, Karl, 7, 16–18, 35, 51–2,
    142–50, 154, 179, 267, 276, 281
Means, Gardiner, 20–1, 176, 270, 282
megacorp, 16, 20, 23, 30–1, 40, 260
Mejprombank, 108–10, 142, 280
Menshikov, Stanislav, 84, 88, 90, 126,
    161–2, 281

minority shareholders, 11, 93–4, 97,
    101, 105–6, 133–4, 136–7, 158,
    167, 174, 257–9
Modern Corporation and Private
    Property, The, 20, 270
Modernisation
    Tsarist, 44
    Soviet, 46, 53–4, 58, 64, 263
    in modern Russia, 74, 181–2, 187
    of Russian enterprises and
    equipment, 209–10, 214, 229,
    234, 267

nature of the USSR and the Soviet
    bureaucracy, Trotskysts'
    controversies, 49–50
    see also 'Thermodor' and Revolution
    Betrayed
Neimann, von, 176

Ofer, Gur, 53–4, 282
'Offshore cloud', 110–1, 121, 231, 238,
    259
    see also chains of firms and offshore
    companies
Offshore companies, 111, 138, 144,
    154, 165, 230–1, 233, 238, 243,
    259
    see also chains of firms and 'offshore
    cloud'
over-accumulation of capital, 22, 35,
    37–8, 41

Patarkatsishvily, Badri, 5
'Perestroika,' 9, 42–3, 56, 63–4, 78
Peter the Great, 44
Pirani, Simon, 50, 71, 115, 153, 166,
    273, 283
plan-market economy, 257
'Planomernost'
    the essence of the concept, 52,
    256–7; the crisis of, 58
Pozner, Vladimir, 1
price disparity, 12–14, 187, 189–95
privatisation
    brief description of, 1, 3–4, 9–10
    spontaneous and informal, 67–8
    and 'Shock Therapy', 69–72
    and emergence of Russian business
    elite, 80, 83–5
    flaws of, 87–9, 91, 131

and ownership and control over the Russian corporations, 91, 93, 97, 102, 118, 122, 131, 222, 247
and 'state capture', 114–15
and instability of insider control, 123, 126
and control over financial flows, 135–7, 189
and social conflicts, 157, 165
Pro-capitalist bloc of social forces, 9, 42, 66–7, 69–70, 78
Protection of 'property rights'
external, 114–17
internal, 117–20
Pugh, Geoff, 171–2, 284
Putin, Vladimir, 5, 272, 278

qualitative non-homogeneity of resources, theory of, 179–80, 192, 194

raiding, 10, 125–6, 129–30, 132, 189, 270, 276, 282, 287–8
Rakovsky, Christian, 50
Rawlinson, Patricia, 117, 284
rent-seeking behaviour, 117, 134, 152, 154, 171
restrictive monetary policy, 36, 70, 73–4, 78
Revolution Betrayed, The, 47–50, 288
see also 'Thermodor'
Rizzi, Bruno, 49, 284
Rozmainsky, Ivan, 62, 96, 286
Russian Revolution, 8–9, 42–3, 45, 47, 50, 77, 79, 263, 274, 281, 283, 288
bourgeois degeneration of, 8, 77
Ryutin, Martem'yan, 264, 286

Sachs, Jeffrey, 71
Sarbanes-Oxley Act, 258–9, 272
semi-periphery (semi-peripheral), 13–14, 150, 193
separation of ownership and control, 7, 15–16, 20–1, 24, 40, 92–3, 97, 102, 113, 197, 251
Serfati, Claude, 32, 267
Serge, Victor, 262
Shachtman, Max, 49–50
'Shareholder revolution', 7, 15–16, 22–3, 26, 30, 34, 40, 197

shareholder value, 7, 16, 24, 30 Shareholder revolution, 1, 33, 40, 255
Shatalin, Stanislav, 1
Shiller, Robert, 34
Shleifer, Andrei, 71, 82, 276, 287
Shock therapy
the concept and principles, 69–72
the main directions, 72–7
'Social structure of accumulation' (SSA) approach, 55
and the Soviet bureaucracy, 55–8
socialism, 1
'Real socialism', Breznev's, 57
European socialism, 60
State socialism, 66, 261, 263
World socialism, 264
see also Trotsky on Soviet system and 'Thermidor'
Soviet society, 8–9, 42–3, 48, 55, 57, 77–8, 151, 261, 286
Soviet system, 6, 8–9, 43, 49–50, 54, 58, 60, 63, 66–7, 71, 77–80, 89, 117, 131, 155, 261, 263, 278
Sraffa, Piero, 176–7, 179, 279, 289
'Stagflation', 7, 23, 37, 40
Stalin, 46–8, 55–6, 263, 287
'State capture', 114–16
substitution, effect of, 180, 192, 194
surplus value, 14, 21, 26, 37, 176–7, 262, 266
and accumulation by dispossession, 23, 40
transformation into profit, 17–18
as an essence of insider rent, 11, 149–59, 154–6, 173, 176, 255, 267
and conditions of growth, 190–1, 193

technological condition of growth, 179–80, 194
technological structure of economy, 75, 176, 180–2, 186, 194
see also Yaremenko, Yuri; compensation effect; substitution effect; technological condition of growth; qualitative non-homogeneity of resources
'Thermidor', 8, 45–6, 60, 77
see also Revolution Betrayed, The
TNC, 6–7, 26, 28, 32, 36, 40

Trotsky, Leon, 8, 45–50, 56, 63, 77, 263, 272, 288
 see also Revolution Betrayed, The, 'Thermidor'
Tsagolov, Nicolas, 51–2, 58, 264
 see also 'Planomernost'

USSR, 2, 6, 27, 35, 42, 47–8, 58–9, 62, 66, 68, 204, 261–4, 277

value chains, 16, 32, 36, 191
 the concept of, 26
 and accumulation by dispossession, 26–30
 'Value condition of growth', The, 12, 177–9, 181, 194
Veblen, Thorstein, 7, 16, 18–19, 21, 23, 33, 190, 289
 Concept of the capitalist business enterprise, 15, 18–19
Vitte, Sergey, 44, 263
Volkonsky, Victor, 88, 183, 289

Wall Street, 24–5, 30, 33, 276

'Washington Consensus', 9, 43, 69–70, 78, 181, 287
Weir, Frederic, 9, 60, 66, 75, 153, 278
Whitefield, Stephen, 61–2, 68, 289
Williamson, John, 69
Woodruff, David, 73–4, 289
World-system, capitalist, 6, 8, 15–16, 18, 22, 30, 36, 39, 41–3, 45, 54–5, 77, 151, 156, 191–3, 261, 264, 276

Yaremenko, Yuri, 9, 58, 267, 290
 on the nature of the Soviet-type economies, 58–60, 182, 201
 on the crisis of central planning, 61
 on 'Shock therapy', 75, 182, 189
 on US-USSR economic competition, 59
 see also technological structure of economy; compensation effect; substitution effect; technological condition of growth; qualitative non-homogeneity of resources
Yeltsin, Boris, 4, 66–7, 69, 265, 272